Liberty's Jihad

African Muslim Slaves and the Meaning of America

Liberty's Jihad

African Muslim Slaves and the Meaning of America

Munawar Ali Karim

diptote

Published by Diptote Books 2019
www.diptote.com

Copyright © Munawar Ali Karim, 2019

Munawar Ali Karim has asserted his right under the Copyright,
Designs and Patents Act 1988 to be identified as the author of this work.

All rights reserved. No part of this publication may be reproduced,
stored in a retrieval system or transmitted in any form or by any means,
electronic, mechanical, photocopying, recording or otherwise,
without prior written permission of the author.

While every effort has been made to trace the owners of copyright material
reproduced herein, the author would like to apologise for any omissions and will
be pleased to incorporate missing acknowledgements in any future editions.

First published in Great Britain by Diptote™ 2019
Diptote Books
www.diptote.com

ISBN 978-1-912892-23-5 (paperback)
ISBN 978-1-912892-24-2 (eBook)

Designed and typeset by seagulls.net
Project management by whitefox

Contents

Apologia xi

Prologue xiii

Introduction xv

Al-Faatihah — **The Opener** I

1.   Historiography 5
2.   Revisiting Sambo and Resistance 15
3.   'All Men are Slaves' 31

ا *Alif* — **The Relocation of History** 49

4.   New World Rising 53
5.   *Muezzin* and *Hegira* — The First African Muslims 67
6.   Muslim West Africa and the Transatlantic Slave Trade 85

ل *Laam* — **Orisons of the Slave** 97

7.   Job Ben Solomon .... IOI
8.   'Abd al-Rahman Ibrahima 149
9.   Dialogue Between Slave and Master 171
10. Bilali Muhammad and the Mysterious Orison 175
11. Bilali's Key to Emancipation 189

م *Meem* — **The Endless Sea** 195

12. Irony and Meaning 199
13. Postscript: Then and Now 211

Bibliography 225

Index 232

FOR

R., S., and H.

WITH SPECIAL THANKS TO

Nuri Abdussalaam
Julia Koppitz
Asia K.
and my parents

*We bestow of our Mercy on whom We please,
and We suffer not, to be lost,
the reward of those who do good.*

(Qur'an 12:56)

Apologia

'It befitteth men of learning and beneficence—may the evil eye be
far removed from the courtyard of their glory and may the edifices of
nobleness and sublimity be constructed with their being!—that, by way
of kindness, they cover the feebleness and deficiency of my language
and style with the train of forgiveness and cancellation, since for ten
years I have set foot in foreign lands and have eschewed study; and the
leaves of the sciences have become "*woven over by the spider*" and the
pictures thereof erased from the pages of the mind—
Like the writing writ upon the surface of the water;
And that they lay not the finger of criticism upon the false steps,
wherefrom no man remaineth exempt,
"*for every courser stumbleth!*".
If thou perceivest irregularity in my style, my
calligraphy, my ability or my rhetoric,
Question not my understanding: verily my dance is
to the tune of the times
And if in the regions of excess and deficiency I have trodden the
pathway of latitude, let them be pleased to consider the force of the
verse, *And when they pass by frivolous sport they pass on with dignity*
[Koran, xxv, 72]; for the purpose of recounting these tales and declaring
and delineating the shape of events compriseth two objects, viz.
the achievement of spiritual and temporal advantage.'

—Ata-Malik Juvaini, *Ta'rikh-i-Jahan-Gusha*
(*History of the World Conqueror*)

Prologue

How to Read this Book

*Read the book through, undeterred and undismayed by the
paragraphs, footnotes, comments, and references that escape you.
If you let yourself get stalled, if you allow yourself to be tripped
up by any one of these stumbling blocks, you are lost.*

—Mortimer J. Adler, *How to Read a Book*[1]

This is an unusual book that grew in the telling and in the finding out.
It is the first in a series entitled 'Liberty's Jihad' which represents my
personal attempt to make sense of the post-9/11 world and the events that
brought it about. How it came to be published is explained somewhat
in the postscript. The work is divided into four parts. *Al-Faatihah* is an
introductory section dealing with such matters as historiography and the
importance of studying the lives of African Muslim slaves in more detail.
Each of the following parts has been given an Arabic letter and an English
title. *Alif: The Relocation of History* seeks to contextualise the origins of
transatlantic slavery in relation to contemporaneous trends in African

---

1   Adler and Van Doren (1972), 36.

and Islamic history towards establishing the historical (and, to an extent, theological) context for the men and women who found themselves slaves in antebellum America. *Laam: Orisons of the Slave* is the narrative part of the book and tells the stories of three of the best known African Muslim slaves. *Meem: the Endless Sea* is a short concluding section that seeks to show the importance of the lives and legacies of these slaves to contemporary America and the questions confronting us all as global citizens in a troubled world.

Perhaps the most *enjoyable* way to read this book is to begin with the introduction and then skip to the narratives in *Laam: Orisons of the Slave*. After which you may wish to:

1. Go back to *al-Faatihah* and *Alif* before reading the concluding section (*Meem*), or
2. Read the concluding section and then end with *al-Faatihah* and *Alif.*

Alternatively, of course, you may wish to read the sections in the order they are presented, which may require more patience on your part, but may be more rewarding in the end. Each sequence of reading described above promises to reveal different facets of meaning contained within the work. So, if it has not bored you too much, you may wish to re-read it in a different sequence on another occasion to help further understand what is being said. Whichever course you decide to follow, the path you choose is yours. *May it bring you home to safety.*

Introduction

This study is founded on the premise that research into the lives of African Muslim Slaves in the antebellum United States has not been given the scholarly attention it deserves. Whilst most aspects of antebellum slave life and society have been written about extensively, the study of African Muslim slaves and their impact upon various aspects of slave culture, African-American and American culture in general, has remained wanting. This study does not claim to fill this vacuum, but seeks rather to demonstrate the need to do so and moreover to tentatively explore the exciting issues that arise from an open and broadminded approach to the subject matter. Above all it seeks to probe a largely uncharted territory of studies on American slavery, to describe the promising fruits of a journey into this potentially rich field of research and to draw attention to a missing chapter in the received history of an American phenomenon. In this latter purpose it aims to call into question the American self-image of the darker episodes of its own history, echoing the title of Ronald T. Judy's work *(Dis)Forming the American Canon*,[1] and to pay tribute to the courage, creativity, and resilience of the slaves whose lives were inevitably inscribed on the pages of that ill-remembered past.

This book proposes that the study of African Muslim slaves can contribute to the undoing of what may be described as an academic

---

[1]   Judy (1993).

servitude to a received epistemology: dictating the way we understand what we are, who we are, and what we are becoming. The study of African Muslim slaves is uniquely suited to this role because it is a subject which, by reason of its very nature, transcends distinctions between east and west—or rather, orient and occident. When dealt with in the manner suggested in this study, it also transcends established mechanisms of discourse which thrive on distinctions such as 'Afro-American' as opposed to 'American'; 'Arabic African' or 'Moor' as opposed to 'African Muslim'; 'African Muslim' as opposed to 'Muslim': distinctions which delineate, deform and then seek to control discourse and perception at all levels, and which are identified and confronted throughout the course of this inquiry. In connecting Islamic Studies, African History and America's self-perception, it at once challenges the usual approaches to a study of the *Other*, and calls into question the very foundations of Orientalism. It is to be noted that none of this would be relevant at all in a study of Muslim slaves had it not been for the fact that their stories, and the documents which corroborate them, have been—as one writer expressed it—'conspicuous by their absence in American writing'.[2] It is this absence that allows us to call into question the modes of discourse surrounding the study of slavery. Given this background the present study also hopes to demonstrate, in a necessarily modest way, how much we have missed by submitting unquestionably to a narrow-minded approach to knowledge—the 'manufactured' treatment of knowledge produced and bartered in the market places of Academia.

Knowledge is the property of the poor: not the monopoly of any intellectual or political elite. The lives of the literate, intelligent slaves who form the subject of this study, and their endeavours to preserve their learning even under the punishing regimen of slavery, testify to the fact that knowledge is, moreover, the property of the slave and the lodestar of the dispossessed.

---

2   Austin (1984), 20.

I

Al-Faatihah

The Opener

بِسۡمِ ٱللَّهِ ٱلرَّحۡمَٰنِ ٱلرَّحِيمِ ﴿١﴾

ٱلۡحَمۡدُ لِلَّهِ رَبِّ ٱلۡعَٰلَمِينَ ﴿٢﴾

ٱلرَّحۡمَٰنِ ٱلرَّحِيمِ ﴿٣﴾ مَٰلِكِ يَوۡمِ ٱلدِّينِ ﴿٤﴾

إِيَّاكَ نَعۡبُدُ وَإِيَّاكَ نَسۡتَعِينُ ﴿٥﴾ ٱهۡدِنَا

ٱلصِّرَٰطَ ٱلۡمُسۡتَقِيمَ ﴿٦﴾ صِرَٰطَ ٱلَّذِينَ أَنۡعَمۡتَ

عَلَيۡهِمۡ غَيۡرِ ٱلۡمَغۡضُوبِ عَلَيۡهِمۡ

وَلَا ٱلضَّآلِّينَ ﴿٧﴾

The Opener

In the Name of God, the Benevolent, the Merciful
Praise is proper to God, Lord of the universe
The Benevolent, the Merciful,
Ruler of the Day of Requital.
It is You we serve, to You we turn for help.
Show us the straight path.
The path of those You have favoured,
not of those who are objects of anger,
nor of those who wander astray.

—translation of the slave 'Abd al-Rahman Ibrahima's writing in
Arabic presented as 'the Lord's Prayer', actually the *Surah
al Faatihah* or 'Opening' (lit. 'Opener') of the Qur'an

I

Historiography

It is not only that the scheme circumscribes the area of history.
What is worse, it rigs the stage.

—Oswald Spengler, *The Decline of the West*[1]

In an important article entitled 'Muslims in Early America', Michael Gomez, Associate Professor at Spelman College, argues for the detailed study of Islam in early America and its associations with Africans.[2] His is one among a growing number of voices that are beginning to realise the importance of such research. Nevertheless, the study of African Muslim slaves—particularly in North America—is still a relatively underdeveloped area of historical studies. This is not to say that scholars have not been aware of the presence of Muslims in the Americas. As Allan D. Austin points out in *African Muslims in Antebellum America: A Sourcebook*,[3] a steady stream of independent African nations emerging onto the global arena in the late 1950s finally prompted Western writers and historians to pay attention to African perspectives on a wide

---

1   Spengler (2000), 17.
2   Gomez (1994), 671.
3   Austin (1984).

variety of issues.[4] As African nations increasingly overcame the shackles of colonialism, the African experience of slavery found a mouthpiece and an audience in Western academia. Moreover, a growing civil rights movement with young black Americans at the fore turned inevitably eastward to find a cultural and ethnic identity it could build upon. Interestingly this is precisely the time Stanley Elkins first published his influential study—*Slavery: A Problem in American Institutional and Intellectual Life*[5]—challenging the popular racist concept of Africans as savages, which had been used to justify slavery and soothe wounded consciences. Elkins, however, implied instead that the slaves, and therefore their African-American descendants, had lost all memory of their African culture and become simpletons confined within the narrow boundaries of plantation life.

Subsequent studies can be seen as attempts at refuting 'Elkins' thesis' whilst developing and building upon his methodological approach. Nevertheless, little to no mention of Muslim slaves is made in these studies, even when they are most relevant to the point being argued.[6]

The search for a genuine African heritage and the need to articulate a respectable cultural adaptation of African-Americans into the American social milieu found popular expression in Alex Haley's *Roots*.[7] Although a work of fiction, *Roots* is an important starting point for those sections of the current study related to discourse and the lack of writing about African Muslim slaves. Not only does *Roots* reveal the willingness amongst African-Americans of that time to acknowledge the Islamic identity of at least some of their forbears, it also highlights at least some awareness of this aspect of their heritage. The televised version of *Roots* enjoyed wide coverage but the response it engendered from reviewers and academics alike indicates, at best, an uncertainty about the Muslim heritage of some slaves in America (which *Roots* seemed to imply); and at worst,

---

4   Ibid., 4.

5   Elkins (1969).

6   This point is taken up again in detail in the following chapter.

7   Haley (1976).

an outright denial that African Muslim slaves ever existed. The novelist James A. Michener commented:

> To have Kunta Kinte [the Mandingo hero], or one of his fellows, praying to Allah while chained in the bottom of a Christian ship is an unjustified sop to contemporary developments rather than true reflection of the past.[8]

Clearly Michener was ignorant about Muslim slaves such as Job Ben Solomon (Ayyub bin Suleiman) who not only prayed whilst on their way to slavery in America, but also prayed on the plantation itself.[9] As Austin points out, 'his is an erroneous impression; but the absence of any criticism of Michener's comment may indicate how ignorant of Africa and Islam, the people of the United States still are.'[10] What Michener called a 'sop to contemporary developments' refers to the fact that Alex Haley was also the amanuensis for Malcolm X's autobiography. Malcolm X, or al-Hajj Malik Shabazz as he is known to Muslims, remains one of the most famous African-American Muslims to this day. The life of Malcolm X and his initial association with the heterodox Nation of Islam organisation is not entirely without relevance to the present study: Morroe Berger has argued that there is a connection between the Nation of Islam (also known as the Black Muslim Movement) and African Muslim slaves. More recent voices, however, have found reason to believe otherwise.[11] If these writers are correct, the legacy of African Muslim slaves has been an instrumental factor in the popularity of Islam in the contemporary United States. Moreover, given the impact of 9/11 on American–Muslim relations, it is more important than ever for the United States and its peoples to understand the antebellum roots of the American Muslim community.

---

8   Michener (1977).
9   See Chapter 7.
10   Austin (1984), 4.
11   Ibid., 25.

Roots is also important for another reason: it was the inspiration for a detailed investigation of all the available documents and other materials related to African Muslim slaves in the United States. Without this research and the subsequent publication of Allan Austin's *African Muslims in Antebellum America: A Sourcebook*, the current study might never have been possible. As Austin writes in the introduction to his sourcebook:

> This volume is the result of a quite specific attempt to better understand the Old and New Worlds of Kunta Kinte, the hero of Alex Haley's novel *Roots*, in a course I taught at Springfield College and the University of Massachusetts, Amherst in 1977 and 1978. I began to gather notes on historical Africans who had left behind stories of lives in both sides of the Atlantic Ocean … By 1979 these background notes became a foreground obsession and my collection grew. A limit had to be drawn. As the overwhelming majority of the lengthier pieces told of Africans who were, like Kunta Kinte, Muslims, and as the Islamic part of the African diaspora had clearly been neglected by scholars, and as finally, the Africanness of these men had been disputed, the scope of my inquiry was settled.[12]

In this valuable work, published as volume 5 in *Critical Studies on Black Life and Culture* (1984), Austin meticulously gathers almost all the available primary records written 'by and on the Africans in question in Arabic and English.'[13] Although a few of these documents are held at the British Library (principally letters written by and about Job Ben Solomon), most of the documents in question are scattered across various libraries and private collections in the United States. Austin's collection of this material in one weighty volume, including copies of some relevant

---

12 Austin (1984), 25.
13 Ibid., vii.

portraits, maps and illustrations from antebellum times, is therefore the principal source for the majority of the primary materials relied upon in the current study. The complete autobiography of Nicholas Ben Said, probably one of the most widely travelled men of his time (counting Africans and non-Africans), was discovered in 2001 by a Harvard doctoral student and published in the same year. This find and the material referred to or hinted at in the documents gathered in Austin's *Sourcebook* suggest that there are many other works which remain to be discovered.

The material contained in Austin's *Sourcebook* primarily relates to fifteen African Muslims who were brought into North American slavery between 1730 and 1860. Austin also provides documentary evidence related to fifty other African Muslim slaves who were in America during the same period. He summarises his collection as offering:

> [...] fascinating, barely tapped glimpses of (1) African education,
> religion, socio-political and economic practices and attitudes,
> especially schools, Islam, trade, and slavery; of (2) proud people
> reduced to slavery far from their own countries and traditions
> who retained old ways, adjusted to and manipulated new ways,
> or escaped them altogether and returned to their homelands; and
> of (3) the historiography and ethnology on Africans and Afro-
> Americans by Europeans and Americans then and now.[14]

By recognising the value of these documents, both past and present—not only as useful sources about slave life and culture which give us a more accurate picture of the variety, background and sophistication of slaves, but also as important sources about Africa and Islam and crucially about Western historiography and ethnology—Austin has identified the true value of this material and pre-empted the theme of our study. Significantly, however, Austin's *Sourcebook* quickly fell out of print and remains difficult to obtain.

---

14 Austin (1984), vii-viii.

Furthermore, although Austin clearly recognised the value of the material on African Muslim slaves and the importance of studying their lives, little of such study has actually taken place. A further attempt has been made by Austin to bring some commentary and discussion to the subject in his updated and condensed version of the *Sourcebook* published as *African Muslims in Antebellum America: Transatlantic Stories and Spiritual Struggles.*[15] This work contains much less of the primary material and much more of Austin's discussion about the more famous African Muslim slaves identified in his first work. Nevertheless it is a small work and is only intended to be a catalyst for further research, not a comprehensive study on the subject. It does, however, contain useful reading lists of secondary material relevant to an inquiry into the lack of historiography in this area.

Austin's pioneering work in this field has been influential in attracting the attention of a few other scholars, but not as many as one might have expected. Outstanding among these studies is Sylviane Diouf's *Servants of Allah: African Muslims Enslaved in the Americas,*[16] and a lengthy article by Michael Gomez (mentioned earlier) entitled 'Muslims in Early America' published in the *Journal of Southern History.*[17]

Diouf is evidently better informed about Islam in Africa than other writers, and uses her knowledge to make some interesting observations about African Muslim slaves. Although relying on much of the same information as gathered by Austin (it should be noted that the primary sources themselves are much more readily available than the lack of scholarly attention to them would otherwise suggest), Diouf's work is fundamentally different to Austin's in three ways: first, Diouf deals with African Muslim slaves in the whole of the Americas and therefore discusses the well known—but also seldom considered—presence of Muslims in South America (particularly Brazil), and Jamaica. This is important, because a comparison of the heavy Muslim presence and influence in

---

[15] Austin (1997).
[16] Diouf (1998).
[17] Gomez (1994).

South America, with the relative (apparent) lack of equal influence in North America, suggests a useful point of inquiry. Austin may well have recognised this because he includes in his *Sourcebook* a section on 'Six African Muslims in Jamaica'.[18] In a footnote to his introduction, Austin also mentions a study by Marina Wikraminayake entitled *The Free Blacks in Antebellum South Carolina*, which apparently describes a group of American Muslims, 'descendants of pre-Revolutionary War Immigrants' who traced their independence 'back to 1790 and a petition to the South Carolina legislature which recognised them as subjects of the Emperor of Morocco. They did not want to be considered "Negroes", and seem to have been treated as honorary whites, even to the point of their being allowed to fight for the confederacy.'[19] This reference is important as it draws attention to the fact that there were Muslims in America at the time who were not from Africa. There is evidence to suggest, for example, that many Native Americans may have been Muslims, or intermarried with Muslims. In any case, reference to other African Muslims outside of the Old South is noticeably scarce in Austin's later work and the chapter on Jamaican Muslims is completely missing.

The second difference between Diouf's work and Austin's is that Diouf is able to use her specialist knowledge of Africa to build upon the American sources about Muslim slaves. In a sense Diouf is responding to Austin's call for an African perspective on the issues at hand. Third, and related to the former point, Diouf makes use of her knowledge about Islam in Africa to present some interesting theories about the more famous Muslim slaves and the impact of their legacy on surviving African trends in the New World. Particularly interesting in this regard is her discussion of Sufism (Islamic spiritual practice) and the non-Muslim perception and use of Marabouts (African Muslim Sufis) in Africa, and how this may have carried over into a mystical image of the Muslim slaves in the Americas. She also talks about Islamic influences in the surviving non-

---

18   Austin (1984), Chapter VIII.
19   Ibid., 64, note 73.

Muslim religious practices of former slaves and their descendants, in both North and South America.[20] In this sense, Diouf's work reflects those aspects of our study which stress the need for an integrated approach to studies on Muslim slaves in America, and on slave life, culture and society in general. An approach that transcends traditional disciplinary boundaries—considering related disciplines across Islam, African and American studies—is needed for a well-informed and clearer picture of the meaning of African Muslim slaves in America, as well as for understanding all aspects of the phenomenon of slavery in general. Diouf's work is a significant and pioneering step in that direction.

Gomez's article and Judy's book are also both noteworthy for their emphasis on this approach and reflect the final dimension of our study: the need to carefully consider the modes of discourse and conceptual frameworks behind the existing historiography in order to understand the factors which have perpetuated ignorance about the Muslim slave presence; and to understand how notions of the *Other* have been manipulated, then and now, in order to explain away those attributes of Muslim slaves which challenge the stereotypes about all slaves in general. Gomez's article is also important in that it stresses the presence of African Muslims in America from before the arrival of English colonists.[21]

Another particularly important source is the Works Projects Administration (WPA) records—particularly chapters in the Savannah Unit of the WPA Georgia Writers Project entitled *Drums and Shadows: Survival Studies Among the Georgia Coastal Negroes*.[22] Here we find descendants of antebellum Muslims in Sapelo and St. Simon's Islands recalling and reliving an Islamic heritage. Also in this category is a compilation of runaway slave adverts from the 1730s–1790s by Lathan A. Windley.[23] As Austin and other sources suggest, Muslim slaves were frequent runaways and the description of slaves given in these adverts often leave important

---

20 For example see Diouf (1998), 198.
21 Gomez (1994), 683.
22 Savannah Unit, WPA (1940).
23 Windley (1983).

clues about the identity and temperament of the slaves concerned. Lydia Parrish's *Slave Songs of the Georgia Sea Islands*,[24] and to a lesser extent, Margaret Creel's *A Peculiar People*[25] are useful works when investigating whether any African elements found their way into the music, singing, and dancing of the slaves. Related works, some of them actually mentioning the possibility of Qur'anic 'melodies' and Sufi chants influencing the development of blues music, are also worth considering.[26]

---

24 Parrish (1942).
25 Creel (1988).
26 Lomax (1993); Oliver (1970); Kubick (1999).

2

Revisiting Sambo and Resistance

We didn't land on Plymouth Rock; the rock was landed on us.
We were brought here against our will; we were not
brought here to be made citizens.

—Malcolm X, *Washington Heights, NY, March 29th 1964*

When Stanley Elkins first proposed in 1959 that the 'Negro' slave, with his childlike antics and his primitive stupidity, was a unique product of the institution of slavery in the United States, that these so-called 'Sambo' qualities were not inherent in the 'savage' black races of Africa, and that such infantile behaviour was not the manifestation of a racial archetype but rather of the dehumanising process of the closed system of US slavery, he may well have thought his argument would settle a long debated subject.[1] Instead his thesis opened up the entire subject of inquiry into realms that had previously not been imagined.[2] Although

---

1   See Elkins (1969), 89-98.
2   For a good summary of the effects of Elkins' study on subsequent historiography see Kolchin (1993), particularly 134-135.

15

his conclusions may have been anathema to many commentators, the very fact of them being so inspired people to set out to refute Elkins' claims that the 'Sambo' stereotype was genuine and that slaves in the antebellum south essentially became dumb animal-like creatures through an experience not unlike that undergone by victims of Nazi concentration camps. Even a casual look at the works of Eugene Genovese,[3] John Blassingame,[4] Herbert Gutman[5] and a host of other writers reveals some latent spark from the Elkins thesis, which remains burning in the deepest recesses of the authors' minds. That is to say, most of these writers were in some way attempting to address issues raised by the Elkins thesis, which perhaps explains why Elkins felt obliged to publish an expanded edition of his earlier work in a kind of belated response to the new currents emerging from an old debate. No doubt, these writers were also responding to a centuries-old contention—in fact a belief as old as American slavery itself—that '… slavery in the Old South had impressed upon the African savages and their native-born descendants the glorious stamp of civilisation.'[6] Indeed the theories of Ulrich B. Phillips—who (it seems) made this remark in 1918—were far more offensive than anything that Elkins was to say 40 or so years later. Whereas Elkins, in a sense, was blaming 'Sambo' on the institution of US slavery itself, Ulrich B. Phillips was claiming that that very same institution was Sambo's only hope for escaping his primitive African personality. Needless to say it was a stereotype, which we are able to recognise in our current socio-cultural milieu as stemming from a bigoted and racist heritage.

---

3   Genovese (1974).

4   Blassingame (1979).

5   See the reference to his study found in Davis (1982), 3.

6   Mentioned in Davis (1982, 3), where she paraphrases from a number of Phillips' works including an article entitled "The Plantation as a Civilizing Factor", *Sewanee Review* (July 1904), reprinted later in Phillips (1968, 83) where he writes: '1. A century or two ago the negroes were savages in the wilds of Africa. 2. Those who were brought to America, and their descendants, have acquired a certain amount of civilization, and are now in some degree fitted for life in modern civilized society. 3. This progress of the negroes has been in very large measure the result of their association with civilized white people.'

And yet that bigotry is still with us. Or at least the demons of that racist past continue to haunt us intellectually and morally as a civilisation. It is a curious fact that in all the studies of slavery in the antebellum South that have come from the pens of thinkers since Ulrich B. Phillips, almost all have implicitly accepted the notion of a primitive or at least simplistic African background from which these slaves were gathered. Many black writers, from whom we would have expected a greater awareness of the cultural background of their forbears, have themselves fallen into the same errors as their non-black colleagues and have internalised the same perceptions and prejudices as the rest of the writers on American slavery.[7] The problem I am pointing towards is rooted in our perception of the cultural backgrounds of the Africans who became slaves in the New World. A carefully constructed image of who these slaves were seeks to lessen the pain of the guilt that must be borne for the darker chapters of American history. This is precisely what, according to Edward Said, Orientalism as a discipline of study (from which we receive our notions of African culture) attempted to do[8]—justifying and vindicating our treatment of the *Other*. This is precisely what was attempted with writings on slavery from the very outset: they were polemics arguing for the good or condemning the evil in slavery:

> Despite the vast amount of writing on American Negro slavery
> and the great variety of temperaments and talents that have
> been brought to the work, the very spiritual agony inherent
> in the subject itself imposes on the result a certain simplicity
> of organisation and a kind of persistent rhythm. The primary
> categories of 'right' and 'wrong' which characterised antebellum
> discourse on the subject of slavery has retained much of its original
> simplicity and vigor.[9]

---

7   See the insightful comments of Diouf (1998), 204.

8   Said, *Orientalism*, (1995) particularly 38.

9   Elkins (1969), 1.

But Elkins' statement, it would seem, is a little outdated now. Almost everyone nowadays recognises that slavery was wrong. The writings on slavery have shifted from an examination of the institution itself to its victims. Whereas Ulrich B. Phillips was in effect saying that slavery was morally justified because it gave backward savages the gift of culture and civilisation, Elkins essentially argued that it made the noble savages of Africa into babbling fools and simpletons in a world where they did not belong.[10] Elkins had shed few of the ignorant stereotypes about African culture—though he was willing to admit a degree of civilisation where none had previously been acknowledged. What Elkins was doing most of all was making an apology for the way the slaves had supposedly turned out: he was saying that Sambo was truly a slave, but 'Sambo' did not come from Africa—he was made (or born) in America. Almost all writings on the subject since then have been apologies for Sambo or attempts to assert his resilience in weathering the brutality of slavery.

For example, Eugene Genovese in *Roll Jordan, Roll: the World the Slaves Made*, building somewhat on Melville Herskovits' work,[11] argues that traits of various African religions were preserved by the slaves and that they manipulated Christian teachings in order to accommodate their own circumstances and to reconcile the religion of their masters with the few African memories their masters were unable to take away from them.

> For good reason the whites of the Old South tried to shape the religious life of their slaves, and the slaves overtly, covertly and even intuitively fought to shape it themselves ... The religion of the slaves manifested many African 'traits' and exhibited greater continuity with African ideas than has generally been appreciated. But it reflected a different reality in a vastly different land and in the end emerged as something new.[12]

---

10   Ibid., 93-100. See especially page 97, where he admits the existence of an African culture at least 'as sophisticated as that of Anglo-Saxon England.'
11   Herskovits (1941).
12   Genovese (1974), 162.

In highlighting the survival of African religious traits in the Christian practices of the slaves, Genovese is at once challenging Elkins' contention that the shock and detachment process that all slaves had to go through from the time they were captured or sold into slavery to the moment they were released into the isolated system of antebellum plantation life, was enough to completely dismember them from their past. If Genovese's contention is true—that the slaves actively resisted, through 'overt' and 'covert' means, a complete and unquestioning absorption of the religion their masters attempted to feed them—then Elkins' assumption that the docile Sambo slave represents the common slave archetype is thereby also challenged. If these slaves remembered their religious past, and if they incorporated it into their new environment, then they had, to some degree, survived the brutality of the enslavement process and they were actively resisting oppression.

But Genovese, unlike Herskovits, does not give us very much more than a few loose statements as to what that past may have been, and what kinds of real African religions were being preserved. When such information is given, it only serves to reinforce the stereotype that African religions consisted of superstitious beliefs in spirits and ghosts and various magical practices.[13] (A stereotype that Herskovits, for all the praise his work has received, also perpetuates.)

Genovese, perhaps following Herskovits, overlooks the fact that Christianity arrived in Africa long before it did in Europe, that some of the slaves probably had a better understanding of Christian dogma than their slave owners, that some of them were literate, monotheistic, piously devout and came from cultures significantly more sophisticated and therefore 'civilised' (by 'Anglo-American' standards of the time) than antebellum America in terms of trade, commerce, and education.[14]

---

13 Genovese (1974), 244 on 'charms' and magic and 231 on assimilating these into Christianity.

14 See Diouf (1998), 112. Of particular interest is the quote from Mungo Park concerning Christian scriptures in Arabic. See also Chapter 5 where we mention Muslim interaction with the Christian empire of Abyssinia.

Certainly not all of the slaves would have been from such a background, but at least those who were educated members of some of the Muslim societies of West Africa would have been, and indeed were—as we shall demonstrate in the following chapters. A curious silence about the history of African Muslims enslaved in the antebellum south has in fact allowed the Sambo stereotype to continue to maintain some credibility. Whereas an open and detailed study of the lives of such slaves may have at once smashed many of the taken-for-granted assumptions that have plagued the historiography of this subject and thereby led to a better understanding of what the slaves and their slave masters were really like. In a study of African Muslim slaves—or at least the ones we know about—far from making apologies for 'Sambo', we find a need to explain why so little about him has really been made known.

In the current study we shall only look briefly at the lives of three such slaves—focusing on the Arabic writings they left behind. But there are many others we might have mentioned: Lamine Kebe; Umar ibn Said; Bilali's (Ben Ali's) friend, Salih, on nearby St. Simon's Island; Yarrow Mamout. These too are only a few names—Austin mentions over seventy-two African Muslim slaves in the summarised version of his earlier work, *African Muslims in Antebellum America*, published in 1997.

It may of course be argued that these Muslims were a rare exception to the usual background and upbringing of African slaves. But this is simply not the case. Elkins himself recognised that most of the slaves came from an 'area that included the Niger Delta, the gold coast, and Dahomey'—all areas of high Muslim concentration.[15]

> In the United States, South Carolina planters had a predilection toward Senegambians because of their skills in rice and indigo cultivation, and they formed 19.5 percent of the slaves imported between 1733 and 1807, along with 6.8 percent of the slaves imported from Sierra Leone and 3.7 percent from the

---

15 Elkins (1969), 93.

> Benin-Nigeria area. The total percentage for South Carolina of slaves from Muslim areas was thus about 30 percent … Curtin's total figures for North America are 13.3 percent from Senegambia, 5.5 percent from Sierra Leone, 4.3 percent from the Bight of Benin and 23.3 percent from the Bight Biafra—a total of 46.3 percent for regions with significant numbers of Muslims.[16]

All these Muslim communities had a standard of literacy and education similar to or more advanced than that of 'Abd al-Rahman's Futa Jallon (see Chapter 8). It is clear therefore, despite the scarcity of modern scholarship about them, that there was a significant educated African Muslim slave presence in antebellum America. The valuable contribution that a thorough study of these slaves can make to existing theories about slave culture and personality cannot be overemphasised. How easy it would have been, for example, to demonstrate the flaw in Elkins' thesis by simply recounting a few of the stories of these Muslim slaves— stories which are easily corroborated with source materials from the Old South as well as manuscripts written by the slaves and, in certain cases, government correspondence. Although by the 1970s Elkins' ideas had largely been dismissed and—according to one writer—'… the Sambo thesis lay in tatters', it had taken at least a decade of inspired and furious research to drive home a point which could have been made so much more easily. And yet in all that time, a thorough study of African Muslim slaves is still found to be wanting in areas where it is most needed.

For example, attempts to refute what we have called 'the Elkins thesis' led to three broad fields of inquiry: first, an attempt to assert the survival of African traits in slave practices;[17] second, an attempt to demonstrate alternative means of resistance to the oppressive system of slavery;[18] third, an attempt to demonstrate the existence of sophisticated

---

16   Diouf (1998), 47.

17   For example, Herskovits (1941) [note: this study predates Elkins' *Slavery*]; Levine (1977).

18   For example Aptheker (1943) [note: this study predates Elkins' *Slavery*].

slave communities and cultures.[19] In all these fields of inquiry a thorough study of African Muslim slaves would prove invaluable, and yet such a study is lacking in every one of them—even in cases where the authors were exposed to some of the same evidence we shall explore in the following chapters. For example, Herskovits—although aware of Bilali's (Ben Ali's) manuscript on Sapelo Island (see Chapter 10)—hardly takes notice of Muslim practices among slaves in his famous work on African slave retentions in the New World.[20] For the sake of brevity, let us take just one example from each type of inquiry and demonstrate how a study of African Muslim slaves would prove to be enlightening.

With regard to the first field of inquiry—*an attempt to assert the survival of African traits in slave practices*—we have already mentioned Genovese's *Roll Jordan Roll: the World the Slaves Made*. Genovese's emphasis on the superstitious African beliefs of the slaves and the way these beliefs were carried over into Christianity entirely neglects any notion that the slaves may have had a strong knowledge of Biblical stories prior to their arrival in America. Peter Kolchin mentions how slaves tended to use stories from the Old Testament, particularly 'accounts of Moses leading his people out of bondage ...',[21] rather than stories of a pacifist Jesus suffering in silence. What none of these writers seem to realise is that the story of Moses and the Israelites would have been very familiar to even mildly educated Muslim slaves. Moses is repeatedly mentioned throughout the Qur'an (as is Jesus)—and Africans from Islamic societies would have invariably memorised some portions of the Book, if not all of it, in their local communities. Ayyub bin Suleiman (Job Ben Solomon), for example, was able to write out three identical copies of the entire Qur'an from memory.[22] It is not unknown for children as young as seven to be able to repeat from memory the entire Qur'an, regardless of their ability to write it. A particularly apt reference

---

[19] For example White (1985).

[20] Herskovits (1941).

[21] Kolchin (1993), 144.

[22] Austin (1997), 56. We recount Ayyub's story in Chapter 7.

to Moses in the Qur'an, which slaves may easily have identified with, is as follows:

> *103. Then after them We sent Moses with Our signs to Pharaoh and his chiefs; but they mistreated them. Now observe how the corrupt ended up.*
>
> *104. Moses said, 'Pharaoh, I am an emissary from the Lord of the universe,*
>
> *105. 'competent on the condition that I not say anything of God but truth. I have come to you with clarification from your Lord, so release the Children of Israel with me.'*
>
> *106. Pharaoh said, 'If you have come with a sign, produce it if you are telling the truth.'*
>
> *107. Then he threw his staff and lo! It was an apparent serpent!*
>
> *108. And he pulled out his hand and lo! It was white to the onlookers!*
>
> *[...]*
>
> *137. And We caused a people thought weak to inherit the land of the East and the West, which We have blessed. And the good word of your Lord was fulfilled for the Israelites, because they endured patiently. And We destroyed what Pharaoh and his people made, and what they built.*[23]

It is clear that many of the Muslim slaves in the Old South were highly educated religious leaders—Imams (or *almaamy*) and/or Sufi mystics (*marabout*): for example Bilali (Ben Ali) Muhammad.[24] If this is the case, there is little doubt that they would have exhorted their fellow slaves—Muslims or otherwise—to have patience in the face of their suffering and have related to them the accounts of Moses and the children of Israel

---

23 Qur'an 7:103-108 and 7:137. Cleary (trans.).

24 Austin (1997), Chapter 5. See also below, Chapter 10.

related in the Qur'an. If some of these Muslims were indeed *marabouts* it would have been commonplace for non-Muslim African slaves as well as Muslims to have consulted them for 'amulets' of protection and for warding off evil. *Marabouts* and *almaamy* have long been consulted by non-Muslim tribes in Africa for such services—the Ashanti kings actually employing Muslims specifically for this role. Raboteau mentioned this in his work on slave religion:

> Among the amulets, or charms, the principal is a scrap of parchment containing a sentence of the Koran, which the natives purchase from the Moors who visit the country ... Muslim slaves became particularly noted in the New World for the power of their magical charms.[25]

These amulets were in fact 'litanies' or prayers calling on God using certain special formulae from the *sunnah* (traditions) and verses of the Qur'an in Arabic: the same *gris-gris* which we shall mention when talking about Bilali's (Ben Ali's) manuscript (see Chapter 11). It is a common practice for Sufis, especially *marabout* in West Africa, to write down copies of these litanies for people who are unable to recite them. The copy is then folded in a pouch and carried round the neck by the patient. A popular litany of the Shadhili order of Sufis (who also penetrated into West Africa and Mauritania along with the Qadiri order) known as the *Hizb al-Bahr*, or 'Litany of the Sea', contains the following lines:

> The believers have been tried, and mightily shaken, and lo, 'the hypocrites and those with sickness in their hearts say: Allah and His messenger have promised us nothing but delusion': So make us steadfast, give us the victory, and subject to us this sea, as You subjected the sea to Moses ... [26]

---

25 Raboteau (1978), 6.
26 Keller (trans.) (1998), 14.

This Shadhili litany, partially quoted, is well known as an extraordinary prayer with special properties accessible to those who have the right spiritual state and permission to make use of it. In fact the *Hizb al-Bahr* was a favourite invocation of seafarers—perhaps this very litany was made use of by some of the spiritually learned men and women captured as slaves in Africa as they endured the long and terrible middle passage across the 'Sea of Oppression' (*Bahr al-Dhuloom*).[27] In any case the reference to Moses in the chanted prayers and amulets (*gris-gris*) of Muslim slaves in America cannot be assumed to be unusual, especially if they were calling upon God to deliver them from the tribulation of their capture and deliver them from their cruel masters even before they had reached America.

It is known that the slave masters and many of their white preachers emphasised Christian virtues of meekness and submission to an earthly tyrant rather than confrontation along the lines of the Old Testament accounts of Moses. Bearing in mind that most of the slaves could not read or write (at least not in English)—how were they able to identify so quickly with the story of Moses and the struggle of the Children of Israel over and above those parts of the Bible which their white Christian preachers attempted to convey to them?[28] Whilst the African tone in some of the spirituals sung by slaves has been recognised by scholars, that they associated their plight with that of Moses and the Israelites has always been taken for granted:

There is a haunting quality about the spirituals that partly echoes African continuities in their music and performance style and

---

27 The Atlantic Ocean was known in Arabic sources as *Bahr al-Kabir* (Great Sea) and sometimes figuratively as *Bahr al-Dhuloom* (Sea of Darkness/Oppression).

28 See for example the so-called 'Slave Bible': 'It was originally published in London in 1807 on behalf of the Society for the Conversion of Negro Slaves [...] They used the Slave Bible to teach enslaved Africans how to read while at the same time introducing them to the Christian faith ... the Slave Bible contained only "select parts" of the biblical text. Its publishers deliberately removed portions of the biblical text, such as the exodus story, that could inspire hope for liberation.' https://www.museumofthebible.org/exhibits/slave-bible [accessed 12/04/2019].

partly reflects the trials and suffering, the sorrows and tribulations of life in bondage:

God call Moses! (Ay Lord!)
God call Moses! (Ay Lord!)
God call Moses! (Ay Lord!)
Time is a-rollin' on!
Moses free the people! (Ay Lord!)
Moses free the people! (Ay Lord!)
Moses free the people! (Ay Lord!)
Time is a-rollin' on!'[29]

A more thorough study of African Muslim slaves and their role on the plantation may reveal that not only the *music and performance style* but also the subject matter of these 'Christian' slave spirituals and rituals were wholly imported from Africa.

The second field of inquiry—*attempts to demonstrate 'day-to-day' forms of resistance*—could also benefit from a detailed examination of African Muslim slaves. For example, Herbert Aptheker argues in *Slave Resistance in the United States* that slaves deliberately poisoned the food of their masters, or damaged equipment or set fire to curtains and so forth.[30] All this, he says, was a means of resisting the institution of slavery without getting caught—surviving whilst wreaking a form of revenge upon one's oppressors. And yet arson attempts and other forms of vandalism lend support to the notion of Sambo—propagating the image of infantile and simplistic Negroes only capable of expressing anger at their masters through stealing food and throwing tantrums. If, however, Aptheker had taken into account how some Muslim slaves continued to preserve their literacy by writing the lessons they had learned in their schooling in Africa on the sands of the plantations where they laboured,[31] or actually

---

29 Joyner (1985), 164.
30 Aptheker (1971), 64.
31 A technique employed by 'Abd al-Rahman Ibrahima. See Chapter 8.

wrote entire manuscripts on African Islamic legal texts (which Bilali/ Ben Ali may or may not have been doing),[32] or how they manipulated the missionary zeal of Christian well-wishers in order to receive copies of the Qur'an[33]—how much more dignified his portrayal of day-to-day slave resistance would have been. Consider this account of a Muslim lady who continued to pray five times a day, according to the tenets of her faith (despite the punishing schedule of plantation life), and compare it to those methods of slave resistance mentioned by Aptheker:

> Muh gran come frum Africa too. Huh name wuz Ryna. I membuh
> wen I wuz a chile seein muh gran Ryna pray. Ebry mawnin at
> sunup she kneel on duh flo in uh ruhm an bow an tech uh head
> tuh duh flo tree time. Den she say a prayuh. I dohn membuh jis
> wut she say, but one wud she say use tuh make us chillun laugh.
> I membuh it wuz 'ashmnegad'. Wen she finish prayin she say
> 'Ameen, ameen, ameen'.[34]

As Sylviane Diouf points out about Bilali (Ben Ali) Muhammad's slave community:

> The Sea Island Muslims did not hide to pray; they did so very
> publicly in front of the other slaves, and some prayed in front of
> their masters. Thomas Spalding's grandson, for example, mentioned
> that his grandfather had slaves, 'devout Mussulmans, who prayed to
> Allah … morning, noon and evening,' and that Bilali faced east to
> 'call upon Allah'.[35]

The third and final field of inquiry resulting from responses to the Elkins thesis—*attempts at demonstrating the existence of sophisticated slave*

---

32   See Chapters 10 and 11.
33   Diouf (1998) Chapter 2 and especially 56-58.
34   Savannah Unit, WPA (1940), 155.
35   Diouf (1998), 62.

communities and cultures with their own social norms and values—includes the full range of writings from Deborah Gray White's *Ar'n't I a Woman?*[36] through to Angela Davis' *Women, Race and Class.*[37] This is not to say that this category only includes writings about female slaves, but rather any writing that attempts to describe some kind of social structure to slave life containing a family unit and a community of sorts. Needless to say the example above—of African Muslim slaves praying together—is a clear expression of solidarity and community. Likewise, an interesting article by Josephine Beoku-Betts[38] picks up on how some of Bilali's family continued to practise Muslim community obligations—in this case the duty of believers to give '*sadaqa*' or charity to those less fortunate than themselves—especially on certain holy days. It is particularly interesting, in the context of slave resistance, that Bilali's wife should have persisted in this practice. Since such a duty is not normally required from slaves or those in poverty themselves, the African Muslim slave's deliberate attempt to perform this duty—even if only as a mere gesture—indicates an adamant refusal to allow themselves to become the victims of slavery. Unfortunately, Beoku-Betts barely touches upon this point in her otherwise interesting article, and thus the '*saraka* cake' becomes just another quaint African food that survived the long and brutal passage to the New World.

This work focuses on the lives and legacy of just three slaves: Ayyub bin Suleiman, 'Abd al-Rahman Ibrahima, and Bilali (Ben Ali) Muhammad. These slaves produced writings and lived lives that may be taken as representative of the legacy of their fellow Muslim slaves. Their lives are fascinating and worthy of detailed study. But for the same reasons mentioned, we have only briefly detailed aspects of their lives, in order to leave room to focus more extensively on the significance of their writings as a response to slavery. In this sense, following the classification of slave studies we gave in the previous section, the current

---

36 White (1985).
37 Davis (1982).
38 Beoku-Betts (1994).

study may be categorised as emphasising slave resistance, rather than highlighting slave retentions (i.e. aspects of African life and culture that slaves were able to maintain in America). The strength of African Muslim retentions in slavery should, however, be self-evident when we realise the real power and significance of the African Muslim slave's method of resisting slavery: a means of resistance that transcends even its own historical context by confronting the dispossessing force of slavery with the emancipating force of an epistemology that belonged and belongs entirely to the slave (*'abd*).

3

'All Men are Slaves'

It is only as a servant that every being in the heavens and on earth,
without exception, comes to the Benevolent One ...

—Qur'an (19:93)[1]

All creation is in servitude, and likewise, according to Islam, all men are slaves. When the Muslim envoy and companion of the Prophet Muhammad, Rib'ee ibn 'Aamir entered the court of the Persian Emperor in the early days of Islam, he declared the purpose of the Muslims to be as follows:

> God has sent us and has brought us here so that we may liberate
> those who so desire from the slavery of men to the worship and
> servitude of God; And from the narrowness of this world, to the
> vastness of this world and the Hereafter, And from the oppression
> of religions, to the justice of Islam.[2]

---

[1] Cleary (trans.) (2004).

[2] Personal translation from a well-known account related by Tabari in his *Tarikh al-rusul wa'l-muluk*. See Friedmann (trans.) (1992), 67.

In the Qur'anic cosmology one might say that there are really only two types of human being—and both are slaves. There is the slave who deludes himself that he is free, acting in whatever manner he pleases and behaving as if he is master over creation. And there is the slave who acknowledges his helplessness before God, surrenders himself completely to Him and, entering into a state of *islam*—literally 'submission' or 'surrender'—becomes the wilful servant of the Creator and so attains to 'peace' (another of the meanings of the word 'Islam'). Since God is free from all wants and needs (*ghaniyy-ul-hameed*) the secret of slavehood to God manifests as emancipation from slavery to creation and liberation from the tribulations of existence and acceptance into God's loving care. Such a slave strives to use his attributes in a manner pleasing to his Master, is afraid to overstep the limits that God has proscribed, always seeking His good pleasure and observing the proper etiquette (*'adab*)— knowing that though he cannot easily perceive it, his Lord is observing his conduct and controlling all his affairs.

Both types of slaves live on earth (*al-'ard*), to which, in the Qur'anic world view as in the Biblical, their great ancestor, Adam, was assigned. But the earth—which being a creature is itself a slave—manifests differently before the two types of men. For the truly 'Adamic' slave the world is *'aalam*—an abode of signs, a place of symbolism and indication, by which the astute and literate wayfarer can trace his way back home. Thus the learned scholar in Islam is called *'aalim*, and knowledge itself *'ilm* from the same tri-literal Arabic root: *'a_la_ma*. For the ignorant slave who acts as if he is free and does as he pleases, the world is *dunya*— literally an abode where people 'reach out for grapes they can never grasp': always the pleasures of the *dunya* seem near at hand, and yet always they prove to be just out of reach; a fleeting and deceptive realm where:

1. *Vying for more diverts you,*
2. *until you go to the graves.*[3]

---

3   The Qur'an (102:1-2). Cleary (trans.) (2004).

The slave who has entered into a state of *islam* (i.e. self-surrender)—a state that can only be realised consciously and voluntarily—has rejected the sovereignty of creatures over himself, and accepted only the sovereignty of the One who does not require servants. All are already His servants and engaged in His worship:

> 49. *And all in the heavens and all on earth bow to God,*
>   *from animals to angels,*
>   *without being proud;*
> 50. *they are in awe of their Lord above them, and they do what they*
>   *are directed.*[4]

Thus Allah makes such a servant master of all creation and gives him true freedom, which, like existence, is contingent upon the Creator. At the same time Allah has left the slave who 'rejects'—i.e. the *kaafir* or 'concealer of the truth'—in his delusion, and so he is enslaved by whatever he pursues and fears, and is the lowest of all creation. For whereas all creatures, apart from *jinn* and men,[5] worship God involuntarily in that they lack the ability not to do so, the human *kaafir* rejects God voluntarily: all creation is therefore made superior to him, and he is the slave of all of them.

> [...] from 'Aaishah [the Prophet's wife] may Allah be pleased with
> her, that the Prophet upon whom be the peace and blessings of
> God said: 'An angel came to me and said: God sends blessings
> upon you and says: If you wish you may be a Prophet–King or a
> Slave–Messenger. So Jibreel (the angel Gabriel)—upon whom be
> peace—indicated to me that I should humble myself. So I said:
> 'A Prophet–Slave.' 'Aaishah said: So after that day the Prophet upon
> whom be the blessings of God and Peace never ate whilst reclining,

---

4   The Qur'an (16:49-50). Cleary (trans.) (2004).
5   For a brief discussion on Jinn see Chapter 10.

saying: 'I eat as a slave eats and I sit as a slave sits. Since indeed I am a slave.'[6]

Thus slavery in Islam takes on a special meaning and the slave (*'abd*) is associated linguistically with the concept of worship through the words *'uboodiyyah* (the state or 'station' of worship) and *'ibaadah* (worship). The condition of a slave in the *dunya* in relation to his earthly master is the same as the relationship between the believer and God, but with some crucial exceptions: God is not in need of slaves and so elevates them to stations of intimacy with Himself to the extent and in the manner He pleases; the slave is in need of God and petitions Him constantly; God loves His slaves and His slaves are in love of God. As the following narration reveals, the reality of slavehood to God is love itself—the distinguishing feature of slavery to God compared to slavery to man is that the slaves of God are enslaved by their love of God. It is the slavery of a lover for his beloved, the slavery of attraction (*mahabba* or *jadhb*) and ecstasy, not the slavery of compulsion and suffering:

On the authority of Abu Hurayrah, may God be well pleased with him, who reported that the Messenger of God, God's blessings and peace be upon him, said:

Verily God Most High has said: "Whoever shows enmity to a friend of Mine I shall declare war on him. And my servant draws nearer to Me with nothing more beloved to Me than that which I have made obligatory on him. And My servant keeps drawing nearer to Me with supererogatory works until I love him, and when I love him I become his hearing with which he hears, his sight with which he sees, his hands with which he seizes and his legs with which he walks. And if he were to ask

---

6   A well-known *hadith* of the Prophet Muhammad recorded for example in the *Kitaab al-Zuhd* of Ibn Hanbal. See Ibn Hanbal, Ahmad b. Muhammad. *al-Musnad*. Cairo, 1313 AH, Kitab al-Zuhd, Beirut, 1994.

Me [for something] I would certainly give it to him, and if he were to seek refuge in Me, I would certainly grant him refuge."[7]

Since slavery or *'uboodiyyah* to Allah is a rank to be desired, Muslims have always been proud to call themselves 'slaves of Allah'. It may even be said that Islam is seen as the way to perfect one's *'uboodiyyah* to God, which entails perfecting the slave's good manners (*khuluq*) towards the Creator (*Khaliq*) and His creation (*makhluq*). Thus the famous narration quoted by al-Ghazali in which the Prophet Muhammad said: 'I was sent only to perfect the noble qualities of Character.'[8]

Given that Muslims esteemed slavery, in this sense, no Muslim slave could ever perceive himself as 'really' the slave of an earthly master—a Muslim enslaved to a human being remained, truly and always, only Allah's slave. Many African Muslim slaves in antebellum America bore names that identified them as slaves of God—for example, *Ibrahima 'abd al-Rahman*: Abraham the Slave of the Merciful (*al-Rahman* being one of the Names of Allah). As Ibrahima and the other Muslim slaves we shall look at indicated by their states and their actions—i.e. their *khuluq*—no human being (*makhluq*) could convince them that they were the slaves of anyone other than Allah (*al-Khaliq*).

Al-Jurayri said, 'The servants of benefit are many, but the servants of the Benefactor are precious.' I heard Abu Ali al-Daqqaq say, 'You are the slave of the one who holds you in bondage and captivity. If you are in bondage to your ego, you are the slave of

---

7 *Hadith* no. 38 from *Arbaeen an Nawawiyya*. The translation is from: *Guezzou, Mokrane, A Treasury of Hadith: A Commentary on Nawawi's Forty Prophetic Traditions*, Kube Publishing, 2016 p. 154. N.B.: who is the slave here and who the master—as now the slave is guaranteed all he requests from his 'master'? 'Abd al-Rahman Ibrahima and the other slaves who manifested *'uboodiyyah* in its truest sense by accepting their fate and petitioning their true 'master' with *faatihah* were ultimately successful in escaping slavery and returning to their homelands. They sought refuge through *'uboodiyyah* and seem to have obtained it, remarkably! For more on this see Chapter 9.

8 Winter (1997), 7.

your ego, and if you are in bondage to your worldly life, you are the slave of your worldly life.'[9]

And yet not one of the handful of authors that have bothered to consider the case of Muslim slaves in antebellum America have taken this concept of *'uboodiyyah* into due consideration. This is despite the fact that the concept of 'slavery to God' is so deeply ingrained in the Qur'anic world view that no Muslim with even a basic Islamic education before the twentieth century could have failed to appreciate it. To be fair, Sylviane Diouf, both in the title and in the very last paragraph of her excellent work on the subject *Servants of Allah: African Muslims Enslaved in the Americas*, does hint at the undoubtedly important role of *'uboodiyyah* in the response of African Muslims to New World Slavery. Her summing up is eloquent and to the point:

> [...] They saw their families torn apart and their loved ones killed.
> In the midst of abuse and contempt, they continued to pray, fast,
> be charitable, read, write on the sand, help one another, sing their
> lonesome tunes, and display pride in themselves, their religion, and
> their culture.
>
> The African Muslims may have been, in the Americas, the slaves of
> Christian masters, but their minds were free. They were the servants
> of Allah.[10]

It is important to note that Islam's concept of slavery—in terms of the enslavement of one human being by another—must also have been tempered by its emphasis on *'uboodiyyah*. The phrase *La hawla wa la quwwata illa billah*—'there is no power or authority save God'—is a regular feature of Muslim prayers and litanies and occurs often, in various forms, in the Qur'an. It is a phrase with which Ayyub bin Suleiman—the

---

9   From *al-Risala* of al-Qushayri. Harris, R., (trans.) (2002), 240.
10 Diouf (1998), 210.

African who became a slave in Colonial Maryland (otherwise known as Job Ben Solomon)—ended his correspondence to John Chandler in 1734.[11] If slavery to created things is an illusion and a consequence of an individual's rejection of his true condition of 'slavery' to God—if indeed there is no power or authority other than Allah—then to attempt to enslave another human being in the full sense of the word as used in English, the sense in which it was usually employed in antebellum slavery, is clearly the antithesis of Islam and contrary to what *'uboodiyyah* implies: namely that all creation is dependent entirely upon God, knowingly or otherwise. Precisely for this reason, however, the idea of slavery in the sense of an earthly master owning another human being as property with no human rights is alien to Islam.

Ironically, some writers construe the tem *'abd* as 'servant' (of Allah)—as Diouf translates the word in the title of her book—rather than 'slave' of Allah. Presumably this is because of the negative association the term carries in English, precisely because of our historical memory of the slave trade. But when we consider the term 'slave' as meaning ownership, then, as the Opening Chapter of the Qur'an—the *al-Faatihah*—suggests in its use of the word *Rabb* (Lord) for Allah and in the plea of the worshipper 'thee do we worship' (using the term *n'abudu* from the root *'abada* and *'abd*), the relationship between God and His creatures is more honestly expressed, in Qur'anic terms, as one of Master and Slave—not Master and Servant.[12] Conversely when we examine the relationship of a 'slave' to an earthly 'master' in the Islamic context, we find that the slave is not property as such. Rather the slave is more akin to a 'servant' or indentured labourer, or perhaps serf; and the slave master a 'possessor' or 'employer'—but in any case, categorically not 'owner'. Thus the Africanist Philip D. Curtin describes the status of a slave in Muslim lands as 'a kind of ward undergoing education'.[13] The possibility of 'owning' a human being is reserved strictly for Allah. And yet even in this case, as the

---

11 For Ayyub's story see Chapter 7.

12 See Chapter 9 for more on this.

13 Curtin (1990), 41.

tradition quoted above indicates, the slave of Allah is able to—and indeed supposed to—rise in ranks towards his Lord, until their relationship is transferred from one of Master and Slave to one of mutual love in which the beloved and the lover are no longer easily distinguished. As suggested above, this is only possible because the slavehood of the believer is the slavery of love and attraction, not of compulsion and suffering.

> The *adab* [etiquette] of the slave is abasement,
> And the slave should not abandon *adab*.
> When his abasement is complete,
> He obtains love and draws near.[14]

In choosing to write the *al-Faatihah*, or the Opening Chapter of the Qur'an, at almost every opportunity, slaves like 'Abd al-Rahman were echoing a sentiment felt and often expressed by all Muslim slaves both individually and collectively. To rephrase Diouf's concluding remark quoted above, by drawing attention to the *al-Faatihah*, 'Abd al-Rahman Ibrahima was saying: 'I may be, in America, the *servant* of a Christian master, but I remain forever the *slave* of Allah'. In other words 'Abd al-Rahman and the other slaves who wrote out the *al-Faatihah* (of all the Arabic slave writings the *al-Faatihah* appears most frequently) were declaring their freedom from created beings, and celebrating literally, in the words 'thee do we worship' (*iyyaka n'abudu*), the Lordship of Allah over themselves and indeed over 'all the worlds'—including the 'world' of antebellum America:

> *Praise be to Allah, Lord of the Worlds ...* [15]

---

14 Two lines of poetry quoted in the manuscript of *Sidi 'Ali al-Jamal of Fez*, translated by Aisha 'Abd ar-Rahman (1977), 47. The original Arabic work was until very recently only accessible in manuscript form but is studied amongst scholars of *tasawwuf* to this day. The English translation has been criticised by several of the same scholars, though the author of the incumbent work is grateful to the translator for bringing such a remarkable text to his awareness at a time when his grasp of Arabic was worse than it is now.

15 The Qur'an (1:2). Pickthall (trans.) (2008).

II

It would be easy here to pre-empt the third section of our study and go into a detailed exposition of 'Abd al-Rahman's use of the *Faatihah* at a level of discourse which remained completely outside the cognisance of the white American recipients of this beginning *Surah* or 'chapter' of the Qur'an. In doing this, however, we are in danger of relating 'Abd al-Rahman's story before we wish to: for the story itself belongs not in an introduction, but in the substance and heart of any work about African Muslim slaves in America. But it is with a view to the importance of the *Surah al-Faatihah* not only in Islam generally, but also in the frequent use made of it in Muslim slave writings, that we have labelled this section with the same name, and why we must bring it to bear so early on in this work, a symbolic representation of all that follows. For the *al-Faatihah* is eloquently and unequivocally the African Muslim response to antebellum slavery. Most surprising of all, it is a response directed not, as might be expected and is often believed, at the white Americans who practised slavery, nor at those among them who opposed it; but rather at the real and only cause of the African Muslim's enslavement and humiliation from his or her own perspective:

In the Name of Allah, all praise belongs to Allah, both good and evil are by the will of Allah.[16]

III

For Ronald T. Judy the ambiguity of the Ben Ali Manuscript—another African Muslim slave's writing—allows it to 'elude the [Western] philosophical, historical, canonical, and intentionality readings that would grasp at it and prove its undoing.'[17] In the penultimate section of this

---

16 Al-Badawi (trans.), Habeeb Abdullah, *The Prophetic Invocations*, (Starlatch Press, 2000), 39.

17 Wahneema Lubiano in Judy (1993), xv.

study we address Bilali's (Ben Ali's) manuscript, and Judy's analysis of it in more detail. Although not taken directly from the Qur'an, like 'Abd al-Rahman's *Surah al-Faatihah*, the Bilali text is also a religious one and contains within it Qur'anic verses and formulae. But Judy's analysis, whilst admirable and innovative, still remains methodologically within the very conceptual paradigms which he rightly recognises as being confronted by the text itself. What Judy does not do, though he comes near it, is to break through the epistemology which encapsulates all discourse and writing on slavery: Judy's work, like all the 'philosophical, philological, historical, and canonical' writings that have gone before it, and which for him, the Bilali manuscript challenges, originates—with some qualification—from the same epistemological paradigm. Judy's work is acceptable within the same dialectic as Kant, though for Judy, Kant's views are anathema.[18] Many, if not all, of the classical Muslim scholars from whom these slaves derived their education are categorically unacceptable within that same dialectic as authorities for knowledge *per se*. This is why, given the secular bent of our contemporary epistemology, the present work, laden as it is with Islamic quotations, may appear to some as overly devotional and therefore decadent. And yet, within the Islamic epistemology, secularism—i.e. a *dunya*-based world view—is equally decadent, ignorant and backward.

To truly understand slavery we have to break through the intellectual barriers that enslave us within a received, secular, and Eurocentric approach to knowledge. This applies to slavery as equally as it applies to any other intellectual inquiry about ourselves: for in the final analysis any study of the *Other* is really an unveiling of the *Self*. Judy is right in concluding that the enigma of the Bilali (Ben Ali) text protects it from the canon formation gestures of academia. Since the Bilali text proved

---

18 By this we are not saying that Judy's views would be acceptable to Kant. Quite the contrary! However, Judy's arguments derive from the same epistemological foundations as Kant's. That is: they derive from Western thinking about the '*Other*' filtered through the collective experience of modernity in our times, which in Judy's case means 'post-modernism'.

not to be an 'autobiography' at all, it became difficult to know what to make of it. It was a received wisdom, rather a religious truth, that if slaves ever wrote, they wrote about their miserable lives and their glorious road to emancipation: but Bilali was not only writing in a foreign language, his subject was something other than himself. His work challenged and challenges the acceptable discourse about Negroes and Negro writing; it could not be controlled like Equiano's or Douglass's work—and consequently has been assigned obscurity and anonymity, disappearing almost entirely from consideration. Thus from the viewpoint of the very epistemology it threatens, Judy is quite right in stating that the Bilali manuscript is an enigma and mystery. Likewise, despite our secular pretensions towards understanding the *al-Faatihah* and other verses of the Qur'an written by slaves in the New World, in our current secular milieu there is no room for the sacred.

Having said this, Bilali Muhammad (Ben Ali), 'Abd al-Rahman Ibrahima, Ayyub bin Suleiman (Job Ben Solomon), and the many other slaves whom we do not mention in this study were not writing *from* a Western socio-intellectual milieu; nor were they writing *to* its secular (that is to say '*dunyawi*, not 'irreligious') audience. They were writing *in* a peculiar institution, which their very presence as literate black Africans challenged and confronted. They were heirs to an Islamic cosmology that sees the universe as an abode full of symbolism and pregnant with meaning beyond the surface context: a world view radically different from our contemporary one. For Muslims, speech itself, letters, words and even individual phonemes are creatures. In a sense the writings of these slaves are alive, and reveal oceans of meaning that the passage of time has not been able to smother. But the writing is in a language that is barely understood: an Arabic, yes, but more than that, a Qur'anic Arabic understandable only through the Qur'anic epistemology. And this, as Judy recognises, marks their works as dangerous, because—to the degree that they are unintelligible as Arabic works (as opposed to the English-language works of other slaves), they are able to elude rigid classification and deconstruction within the Western dialectic of knowledge and the neo-European treatment of the *Other*. But more than this, to the degree that they are intelligible as Arabic works from the last remnants of a widespread classical Islamic educational model (before the dismantling of that model by colonialist pogroms)—and therefore a thoroughly Qur'anic cosmology—the original meanings of their writings are preserved against any interpretations that white amanuenses, well-wishers, or friends may have attempted to impose upon them; something which the English-language works of non-Muslim slaves could not escape: i.e. the process of agency. In other words, there is in most cases an original foreign language (Arabic) text against which any attempt at manipulating the *meanings* intended by the Muslim African slaves are exposed.

But Judy seems to emphasise the dual nature of these texts from the point of view of Western academia without mentioning the logical corollary of this fact—probably because his work is rooted in American literary studies—a subject which itself can be traced within a Western intellectual discourse about the *Other*. Although 'Abd al-Rahman's *al-Faatihah* writings, for example, could be labelled the 'Lord's Prayer' by the white Americans surrounding him—'Abd al-Rahman is even able to state that they are the 'Lord's Prayer' and engage in a kind of intellectual counter-offensive—his true intentions, and his response to the potentially dispossessing institution of antebellum slavery, is in fact eloquent and empowering. He actually challenges and confounds the processes of dispossession by placing the foundational texts of an alternative (i.e. Islamic and African) cosmology in direct confrontation with the social and intellectual elite, the 'Imams' and 'scholars' of the society which sought to reduce him to the status of chattel and whose world view actually justified the enslavement and treatment of black Africans in this manner. Moreover, in doing this, 'Abd al-Rahman and the other slaves we mention were actually juxtaposing and thereby challenging the neo-European/Western epistemology—that is, the Western theory of knowledge and the '*dunyawi* world view—against the Qur'anic one: a challenge which defines in many respects, the challenge of modernity—to come to terms with its own shortcomings, to re-evaluate the origins of its own epistemological foundations and to confront, in all honesty, the mythology upon which it has built itself a precarious civilisation.

The African Muslim's enslavement in the New World was thus an encounter between two different worlds: a secular and materialistic world emerging out of a formerly Christian civilisation, and a deeply spiritual Islamic world that would fall into political retreat against the emerging onslaught of colonialism. An encounter which occurred at the threshold of historical time as the old worlds of the Christian and Muslim *'aalam* slipped slowly into the new world of the Christian and now secular *dunya*. In this chapter, as in the entire study, we have only touched the surface of an endless sea of meanings and a limitless horizon of knowledge which the study of the African Muslim encounter with transatlantic slavery promises to reveal.

As one world recedes, another opens up. Allah says:

He has let free the two bodies
Of flowing water, Meeting together
Between them is a Barrier
Which they do not transgress:
Then which of the favours
Of your Lord will ye deny? [19]

Thus the second part of this study (that is, the following section) seeks to represent the historical context behind the emergence of transatlantic slavery from within an Afro–Islamic perspective that emphasises the cultural encounter of the Islamic and African world with European expansionism. Within this context, Muslims from Africa became slaves in the New World, including antebellum America. As the brief remarks in this chapter have sought to indicate, their behaviour—particularly those slaves who left writings in Arabic—was to emphasise their Islamic

---

19 Qur'an 55:19-21. Ali, Abdullah Yusuf, (trans.) (1938).

culture and civilisation as a valid and powerful counter-offensive against the dispossessing processes of antebellum slavery—i.e. those aspects of antebellum slavery and society which sought to deny and erode the African's sense of self, humanity, intelligence, civility, dignity and cultural–religious validity. Moreover, they were, in resorting to this mode of real and effective resistance, not making any appeals to the members of the society and institutions that had enslaved them or sought to free them from one kind of slavery only to use them in another type (where, for example, they might function as missionaries to other 'savage' Negroes in Africa). Rather their writings are direct testimonies to their religious convictions and actual praxis of the requirements of their faith. Their writings, such as the *al-Faatihah*, and their behaviour were in accordance with the Qur'anic injunction:

Remember me. I will remember you ... [20]

Some of their lives are briefly discussed in the third section, which we have entitled: *Orisons of the Slave*.

Where opposites meet, great affairs occur, and so the implications of this juxtaposition between two epistemological traditions—with the emphasis necessarily on the post 9/11 world in which we now live—are discussed in the fourth section entitled: *The Endless Sea*. In the poetry of the Sufis, knowledge is often referred to as an ocean, or oceans, and a favourite aphorism of Muslim learning has always been: 'the one who gives a part of himself to knowledge, knowledge gives him nothing; whilst the one who gives all of himself to knowledge, knowledge gives him only a part'.

I marvelled at an Ocean without shore
and a shore without ocean,

---

20 The Qur'an (2:152). The translation of this verse is taken from Al-Badawi (2000) where it is cited at x.

At a morning Light with no darkness
And a Night with no dawn,
At a Sphere without any location
Known to pagans or priests,
At an azure Dome, raised high, revolving,
All Compelling Power its centre,
And at a rich Earth without dome or location,
The Mystery concealed.[21]

And so we have labelled the following section of this study '*Alif*', the next one '*Laam*' and the concluding part '*Meem*'. For knowledge is overwhelming, and emancipation from the slavery of ignorance is not easily achieved: neither by a Bill of Rights, nor by a Declaration of Independence. So long as we are unaware of shortcomings within ourselves, we are bound to the shackles of the Self. This is as true for the family, the city, the society, the country, and the civilisation. If some of the major figures of our intellectual tradition could remark so easily that a human is savage or stupid, or even sub-human, by reason of his colour, and that that justifies his being brutalised by those more 'human' than he;[22] that it has taken us so long and so much effort to recognise the fault in such remarks, but without acknowledging what else might be wrong in the tradition that celebrates the authors of these remarks as geniuses of the first order, means that we have yet to confront our own demons— demons that we have cast, and continue to cast upon the *Other*:

---

21 Hirtenstein (1999), 16.

22 See for example Immanuel Kant, 'Of National Characteristics, so far as They Depend upon the Distinct Feeling of the Beautiful and Sublime' in *Observations on the Feeling of the Beautiful and the Sublime*, where amongst other things we are treated to an example of the 'great' philosopher's reasoning: 'Of course, Father Labat reports that a Negro carpenter, whom he reproached for haughty treatment towards his wives, answered: "You whites are indeed fools, for first you make great concessions to your wives, and afterward you complain when they drive you mad." And it might be that there were something in this which perhaps deserved to be considered; but in short, this fellow was quite black from head to foot, a clear proof that what he said was stupid' (trans. Goldthwait, 1991, 110-114).

Say to those who see what they reject in us;
By the Purity of our drink,
You see yourselves in us.[23]

The story that these slaves tell us as articulate *Others*—speaking not only for their fellow Muslims, but for all Africans and all *Others* in any context—the message that they bring, the cry that they make, like so many *Muezzins* calling from their minarets in the East and in the West, is a call to an emancipation that has yet to come. The legacy of the African Muslim slaves in antebellum America, when considered as an encounter of epistemological consequences, is therefore, if we may be so bold as to play on the self-applauding title of Kant's work, a *Prolegomena to Any Future Emancipation*.

And Allah alone knows the truth.

---

23 'Abd ar-Rahman (1977), 139 and 234.

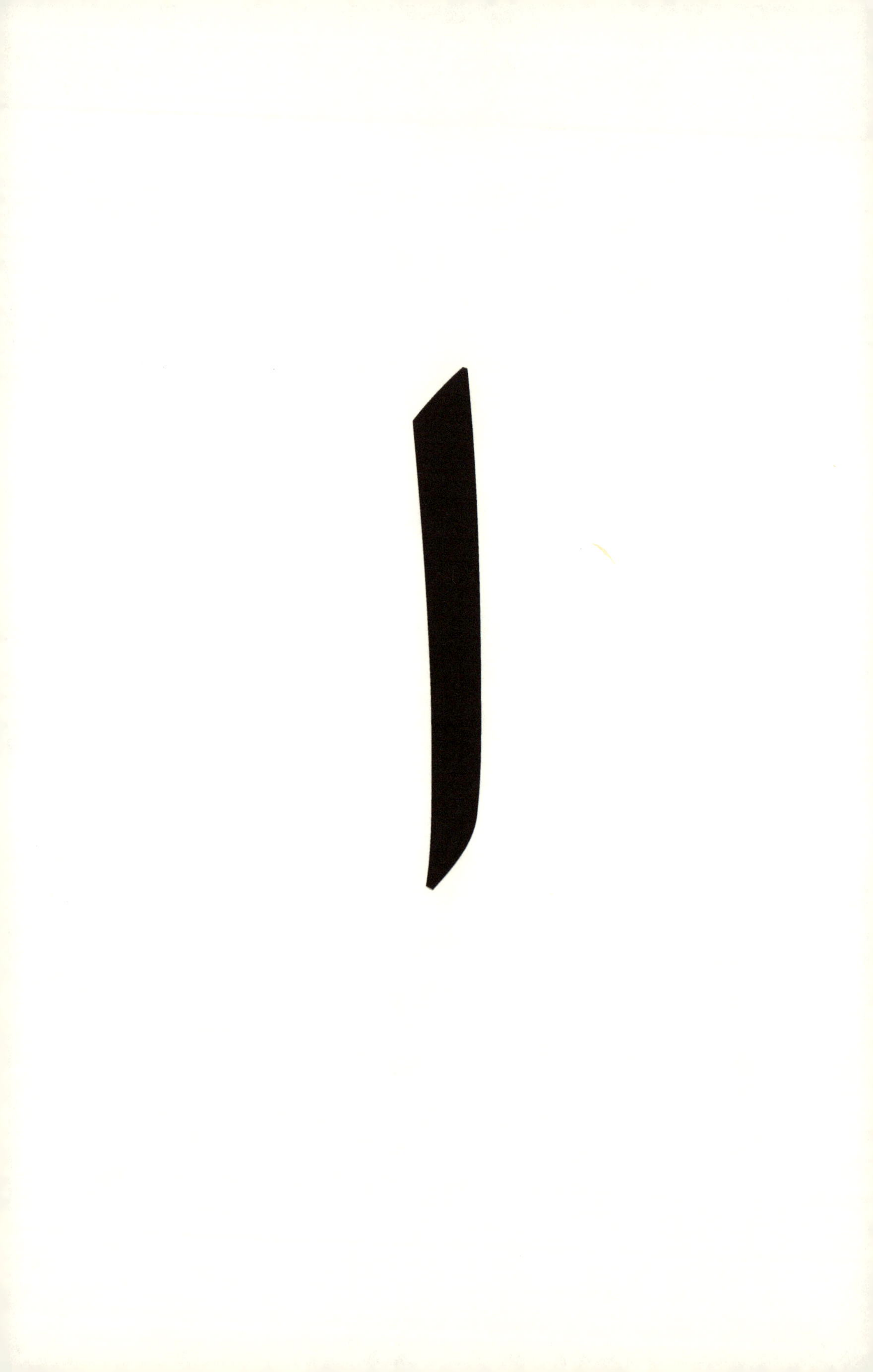

II

Alif

The Relocation
of History

This part of the study seeks to contextualise the origins of transatlantic slavery in relation to contemporaneous trends in African and Islamic history.

Having begun in the previous section with a look at existing studies on African Muslims enslaved in the Americas, and having described the major themes of the current study, there now follows in the next chapter a general overview of the origins of the slave trade and colonialism in relation to Islamic history. Here we deliberately seek to disengage (as far as possible, and appropriate) the issue of antebellum slavery from a Eurocentric perspective. At the same time, Chapter 4 seeks to redefine the subject of inquiry within the conceptual framework of a dynamic cross-cultural encounter between a 'West' in the infant stages of its colonial expansion into a much wider world and a once rich Muslim civilisation showing signs of decay. An important result of this encounter is apparent in the current trend towards an increasingly homogenous, secular and 'quasi-Western', global corporate culture. In this chapter the Muslim slaves are seen as the first peoples of the Islamic world to experience and deal with the pressures of this wholesale export of the European world view—a view which, until very recently, denied non-European cultures any legitimate form of self-expression as equals. We suggest here a useful comparison between the Muslim slave and the non-Muslim slave's manner of coping with American slavery, as a paradigm for later Muslim and non-Muslim people's responses to colonialism and the pressures to adopt the foreign and therefore alien world view of the 'Western' powers.

Chapter 5: *Muezzin and Hegira*, goes on to look at the extent of Islamisation in those parts of Africa from which the majority of slaves derived. This includes a look at the position of slavery in Islam and the socio-political background of African Muslim and African non-Muslim interaction in the African context, which undoubtedly affected the behaviour of the two groups towards each other as slaves in the New World.

4

New World Rising

Corruption has appeared on land and sea because
of what people have earned by their acts,
To make them taste Some of what they have
done that they might turn back.

—The Qur'an (30-41)[1]

In confining our inquiry to African Muslims as opposed to Muslims in Africa, in looking at slaves rather than slaves and freemen, in looking only at antebellum America rather than the Americas as a whole, we have deliberately limited our study to a small aspect of a much wider theme: the theme of non-Europeans, principally Muslims from Africa, in the New World as travellers, explorers, traders and settlers from as early as the thirteenth century. To this category of Muslim presence in the New World we must add slaves, and it is with these men and women we are concerned. They were amongst the last of the Muslims to arrive in the Americas before colonialism completely ravished the vast Islamic world of which they were a part: stretching from the Malay archipelago in the Pacific Ocean to the

---

[1] The Qur'an (30:41), Cleary (trans.) (2004).

shores of West Africa and the Gold Coast, where Islam met the Atlantic. They came across this 'Sea of Darkness', as Muslim geographers sometimes called it, involuntarily—often having been abducted or taken prisoner in an African war and sold off to white slave traders on the coast. Their African homelands were already at the threshold of two different worlds, the *Dar-al-Islam* or 'Abode of Peace' where they lived, and the *Dar-al-Kufr* or the 'Abode of Infidelity' with which they often had close commercial, political and cultural contact. There was a subtle spiritual and physical barrier between these two worlds, even when they appeared to coexist in locations of mixed Muslim and non-Muslim residence or interaction. Nevertheless these Muslims were all Africans, and all black. Not one of the slaves we shall consider in this study was an Arab or a Moor—although in almost every case they were labelled as such by the white Europeans and Americans who met them. To this day, for the most part—though not entirely—even African-American scholars and writers have ignored them, as if these Muslims did not properly belong to Africa.

But just as Africa was not, and is not to this day, exclusively Muslim, the African Muslim was not, and is not, exclusively African. He shared and shares in a much wider world of like-minded believers, each engaged in the same spiritual quest, each demonstrating through symbolism, speech and action the same world view. Every Muslim, regardless of race, culture and language, would have awoken in the old Muslim world to the same call to prayer—the *adhan*, echoing from the *Muezzin*'s voice in the same deep Arabic melodies (though not without local interpretations of the sounds) from the minaret of every mosque in all the lands from Timbuktu to Xian and beyond. Every one of them from Africa to the furthest reaches of Asia would have greeted his fellow Muslim with the same greeting *asalaamualaikum* 'peace be with you' and heard the same reply, *wa-alaikum-as-salaam wa rahmatullah*: 'and with you be peace and the mercy of God'. This vast mass of humanity, speaking different tongues and enjoying different foods, but yet observing the same dietary requirements, would all have fasted during Ramadhan, paid the obligatory alms due (*zakah*), recited and memorised the same book (*al-Qur'an*) and dreamt the same dream—for some a dream manifested in reality—of travelling to the Sacred Mosque (*Masjid al-Haram*) in Mecca and performing the great pilgrimage (*al-Hajj*) in symbolic manifestation of the unity of mankind (*ummah*) and the Unicity (*tawheed*) of God.

> The close view [of Muslim prayer] is of a man or a line of men oriented in one direction bowing and prostrating. The distant view reveals not a line of men, but seen globally, a circle of devotion centring on the point of the *Ka'bah*. So that what we have is a series of concentric circles moving towards the Makkan focus of adoration. There is another dimension that must be considered to make this a moving and living picture—and that is time. Qur'an specifies that *salah* [i.e. the Muslim ritual prayer] is fixed at appointed times, the times being taken very simply from the sun's position in the sky. There are five necessary sets of prostration, the first being at dawn when the first thread of white light appears on the horizon and lasting until the sun's disc is about visible—the second is at noon immediately following the meridian—the third is mid afternoon—the fourth, the sunset, after the descent of the sun's disc—and the last, the night prayer, when the light leaves the sky. Thus, in the global picture, it follows that what you have is an endless rippling movement of circle upon circle, in to the centre point of the *Ka'bah*, that virtually never ceases, as the sun is constantly rising and setting across the world. At the centre is the Ancient House, of which the Qur'an says:

> > 'The first House established for the people was at Makka, a pure place, and a guidance to all beings.' (Qur'an 3:96)

> So the focus of this worship and opening to the Universal Reality is a place that has been celebrated from the beginning of man's story as a place of meeting between the slave and the Lord.'[2]

---

2   Sufi (2002), 76–77.

And yet the African Muslims, as with Muslims everywhere, were not devoid of cultural and customary differences that distinguished them racially and geographically. The ocean of Islam, with its Mecca-centric rhythm, is rainbow coloured and its waves—all rising and falling—have their own peculiar shapes and movements and dance. Islam has always been able to foster in its adherents the ability to transcend racial differences in a common celebration of universal humanity, without destroying the positive aspects of cultural diversity. Testifying to the two-fold creed of *la-ilaha-illallah muhamadu-rasoolullah* ('there is no god save God [Allah] and Muhammad is His Messenger') is the only requirement to enter into its family of believers and to experiencing what Muslims call the 'sweetness of faith' or *hilaawatul-Imaan*.

Colonialism, however, has bred contrary tensions in the Muslim world that reverberate to this day. Strands of modernist Muslims, unable to cope with differences in a once rich Muslim world now stripped of its former glory, unable to come to terms with the vibrant expressions of the Islamic teaching within the sanctuary or *furqan* (criterion) of the Qur'an and *Sunnah* (Prophetic example) and the guiding principles articulated by the *fuqaha* (jurisprudence) of the traditional *madhaahib* ('Schools of Law'), have invented an Islamic model which internalises the world view of the colonialist, rather than the traditional (transmitted) epistemology of Islam.

> Self-evidently, the belief that terror can remake the world is not a result of any kind of scientific inquiry. It is faith, pure and simple. No less incontrovertibly, the faith is uniquely western. Western societies are ruled by the myth that, as the rest of the world absorbs science and becomes modern, it is bound to become secular, enlightened and peaceful—as, contrary to all evidence, they imagine themselves to be. With its attack on the Twin Towers, Al Qaeda destroyed this myth; and yet it continues to be believed.[3]

---

3   Gray (2003), 118.

It is significant that a major effect of colonialism in the Muslim world has been the dismantling of traditional Islamic education—the kind of education that many of the slaves received—and which they were able to put to good use in liberating themselves in the hostile environment of slavery in America. It was this education which allowed them to be free even when confined to the plantation, which earned them a reputation for uprightness, and even magical abilities in the eyes of their fellow slaves and their 'owners'—both of whom sought their assistance for protection and aid in times of need. The Muslim slaves seemed keenly aware of the importance of their Islamic education, many of them—as we shall see—going to great pains to preserve their learning in an environment that was hardly conducive to living, let alone learning. Other slaves, lacking pen and paper, would copy the lessons acquired from their Islamic schooling in Africa on the sands of the plantations where they were kept, using sticks as writing instruments.[4]

In the absence of this traditional Islamic education system and the subsequent decline of Islamic epistemology in the Muslim world, some Muslims have resorted to a quasi-Western 'ideology', outwardly Islamic but inwardly thoroughly Western in its militant and radical dimensions. The celebrated political philosopher Professor John Gray unequivocally draws attention to this fact when he writes:

No cliché is more stupefying than that which describes Al Qaeda as a throwback to medieval times. It is a by-product of globalisation. Like the worldwide drug cartels and virtual business corporations that developed in the Nineties, it evolved at a time when financial deregulation had created vast pools of offshore wealth and organised crime had gone global. Its most distinctive feature— projecting a privatised form of organised violence worldwide—was impossible in the past. Equally, the belief that a new world can be hastened by spectacular acts of destruction is nowhere found in

---

4   See Diouf (1998) Chapter 4 where she cites several examples of all these practices.

medieval times. Al Qaeda's closest precursors are the revolutionary anarchists of late nineteenth century Europe.[5]

Whereas Muslims in pre-colonial times would have been able to communicate with each other wherever they met in the world quite easily, through the medium of classical Arabic, with some exceptions the new international language of communication among Muslims is English and their intellectual pursuits in almost every dimension are epistemologically founded within Western paradigms. Interestingly enough one of the most crucial exceptions is in Africa itself, where the classical Islamic education system is preserved somewhat in nomadic and sedentary communities found in sub-Saharan Africa and neighbouring lands.

The lives of the Muslim slaves in this study are therefore deeply significant from the perspective of cross-cultural Muslim–Western interaction, for they represent one of the first, if not the first, encounters of the Muslim world with an emerging secular—as opposed to Christian—West. The Muslim slaves were able to make use of their Islamic education not only to communicate with their fellow Muslims through the medium of Arabic, but also to maintain their Islamic identity in spite of the damaging regimen of slave life, and to impress their slave 'masters' with their learning (which is not to say that they necessarily sought to impress their white masters by engaging in acts of worship and writing). They left important signs of their presence, the strength of their traditions and the sophistication of their peoples wherever they were taken or travelled in America and Europe. With hindsight we can understand an important symbolism which manifests from the story of these early captives of a Western institution: Muslims with their Qur'anic cosmology would never easily submit to outside influence, would never easily bend to foreign coercion, and would—through their ways of worship and scholarship—strive to retain their identities even in

---

5   Gray (2003), 1-2.

the most hostile of environments. Following the footsteps of the African Muslim slaves in antebellum America we can see a small drama of a greater and more devastating struggle that would come after they had passed from the world, and which still continues, to a certain extent, to this day: Islam would be the greatest adversary of the colonial powers, and the Muslim world their most difficult venture. For the Muslims themselves, colonialism would hail the rupture and fragmentation of a previously well-preserved and intelligible legacy.

The point of rupture cannot easily be defined—if indeed we accept at all that there was a singular moment in time at which this change occurred. Nevertheless the history of the West in the 'New World', and of the colonialism which followed it, and of the modern drive towards a secular world culture (*novus ordo seclorum*) which it has produced, begins with a major Muslim defeat at the hands of Christian powers in the Old World in 1492. This is a useful starting point: the tidal waves of history which were unleashed in that year in the Iberian peninsula still influence the subtle trends of early twenty-first-century geopolitics.[6] In the West 1492 is celebrated as the year Columbus discovered the New World, launching centuries of European discovery, trade, conquest, and imperialism. Atlantic slavery was a direct consequence and an important source for the European subjugation of the world—politically but also, more importantly, culturally and intellectually.[7] Only in the closing years of the twentieth century was there an indication of this inexorable march towards a surrogate-European cultural milieu slowing down and finally exhausting itself against a few tattered remnants of 'Old World' cultures: principally China and what is left of the 'Islamic World'. Following the attacks in New York on September 11th 2001 and the neo-conservative imperatives driving White House policy, the world is ever-increasingly embroiled in what seems a desperate and ultimately disastrous attempt to maintain the West's colonial hegemony over the rest of the world. And yet

---

6 See for example Chomsky (1992).

7 See Curtin et al. (1978), 215-222 and especially Curtin (1990), 8-16.

the 'Old World legacy' (so to speak) is chronically ill and increasingly at a loss to hold off the ever-encroaching influence of what we call 'modernity' (i.e. the status quo). China turned Communist a long time ago and now is busy transforming itself into a Capitalist super-state—both ideologies being Western imports and arising under Western pressure. The 'Islamic world' ceased to be politically Islamic with the end of the Ottoman Empire in the early twentieth century and has ever since remained socially and politically, though not yet spiritually, in disarray. There are loud voices calling for a return to the golden age of Muslim history, but they lack any real thought or willpower. Lunatic fringes—themselves a modern manifestation—have taken up the symbols of the past, without any of its morals, manners, or methodologies. Everywhere the contemporary icons of what might be called the 'neo-Roman' and 'Surrogate-European' (i.e. 'American') cultures—Spengler's aptly-named 'Faustian' culture-form—dominate. From the walls of the Forbidden City in the heart of Beijing right up to the gates of the Sacred Mosque (*Masjid-al-Haram*) in the City of Mecca: McDonald's and Colonel Saunders, Mickey Mouse, Madonna and Hollywood have found themselves a home, shopping precinct, or heart in which to reside. The largest clock face in the world now looms over the Sacred Mosque and casts its mechanical shadow over Islam's most ancient building: the Ka'bah. In Spengler's schema Islamic civilisation is the ultimate expression of the Magian culture-form (which embodied the spirit of early Christian, Jewish, and even more ancient peoples). But within the ancient heartland of this spiritual tradition it is now the Faustian culture-form that dominates the skyline and towers over the mountains.[8]

And yet in the Euro-American sphere young men and women passionately seek out the lost treasures of the East: the former pop star turned Muslim philanthropist, the Cambridge professor and Sufi, the prince and his School of Traditional Arts, the doctor who treats patients

---

8   For the 'Faustian culture-form' see Oswald Spengler (Reprint 2000). For Neo-cons see Fukuyama (2006). For the destruction of Mecca see https://interactive.aljazeera.com/aje/2015/man_who_dreams_of_old_mecca/index.html (accessed on 22/02/19).

with acupuncture and *shiatsu*, the former Catholic girl who now recites from the Qur'an and prays five times a day, the musician who sings Rumi in English, the Christian composer who writes a work meditating on the ninety-nine names of Allah—all of these are familiar and current themes in the West. And all these rivers and streams of socio-cultural upheaval, assimilation, resistance, transformation, transmutation, and change find some way back to the events of 1492 and the complicated history of the Islamic–Christian encounter. The Muslim slaves who found themselves transported from their African homes to lives of servitude in America were only a brief part of this wider history: but they, along with their fellow non-Muslim Africans, the Inca people, and other natives of the Americas were to different degrees and with different consequences (some more horrific than others) parts of the spoils of war the Europeans exacted from their conquest of Andalusian civilisation. In 1492, just before Columbus sailed across the Atlantic, Granada, the last Muslim city in Spain, surrendered to the combined forces of Aragon and Castile, finally bringing to a close almost a thousand years of Islamic civilisation in the Iberian Peninsula. Inquisition, conquest, and the Conquistadores followed: and the African world, at long last, became fully accessible to the European powers.

With Muslim strength temporarily checked along the western shores of the Mediterranean and the North African (*Maghrebi*) coast, and a gradual rise in the strength of Islam in Eastern Europe (with the powerful Ottoman dynasty),[9] Portuguese and Spanish attention naturally inclined towards Africa, and subsequently with Columbus, westward across the Atlantic.[10] As early as 1444 Portuguese vessels were able to avoid Muslim ships and reach as far down the West African coast

---

9   The Ottomans under the leadership of a very young Sultan Muhammad conquered Constantinople in 1453—just 39 years before the Muslim surrender of Granada. Constantinople was renamed Islambul, the City of Islam, and remained the capital of an Islamic civilisation until approximately 1922. Islambul is now of course better known as Istanbul. It appears that both names, and a host of others, were used even by the Ottomans themselves.

10   Curtin (1990), 8-16.

as Senegal. Tellingly these first contacts between Africans and European Christians were characterised by kidnappings and abductions.[11] One of these early African victims was a Muslim by the name of Adahu who managed to convince the Portuguese to let him return to Africa, where, he promised, he would supply them with many more and stronger 'blackamoors' than himself who were not Muslims. On returning to Africa, however, Adahu refused to sell any Africans at all and disappeared.[12] As this incident suggests, Curtin's assertion that the earliest Portuguese interests in Africa were for its gold and not for slaves is not entirely accurate. When subsequent attempts to 'steal' Africans failed, due to organised military resistance on the part of local African nations, the same Europeans resorted to trade—building commercial outposts along the coast.[13] In later years this would become a central theme of colonial expansion and conquest the world over.

II

We have already mentioned how slaves in Muslims lands—including Andalusian Spain—were not considered as units of production but rather, as Curtin points out, as wards undergoing education: 'His or her status was assimilated to that of a child in the same society, but still as a person—not just a possession … nor was a slave restricted to hard agricultural labor.'[14] Muslim history testifies to the subordinate but nevertheless influential position of slaves in Islam; in Egypt the ruling Mamluks, a powerful dynasty founded by slaves, were able to turn back the Mongol armies of the east and patronised medicine and the arts until the Napoleonic invasion in the nineteenth century. The Ottomans staffed many of their key bureaucratic positions and the Janissary guards with

---

11 Diouf (1998), 15-16.

12 *The Chronicle of the Discovery and Conquest of Guinea*, 95 (London: Hakluyt Society, 1896) quoted in Austin (1984), 58.

13 Ibid., 16.

14 Curtin (1990), 41.

slave recruits specially selected for the purpose. As in the rest of the Islamic world, in Muslim Africa, from the Maghreb to Timbuktu—slaves found themselves commanders of armies, guards, palace servants, administrators, and concubines.[15] In these roles they wielded power and influence that later slaves across the Atlantic and in Africa would never enjoy. More often than not, the opportunity for a slave to obtain freedom was almost inevitable in Muslim society and, as we shall see in the following chapters, Islamic law seemed to encourage their good treatment and liberation. Writing about slavery in Muslim sub-Saharan Africa in the nineteenth century, Fisher and Fisher point out that the distinction between slave and freeman was not always very obvious in Muslim societies:

> In certain respects slaves and freemen were outwardly much alike. A slave often had, like a free man, the right to earn something for himself, and to own property, even to own other slaves.[16]

Although black slaves (along with their white counterparts) had been present in Spain since the thirteenth century when it was under Muslim rule, the kind of positions that slaves filled in Muslim societies were certainly not the kinds of positions the new Catholic power of Spain was willing to entrust to the heathen Moor, or his brethren, in the Americas. The use of slaves for plantation labour, however, was more acceptable to the Church, especially since there was a precedent for this in other parts of Europe.[17] Sylviane Diouf mentions how the papal bulls of Nicholas V (1454) and Caxlitus III (1456) justified slave trading as a crusade to turn the pagan and Muslim Africans into Christians.[18] Nevertheless, as the following example shows, the Spanish and Portuguese seemed to meet with little success in those parts of Africa where the natives shared the same faith as their recently expelled brethren from Spain:

---

15 Fisher and Fisher (1970), 36.

16 Ibid.

17 Curtin (1990), Chapter 1 and Curtin (1978), Chapter 7.

18 Diouf (1998), 16.

A letter sent by a Spanish Capuchin to his superior illustrates the Senegalese Muslim's unwillingness even to consider conversion. Father Francisco de Valleca reported around 1646 that he and other priests were 'doing everything possible to attempt to convert these people. We talked to the kings of Dencallor and Lambaya; we showed them the truth of the Holy Gospel and the falsity of the sect of Mohama which is followed by all the natives of these coasts, and after several retorts, they ordered the interpreters to remain silent, and without them it was impossible to do any fruitful work.' Portuguese, Spanish, and French missionaries who visited Senegambia noted repeatedly the refusal of the Muslims to convert. The profound impact of Islam on its followers and their rejection of Christianity in Africa is important in view of how the 'followers of the sect of Mohama' later reacted to forced conversion in the New World and what they did to preserve their own religion ... [19]

It is likely that much of the animosity and hostility towards the Muslims which the Inquisition engendered in its Spanish subjects, who had to clearly show their allegiance to Christianity—especially in former Muslim strongholds—coupled with their awareness of the presence of Islam in sub-Saharan Africa, contributed to the European ill-treatment of black Africans. The potential for Islamic civilisation to achieve extraordinary heights of sophistication, as witnessed in Spain, had clearly frightened and inspired Christian Europe. The majesty of this flourishing, cosmopolitan, and enlightened Muslim realm had been a constant embarrassment for the rest of Europe under Catholic hegemony, and its defeat was an opportunity for European Christendom to prove its superiority over all non-Christian and non-white peoples.

Clear evidence of associating Muslims with 'blackness' is found in Shakespeare's *Othello*. In one scene, Iago describes Othello as being a Moor, being black and a devil. (It is to be noted that Shakespeare uses Iago as a

---

[19] Ibid., 17.

'noble savage' character who fights against the Turk. Likewise Ayyub bin Suleiman was described as a more civilised 'Mohammedan' than the Turk):

> Iago: Zounds, sir, you're robbed; for shame, put on your gown;
> Your heart is burst, you have lost your soul.
> Even now, now, very now, an old black ram
> Is tupping your white ewe. Arise, arise
> Awake the snorting citizens with the bell
> > Or else the devil will make grandsire of you.
> Arise, I say!
> … I am one, sir, that comes to tell you, your daughter and the
> Moor are now making the beast with two backs.[20]

It is noteworthy that only 100 years after Shakespeare wrote *Othello*, beginning in the early 1730s, if not earlier, attempts would be made by Englishmen and Americans to portray literate, black African Muslim slaves as being 'light-skinned' Moors rather than 'black Negroes'. In one such instance, North African Muslims ('Moors') or rather Berbers, who in fact are generally fair or brown-skinned, are described as 'black' in order to discredit them and associate them with 'devilish' qualities; in the other instance, as we shall see later on with slaves like Ayyub bin Suleiman (Job Ben Solomon) and 'Abd al-Rahman Ibrahima, genuinely black African Muslims are portrayed—because of their learning and sophistication—as being more 'white' than 'black' and therefore Moors from North Africa! In both cases 'blackness' is portrayed derogatorily—but in the first case it is used to present a light or brown-skinned North African Muslim as a savage; and in the second case, blackness is denied to a genuinely black-skinned sub-Saharan African Muslim in order to 'explain' his education and civility. What changes in each case is the definition of the Moor or Muslim: in one case he is portrayed as black and evil, in the other as almost 'white' and Christian; in one case he is

---

20 Shakespeare (reprint 1996), 54-55.

denied noble qualities by being labelled black, in the other his undeniable virtues must be disconnected from his blackness—and so he is denied his race. Here we have early examples of discourse being manipulated to pacify the dangerous significance of the Muslim '*Other*'. We shall turn to this theme again throughout this study.

Let us say for now that the *Other* in every case bears a message which challenges or confirms the observer's cultural self-perception. With its close ties to Christianity and its historical role in Spain and in the Renaissance, Islam has always been European civilisation's greatest 'Other'. It is the Christian world's close brother, the secular West's obstinate spiritual neighbour to the East, and the constant mirror in which it finds its own self-image. Perhaps for this reason, when Muslim slaves were brought to antebellum America, some of them, at least, were able to show their slave masters a humanity in the African that the usual justifications of slavery worked so carefully to deny. At times—as we shall see—the Muslim slave exposed the savagery of the slavemaster; always he demonstrated the evil of antebellum slavery as an institution. But in most instances the slave master responded by admitting, in part, the Muslim slave's civility or humanity but denying, in turn, his Africanness and his blackness.

For this reason, before relating the stories of some of the more famous Muslim slaves in antebellum America, we shall briefly explore, in the following chapter, the depth of Islamic presence in sub-Saharan and tropical Africa. This is in order to clarify how Islam had already embraced African peoples by the sixteenth century in the same way as it had Berbers, Turks, Persians, Indians, Malays, and the Hui and Uighur peoples of China. This is followed by a look at Muslim and non-Muslim relations in Africa and the principal African sources for the transatlantic slave trade, which would have jointly determined the amount of Muslims likely to have been taken as captives into the Old South. In Part 3 (*Laam*) we relate some of the stories of these slaves based on primary sources. In Part 4 (*Meem*) we attempt to look at the broader implications of their remarkable legacy in line with the issues raised in this chapter, and other matters that arise in due course.

5

Muezzin and Hegira— The First African Muslims

Ye may go, for by God I will not deliver them unto you;
they shall not be betrayed.

—The Negus (King of Abyssinia)[1]

'*Muezzin*' as defined in the Oxford English dictionary means 'a Muslim crier who proclaims the hours of prayer.'[2] The dictionary entry goes on to explain that the word is derived from an Arabic term *muadhdhana*, which means 'to proclaim'. Of course an Arabic dictionary would go into far more detail, indicating that the word also means an 'invitation', a 'call', 'a warning', 'permission', 'a declaration', 'to cry aloud', 'to cause to be declared', and (among other things) 'to ask leave to be excused'.[3] In more than one way, all of these terms correctly define aspects of the lives of Muslim slaves in antebellum America. In some respects they also relate to the behaviour of some

---

1   Lings (1991), 83.

2   OUP (1996).

3   See for example Penrice (1873).

67

of the more famous non-Muslim slaves.[4] The Muslim slaves we know about, for example, more than once proclaimed the dignity of their fellow countrymen: asserting, against the more politically correct view of the time, that their African homes were far more civilised than the slave-holding elite would have everyone believe. Consider for instance, the following entry in the diary of a Quaker merchant who met a slave on the Mississippi River in 1822:

> He will not allow that the Americans are as polite and hospitable a people as the Moors [Muslims]—nor that they enjoy a tenth part of the comfort they do—and that for learning and talents [Americans] are far behind them.[5]

Muslim slaves seem to have often demanded and/or been given special consideration by the slave owners who recognised the differences between them and their other slaves. Many Muslims, for example, seem to have been identified by plantation owners who exploited their skills in some kind of mutually beneficial arrangement—for example by employing their Muslim slaves as drivers or overseers. The idea of the *Muezzin* as a 'warner' and the meaning 'to ask leave to be excused', stemming from the related root word *muadhdhana*, is very eloquently expressed by slaves such as the one described by a certain Miss Leach in a letter to Joel Chandler Harris.[6] This slave, by the name of Aaron [Harun], and described as having a 'personality which cowed black and white alike …' had, after several years in slavery, 'boldly declared that he wanted no more of slavery and was allowed to leave, even helped with his master's money to walk away from it to Canada. From there, from

---

4   E.g. Frederick Douglass. Interestingly he may well have had Muslim parents, as has been suggested by some commentators.

5   Quoted in Austin (1997), 16.

6   Interestingly, when mentioning this letter, Austin points out that Harris had once written that '"Arabic-Africans" … [were] not the most numerous, but the most noticeable type of slave along the coast of Georgia'. Austin (1984), 42.

time to time, he wrote properly respectful and yet independent letters to his former owner.'[7]

A third connection with the word *Muezzin* is perhaps the most obvious one: almost all of the Muslim slaves we know about were meticulous in observing the ritual Muslim prayer at least three or five times a day and performing as many other of the usual duties of their faith as they were able to.[8] As an article by Beoku-Betts indicates, sometimes they went beyond the bare minimum requirements of their faith by performing tasks that were not strictly demanded of them according to Islamic Law (such as giving charity), given their poor circumstances and their status as captives.[9] Slaves such as Salih Bilali, on St. Simon's Island, seem also to have been successful in inviting non-Muslim Africans to their faith: once again echoing the meaning of the *Muezzin*, who in the most simple use of the word is the one charged with calling people to prayer and to the benefits of the belief in God (Allah) and His final Prophet (Muhammad). As the words of the *Adhan* (Prayer Call) indicate: 'Come to Prayer! Come to Prayer! Rush to felicity! Rush to Success! There is no God but Allah and Muhammad is His Messenger.'

The most significant connection between the word *Muezzin* and African slaves relates to the history of that office in Islam. The first ever Muslim to be given this title of respect, and the function of calling people to the five-time ritual prayer was a black African man by the name of Bilal. His story is well known among Muslims the world over because he was chosen for this office by the Prophet Muhammad himself and remained one of his most dedicated companions. Many Muslims continue to name their children after Bilal and several of our Muslim

---

7 Ibid.

8 There is a special dispensation under Islamic Law for travellers to combine the five daily prayer times into three prayer times. Interestingly this rule only applies to people when they are in an area that is not their permanent residence. Was the practice of praying three times a day an indication that these slaves held out hope of a return to their homeland? And perhaps a type of symbolic resistance to the circumstances of slavery?

9 Beoku-Betts (1994).

slaves in antebellum America had this name (e.g. Salih Bilali). Bilal is one of a limited number of early Muslims who was actually given the good news of his acceptance into paradise by the Prophet Muhammad during his lifetime, as the following report indicates:

> Abu Huraira reported that Allah's Messenger (may peace be upon him) said to Bilal: Bilal, narrate to me which act at the time of the morning prayer you did in Islam for which you hope to receive good reward, for I heard during the night the sound of your steps before me in Paradise ... [10]

It should now be apparent why we have laboured so much on the meaning of a single Arabic word: in the multiple facets of its meaning, *Muezzin* describes much of the spirit and struggles of the African Muslim slaves who are the subject of our inquiry. Crucially it identifies the historical significance of these slaves as a voice or proclamation which, though largely ignored, has survived the long passage of time right into the twenty-first century: a proclamation which emphasises the essential dignity of all African slaves, and by extension all African peoples, and completely demolishes any latent shadows of the 'Sambo thesis': a perspective that portrays Africans as simpletons and savages who benefitted from a rudimentary schooling in civilised society as slaves in America (see Chapter 2). By connecting Islam and Africans by association with Bilal, one of the first people to accept Islam and moreover a black man and holder of the distinguished rank of the first ever *Muezzin*, we can eloquently highlight the theme of discourse and ethnology in slave writing to which the study of Muslim slaves particularly draws attention.

Most of the writers we have mentioned thus far—including Austin

---

10 *Sahih Muslim*, vol. 4, *Hadith* 6015 from the Chapter on 'The Virtues of Bilal'.
The translation is taken from Abdul Hamid Siddiqui (trans.), *Sahih Muslim: Being traditions of the sayings and doings of the Prophet Muhammad as narrated by his companions and compiled under the title Al-Jami-us-Sahih by Imam Muslim*, Dar Al Arabia, Beirut, 1971.

and Gomez—have failed to acknowledge the involvement of Africans in Islam from its very inception in Arabia at the time of the Prophet Muhammad himself.[11] This may well be because their concern has been to highlight the involvement of Islam in West Africa—which was the major supplier of slaves to the New World—rather than Africa as a whole. Diouf states that Islam, 'the religion revealed to … Muhammad between 609 and 632 CE had been introduced to North Africa as early as 660. South of the Sahara it had been known since the eighth century through contacts with merchants from the north'.[12] But Islam made contact with East Africa long before it reached the North, and its route into West Africa (south of the Sahara) was therefore not exclusively via the Maghreb. At the very least, Africans in some form or other had already been exposed to Islam well before the first Muslim traders came across the Sahara; in fact a small Muslim community had arrived in Abyssinia in the very early days of Islamic history, the days when the Arabs of Mecca violently opposed the new faith, and before the Qur'an had been completely revealed to the Prophet Muhammad and the teaching of Islam perfected.

> Some of the victims of the Makhzum and of other clans could not
> endure what they were made to suffer … And when the Prophet
> saw that although he escaped persecution himself many of his
> followers did not, he said to them: 'If ye went to the country of
> the Abyssinians, ye would find there a king under whom none
> suffereth wrong. It is a land of sincerity in religion. Until such time
> as God shall make for you a means of relief from what ye now are
> suffering.' So some of his companions set off for Abyssinia, and this
> was the first emigration [hegira] in Islam.[13]

---

11 Austin does mention Bilal but inaccurately (1997, 19). Moreover the criticism here in no way detracts from the work of the authors mentioned. Indeed the current author is indebted to them.
12 Diouf (1998), 4.
13 Lings (1991), 80.

This very first Muslim *hegira* ('flight' or 'emigration') to Africa is noteworthy given the streams of discourse that plagued early Orientalist perceptions of Islam, and which allowed white slave owners to see in the African Muslim slave's erudition and virtue only an Arab phenomenon. Even if Islam had only reached West Africa from the North, and even if most of the Muslim slaves to be transported to America were 'West Africans', there was clearly a strong intimacy between Islam and black Africans from the very beginnings of the faith—an intimacy that the Muslim slaves would have shared, and which would have contributed to the total self-identification of Muslim Africans with a wider Islamic milieu. And so Diouf quite correctly writes that 'Africans themselves considered Islam an African religion.'[14] In looking at Africa from the perspective of Muslim history, albeit East Africa at the time, we see a profound warmth and love for the Christian, black, king of Abyssinia (the Negus), in the heart of the Prophet Muhammad. This in itself is a vision of universal brotherhood startling in its implications when compared to the usual stereotypes of religion, Africa, and Islam which have been the hallmark of Orientalism up until, and including, modern times. The following account of a significant and direct encounter between the first Muslims with an African and Christian kingdom is important in highlighting several fascinating points:

First, Christianity was present in Africa centuries before Europeans 'discovered' the continent and attempted to use slaves, including Muslim slaves, as missionaries to their fellow Africans. Second, the Christian king not only tolerated, but was impressed by Islam—this would be very different from the subsequent history of Muslim encounters with European Christians, although Christian slave owners in some cases evinced a peculiar admiration for their Muslim slaves' piety. Third, Africans had produced a powerful and sophisticated civilisation in Abyssinia, which maintained diplomatic and trade ties with other nations. Fourth, Muslims—both Africans and non-Africans—were

---

14 Diouf (1998), 4.

deeply familiar with the major figures of Christianity such as Jesus and Mary, and had their own strong beliefs concerning these personalities from well before their contact with Christian civilisation. This means that when Muslim slaves entered the world of American slavery, they were already in a strong position to contend with Trinitarian Christian dogma and attempts by Americans to convert them to Christianity. This point is of great importance when looking at how these Muslim slaves behaved in the 'New World', and will be taken up again in Part 3.

Let us now turn to the historical encounter itself, as described by Martin Lings from an account recorded in early Arabic sources. Although it is a lengthy episode, given its importance and the fact that it is based on a primary Arabic source from an eyewitness report, we have omitted nothing of the essential points:

The emigrants were well received in Abyssinia, and were allowed complete freedom of worship. In all, not counting the small children they took with them, they were about eighty in number; but they did not all go at the same time. Their flight was secretly planned and carried out unobtrusively in small groups ... Their families ... failed to realise what had happened until the believers had all reached their destination. The leaders of Quraysh [the Prophet Muhammad's tribe—and the most respected of Arabs due to their descent from Abraham] however, were none the less determined that they should not be left in peace, to establish there, beyond their control, a dangerous community which might be increased ... So they speedily ... made ready a quantity of presents of a kind that the Abyssinians were known to value [mostly leathers] ... enough to make a rich bribe for everyone of the Negus's generals ... [and] gifts for the Negus himself. Then they ... chose two men of Quraysh [who] took their presents to the Negus asking that the emigrants should be given into their hands ... 'The nobles of their people, who are their fathers, their uncles and their kinsmen, beg thee to restore them unto them.' The generals ... urged the Negus to comply with their request and give up the refugees, inasmuch kinsmen are the best judges of the affairs of their kinsmen. But the Negus was displeased and said: 'Nay, by God, they shall not be betrayed—a people that have sought my protection and made my country their abode and chosen me above all others! Give them up I will not, until I have summoned them and questioned them concerning what these men say of them ...'

Then he sent for the companions of the Prophet, and at the same time he assembled his bishops, who brought with them their sacred books and spread them open round about the throne. [The Quraysh] envoy[s] had hoped to prevent this meeting between the Negus and the refugees ... [but] they were unaware that while the Abyssinians tolerated them for commercial and political reasons they looked down upon them as heathens and were conscious of a barrier between them. They themselves were Christians, many of them devout; they had been baptised, they worshipped the One God, and they carried in their flesh the sacrament of the Eucharist ... So much the more were they receptive—none more than the Negus himself—to the impression of holy earnestness and depth which was made on them by the company of believers who were now ushered into the throne room, and a murmur of wonderment arose from the bishops and others as they recognised that here were men and women more akin to themselves than to such of Quraysh as they had previously encountered. Moreover, most of them were young, and in many of them their piety of demeanour was enhanced by a great natural beauty.[15]

This initial reaction from the Negus and his clergy on seeing the believers has a peculiar parallel—though less marked—in the description of young Muslim slaves, particularly Ayyub bin Suleiman, which are found in the sources mentioned in Part 3. In a sense the reaction of the wealthy

---

15   Lings (1991), 81-82.

philanthropic Christians in America who helped some of the Muslim slaves was likewise one of fascination with their devotion, piety, and 'beauty'; a beauty that they acknowledged in spite of their prejudices towards what they called 'Negro features'. An interesting aspect to this is the almost reciprocal notion of beauty which was recognised in the countenance of a visiting Christian deacon in Mecca, and after whom one of the delegates of the Muslim refugees was named:

the refugees needed a spokesman and Ja'far … [had been] chosen to preside over the community of exiles … Likewise remarkable [among the Muslims] was a young Makhzumite known as Shammas, whose mother was the sister of 'Utbah. His name, which means 'deacon', was given him because on one occasion Mecca had been visited by a Christian dignitary of that rank, a man so exceptionally handsome as to arouse general admiration, whereupon 'Utbah had said 'I will show you a shammas more beautiful than he,' and he went and brought before them his sister's son … It is from the beautiful Umm Salamah that most of the accounts of this first emigration have come down.

When they were all assembled, the Negus spoke to them and said: 'What is the religion wherein ye have become separate from your people, though ye have not entered my religion nor that of any other of the folk that surround us?' And Ja'far answered him saying:

'O King, we were a people steeped in ignorance, worshipping idols, eating unsacrificed carrion, committing abominations, and the strong would devour the weak. Thus we were, until God sent us a Messenger [Muhammad] from our midst, one whose lineage we knew, and his veracity and his worthiness of trust and his integrity. He called us unto God, that we should testify to His Oneness and worship Him and renounce what we and our fathers had worshipped in the way of stones and idols; and he commanded us to speak truly, to fulfil our promises, to respect the ties of kinship and the rights of our neighbours, and to refrain from crimes and from bloodshed. So we worship God alone, setting naught beside Him, counting as forbidden what He hath forbidden and as licit what He hath allowed. For these reasons have our people turned against us, and have persecuted us to make us forsake our religion and revert from the worship of God to the worship of idols. That is why we have come to thy country, having chosen thee above all others; and we have been happy in thy protection, and it is our hope, O King, that here, with thee, we shall not suffer wrong.'

The royal interpreters translated all that he had said. The Negus then asked if they had with them any Revelation that their Prophet had brought them from God and, when Ja'far answered they had, he said: 'Then recite it to me,' whereupon Ja'far recited a passage from the *Surah* [chapter] of Mary, which had been revealed shortly before their departure:

> *And make mention of Mary in the Book, when she withdrew from her people unto a place towards the east, and secluded herself from them; and we sent unto her Our Spirit, and it appeared unto her in the likeness of a perfect man. She said: I take refuge from thee in the Infinitely Good, if any piety thou hast. He said: I am none other than a messenger from thy Lord, that I may bestow on thee a son most pure. She said: How can there be for me a son, when no man hath touched me, nor am I unchaste? He said: Even so shall it be; thy Lord saith: It is easy for Me. That we may make him a sign for mankind and a mercy from Us; and it is a thing ordained.* (Qur'an 19:16-21)

The Negus wept, and his bishops wept also, when they heard him recite, and when it was translated they wept again, and the Negus said: 'This hath truly come from the same source as that which Jesus brought.' Then he turned to the two envoys of Quraysh and said: 'Ye may go, for by God I will not deliver them unto you; they shall not be betrayed.'[16]

This remarkable initial encounter of Muslims with an African nation is full of revealing information about Islamic and African-Christian, as well as Abyssinian, history and culture. We have already mentioned several key points that arise from this account, but we should mention two more important points before leaving this story. First there is in the above account a hint that the non-Muslim Arabs were afraid that Islam might gain converts in Abyssinia. It is difficult to say unequivocally whether or not a very early Muslim community was established there in the lifetime of the Prophet Muhammad, but it does seem highly likely. Later on news would reach the refugees in Abyssinia that Islam had gained strength in Mecca and they would return to be with their beloved Prophet. But at least one Abyssinian—the Negus himself—was so moved by the teachings of Islam that he accepted the faith, almost losing his authority in the process. His belief in Islam is testified to by the fact that the Prophet Muhammad actually performed the funeral prayer for him when he died. It is also apparent that several delegations from Africa/Abyssinia came to meet the Prophet Muhammad in Medina and became Muslims before returning home.

The story of the Negus becoming a Muslim is also important because it indicates the Muslim attitude to slavery and the Muslim concept of Prophethood—particularly that of Jesus. As we mentioned earlier (Chapter 3), generally speaking the Muslim sees the world as a domain of servitude. All human creatures have a choice: either to be slaves of created things by denying their real state of slavery to God, or to be wilful slaves of God (who is not in need of slaves) and therefore to be free in reality. For this reason Muslims ascribe the title 'slave of God' to His Prophets, messengers and the spiritually elect. Again, Muslim slaves who ended up in America would have been very familiar with these concepts and

---

16 Lings (1991), 82-83.

we can only speculate as to how it affected their behaviour in the New World. As mentioned earlier, Diouf hints at this in the title of her work and explicitly states in its completion that even as slaves of 'Christian masters' the Muslims, were, from their own perspective, 'the servants of Allah', not the servants of any his creatures.[17] This knowledge no doubt gave them a degree of freedom, which cannot be expressed outside of the experiential 'life-transaction' (*deen*) in which the Muslim is engaged, but which is represented in the verses (*ayah* lit. 'signs') of the Qur'an, the utterances of the Prophet and the sayings of the people of 'inner purity' (*tasawwuf*) often called 'Sufis', or *marabouts* in Africa. As Diouf suggests, the Muslim slaves in America were no doubt imbued with this deep cosmological understanding, albeit to different degrees. No doubt they would have understood the meaning of such Sufi aphorisms as 'You have not loved anything without being its slave, but He does not want you to be someone else's slave.'[18] The pagan Arabs were also aware of Muslim references to Jesus as a 'slave of God' and not content with the Negus's decision about the Muslim emigrants, decided to employ a new tactic to secure their captivity. The plan backfired and resulted in the Negus accepting Islam:

> 'Amr [one of the Qurayshi envoys] said to his companion:
> 'Tomorrow I will tell him a thing that shall tear up this green
> growing prosperity of theirs [i.e. the Muslim's] by their roots.
> I will tell him [the Negus] that they aver that Jesus the son of Mary
> is a slave.' So the next morning he went to the Negus and said:
> 'O King, they utter an enormous lie about Jesus the son of Mary.
> Do but send to them, and ask them what they say of him.' So he
> sent them word to come again and to tell him what they said of
> Jesus, whereupon they were troubled, for nothing of this kind had
> ever yet befallen them ... when they entered the royal presence,

---

17 Diouf (1998), 210. See also our discussion in Chapter 3.
18 Ibn Ata'illah. Danner (trans.) (reprint 1999), Aphorism 210, 53.

and it was said to them: 'What say ye of Jesus, the son of Mary?' Ja'far answered: 'We say of him what our Prophet brought unto us, that he is the slave of God and His Messenger and His Spirit and His Word which He cast unto Mary the blessed virgin.' The Negus took up a piece of wood and said: 'Jesus the son of Mary exceedeth not what thou hast said by the length of this stick.' And when the generals round him snorted, he added: 'For all your snorting.' Then he turned to Ja'far and his companions and said: 'Go your ways for ye are safe in my land. Not for mountains of gold would I harm a single man of you'; and with a movement of his hand towards the envoys of Quraysh, he said to his attendant: 'Return unto these two men their gifts, for I have no use for them.' So 'Amr and the other man went back ignominiously to Mecca.

Meantime the news of what the Negus had said about Jesus spread among the people, and they were troubled and came out against him asking for an explanation, and accusing him of having left their religion. He thereupon sent to Ja'far and his companions [i.e. the Muslims] and made ready for them boats for them and told them to embark and be ready to set sail if necessary. Then he took a parchment and wrote on it: 'He testifieth that there is no god but God and that Muhammad is His slave and His Messenger and that Jesus is His slave and His Messenger and His Spirit and His Word which He cast unto Mary.' Then he put it beneath his gown and went out to his people who were assembled to meet him. And he said to them: 'Abyssinians, have I not the best claim to be your king?' They said that he had. 'Then what think ye of my life amongst you?' 'It hath been the best of lives,' they answered. 'Then what is it that troubleth you?' he said. 'Thou hast left our religion,' they said, 'and hast maintained that Jesus is a slave.' ' Then what say ye of Jesus?' he asked. 'We say that he is the Son of God,' they answered. Then he [the Negus] put his hand on his breast, pointing to where the parchment was hidden, and testified to his belief in 'this', which they took to refer to their words. So they were satisfied and went away, for they were happy under his rule, and only wished to be reassured and the Negus sent word to Ja'far and his companions that they could disembark and go back to their dwellings, where they went on living as before, in comfort and security.'[19] [Ibn Ishaq, the eighth century historian of early Islam adds: 'News of this reached the Prophet, and when the Negus died he prayed over him and begged that his sins might be forgiven.'[20]]

If other Abyssinians later followed the example of their king and accepted Islam, as the following incident suggests, then we can be sure that an indigenous Muslim community was present in Africa in the early seventh century in the lifetime of the Prophet Muhammad himself and before all of Arabia had accepted Islam. Indeed, it can be said without hesitation that Africans were amongst the earliest supporters of Islam and the Prophet Muhammad—a delegation of Abyssinians actually returned with Ja'far to Mecca in order to meet the Prophet and declare their faith in him:

In the midst of the suffering and persecution which was being endured by the Prophet (peace be upon him) and his Companions, a delegation came from outside Mecca to meet with the Messenger of God (peace be upon him) and gain some understanding of Islam. The delegation was made up of about thirty Christian men from Abyssinia who had come with Ja'far Ibn Abi Talib upon his return to Mecca. When they sat with the Messenger of God (peace be upon him), they became familiar with his character and the conditions in which he lived and heard the Qur'an recited to them, all of them believed.

When Abu Jahl [an arch-enemy of Islam] learned of it, he approached them, saying, 'Never have I seen a more foolish

---

19 Lings (1991), 84.
20 Guillaume (1978), 155.

bunch of riders! Your people sent you to find out more about this man, and no sooner had you sat with him for a while than you abandoned your religion and believed the things he said!'

'Peace be upon you,' they replied. 'We have no intention of insulting or discrediting you. It is simply that we have chosen this path, and you have chosen another. Nor have we done any injustice to ourselves.' It was in regard to these men that the following verse was revealed:

As for those unto whom We have vouchsafed revelation aforetime—they (are bound to) believe in this one (as well); and whenever it is (clearly) conveyed unto them, they (are bound to) profess, 'We have come to believe in it, for, behold, it is the truth from our Sustainer—and verily, even before this have we surrendered ourselves unto Him!' These it is that shall receive a twofold reward for having been patient in adversity, and having repelled evil with good, and having spent on others out of what We provided for them as sustenance, and, whenever they heard frivolous talk, having turned away from it and said: 'Unto us shall be accounted our deed, and unto you, your deeds. Peace be upon you—(but) we do not seek out such as are ignorant (of the meaning of right and wrong).' (Qur'an 28:52-55)[21]

There are plenty of other narrations in the *hadith* literature (oral and recorded tradition) that testify to the presence and active involvement of African Muslims from the very beginnings of Islam.[22] For our purposes, the examples we have already quoted should suffice to show that Islam

---

21 Roberts (trans.) (2007), 175-176 citing a *hadith* from Ibn Ishaq, Muqatil, and al-Tabari on the authority of Sa'id Ibn Jubayr. The reference in this work also refers readers to commentaries by Ibn Kathir, al-Qurtibi and Naysaburi. Some accounts state that there were more than forty men in the Abyssinian delegation (c.f. ibid., 176).

22 For examples the reader may wish to consult the *Sahih* collections of Bukhari and Muslim, which contain, among other mentions of Abyssinian Muslims, an account of a delegation of Abyssinians who danced in adoration of the Prophet before his house in the Mosque of Madinah whilst he looked on, along with his wife, Aisha.

came to Africa at more or less the same time it came to Arabia. In other words, Islam in Africa is as old as Islam in Arabia; and just as Islam is native to Arabs, it is and always has been native to Africans. Moreover, given that Islam entered the Maghreb in the latter part of the seventh century, it is clear that the first African peoples to have Muslims among them were so-called 'Negroes' as opposed to Berbers or Moors.

In the conversion of the Negus to Islam we also have an example from the very beginning of Islamic history of a black African Muslim—a king no less—hiding his Islamic convictions from Christians by giving them the false impression that he was in agreement with their version of Christian doctrine. In times of danger this is an acceptable response in Islamic law as long as one does not state an untruth. And, furthermore, it explains clearly the behaviour of those Muslim slaves—such as 'Abd al-Rahman Ibrahima (also of royal descent)—who sent mixed messages of conversion to Christianity for the benefit of their American audiences, only to immediately recant their gestures upon touching foot once more in Africa. We shall encounter several such examples in Part 3.

Before proceeding to the next chapter where we shall look briefly at Islam as it appeared in West Africa—the source of the majority of slaves shipped to America in antebellum times—we should emphasise the fact that whether or not the first Muslim community in Africa emerged in the lifetime of the Prophet Muhammad in Abyssinia or otherwise, there is no doubt that there were more than just a few African Muslim companions of the prophet Muhammad in the Arabian peninsula itself. The following report cited in an Arabic work attributed to one of the foremost Sufi masters of Muslim Spain and North Africa—Abu Madyan al-Gawth—describes one such African Muslim as being someone singled out by the Prophet as an exemplar of true repentance and one of the people of Paradise. It is representative of a whole body of *hadith* literature about the Prophet's words and deeds and those of his early companions, in which black men and women feature alongside Arabs and others from the first generation of Muslims.

> An Abyssinian said, 'Oh Messenger of God, verily I have performed
> immoral acts and desire to repent. Do I have repentance?' 'Yes,'
> said [the Prophet]. Then [the Abyssinian] returned and said,
> 'Oh Messenger of God, did God see me while I was doing [these
> immoral acts]?' 'Yes,' he replied. At this the Abyssinian let out a cry
> and his soul departed with it, may God have mercy on him. Said
> the Messenger of God: 'This one is of the Folk of Paradise and this
> is true repentance.'[23]

We began this chapter with mention of Bilal—the first *Muezzin*, and
an African. It is worth pointing out that he had chosen Islam whilst
still a slave under a very cruel pagan master and before the Muslims
made their *hegira* to Abyssinia. Bilal, it seems, did not accompany this
group of early emigrants to his homeland, preferring to stay with the
Prophet Muhammad in Mecca. The following episode in Bilal's life also
highlights Islam's approach to slavery from the outset—before much of
the religion had been codified in laws (most of which were revealed to
the Prophet Muhammad in the Medinan phase—i.e. after the *hegira*—
and not in Mecca). It is clear that Islam's approach to slavery was to
encourage the liberation of slaves—especially if he or she was a Muslim.
This pattern would be repeated centuries later in West Africa, as we
indicate in Chapter 7.

> Each clan dealt with its own Muslims: they would imprison them
> and torment them with beating, hunger and thirst; and they would
> stretch them out on the sun-baked earth of Mecca when the heat
> was at its height, to make them renounce their religion.
>
> The chief of Jumah, Umayyah, had an African slave named Bilal
> who was a firm believer. Umayyah would take him out at noon into
> an open space, and would have him pinned to the ground with a

---

23 From a manuscript entitled *Bidayat al-Murid (Basic Principles of the Sufi Path)* by Abu
Madyan al-Gawth translated in Cornell, (1996), 106.

large rock on his chest, swearing that he should stay like that until he dies, or until he renounced Muhammad and worshipped al-Lat and al-Uzzah (two Arabian goddesses). While he endured this Bilal would say: 'One, One'; and it happened that the aged Waraqah came by when he was suffering this torment and repeating 'One, One.' 'It is indeed One, One, O Bilal,' said Waraqah. Then turning to Umayyah, he said: 'I swear by God that if ye kill him thus I will make his grave a shrine.'[24]

'It was through … [Abu Bakr] that Bilal had entered Islam; and when he saw how they were torturing him, he said to Umayyah: 'Hast thou no fear of God, to treat this poor man thus?' 'It is thou who hast corrupted him,' retorted Umayyah, 'so save him from what thou seest.' 'I will,' said Abu Bakr. 'I have a black youth who is tougher and sturdier than he, a man of thy religion. Him will I give thee for Bilal.' Umayyah agreed, and Abu Bakr took Bilal and set him free.

He had already set free six others the first one being Amir ibn Fuhayrah, a man of great spiritual strength, who had been one of the earliest converts … Another of those whom he set free was a slave girl belonging to 'Umar. She had entered Islam, and 'Umar was beating her to make her renounce it, when Abu Bakr happened to pass by and asked him if he would sell her to him. 'Umar agreed, whereupon Abu Bakr bought her and set her free.[25]

---

24 Lings (1991), 79.
25 Ibid.

6

Muslim West Africa and the Transatlantic Slave Trade

*Then that sultan got ready 2,000 ships, 1,000 for himself and the men
he took with him and 1,000 for water and provisions. He left me to
deputize for him and embarked on the Atlantic Ocean with his men.*

— Mansa Musa on how he became King of Mali[1]

The UNESCO-sponsored *General History of Africa*—a vast, eight
volume work covering over 3 million years of African history from
an African perspective—begins Volume IV with the observation that
beginning in the twelfth century,

'… Africa developed its original culture and assimilated outside
influences while retaining its own individuality … [D]rawing on
Arabic texts, Africa was shown to emerge [in the preceding century]
from obscurity with the Muslim discovery of the rich Sudan to the
south of the Sahara …'[2]

---

1   Al-Umari (1337–1338), *Masaalik al-absaar*, cited in Levtzion and Hopkins (2000), 269.
2   Niane (1984), Vol. IV, 1.

As we mentioned in the previous chapter, Islam had entered North Africa as early as 660 CE and had had contact with Abyssinia even earlier when a community of the Prophet's companions sought refuge there, and when the king of Abyssinia embraced Islam. If the twelfth century was indeed as decisive a period for the development of African culture as the UNESCO *History* suggests, then clearly Islam—having been present in Africa for the previous 500 years—was already an integral part of the African experience. Moreover, it is from Muslim sources that we have our earliest and most extensive collection of written information about the history of African civilisations. It is also noteworthy that the UNESCO *History* confirms the contention in the previous chapter that large numbers of black Africans were already an important part of the Islamic milieu before it gained a firm political foundation in West Africa:

> In the eleventh century the Almoravids, setting out from the
> Senegal estuary with armies which included large forces of
> Negroes from Takrur, conquered parts of the Maghreb and of the
> Iberian peninsula and restored 'sunna', a strict Muslim orthodoxy,
> throughout western Islam.[3]

In fact this statement is misleading: Muslims had conquered Spain and the Maghreb long before the eleventh century—Muslim armies had reached France by the eighth century, only losing Narbonne in 759 CE.[4] The Almoravid campaign is better seen from the perspective of a change in the fortunes of one Muslim hegemony over another, rather than as the introduction of Islam to a new geographic area. Understood correctly, this remark from the UNESCO *History* indicates a Senegalese

---

3   Ibid.

4   Lewis (2000), 19. Lewis quite rightly contends, however, that for Muslims the loss of Narbonne was a relatively minor affair—it being considered little more than a distant skirmish in a remote outpost of the Muslim world. The city had previously been successfully defended by its Muslim and Christian Visigothic citizens against the forces of Charles Martel. The latter has become a mythical figure for fascists in modern times: see Chapter 12 below.

(i.e. African) Muslim involvement in the Iberian and Maghrebi parts of the Muslim world: and not, as is usually supposed by non-Muslim commentators, a wholly Arab predominance. The mention here of Takrur is important. Following the conversion of its king, Wardjabi (or *War Diaby*), Takrur became the first West African Muslim state to apply *shar'iah* (Islamic Law).[5] In line with his devotion to Islam, Wardjabi allied himself closely with the Almoravid dynasty and Takrur participated in the Almoravid wars in the Sahara and elsewhere. Takrur became an important trading centre in Muslim West Africa, initiating a common theme in the expansion of Islam in that part of the world.[6] The nearby Songhay people—occupying the Niger Bend—had apparently converted to Islam in 1010 CE and like the Takrur were successful in attracting Muslim trade and scholars. They managed to take control of Timbuktu, an important city in the heart of the later Malian empire where some of the future Africans exported to America as slaves would receive their Islamic education.[7]

> Within fifty years Islam had expanded from the banks of the
> Senegal River in the west to the shores of Lake Chad in the east.
> Malian traders and clerics introduced it to northern Nigeria—
> where the Muslims became known as Male, or people coming from
> Mali—in the fourteenth century.
>
> In contrast to its arrival in North Africa ... the spread of Islam
> [in West Africa] was diffused not by outsiders (except in the early
> years) but by indigenous traders, clerics and rulers.[8]

The conversion of indigenous rulers, mentioned here, is interesting since it parallels the earliest encounters of Islam in Africa, mentioned in the previous chapter, where the king of Abyssinia accepted Islam in spite of

---

5   Diouf (1998), 4; Niane (1984), GHA Vol. IV, 119.
6   Ibid., 120-121.
7   Ibid.
8   Diouf (1998), 4.

his people's disapproval. In West Africa, however, a contrary trend was also manifested in some areas, whereby Islam became the 'religion of the masses in opposition to their "pagan" leaders.[9] The general exponential growth of Islam, wherever it has travelled, is also evident in Islam's spread in West Africa, where by the fourteenth century CE it had become a dominant and indigenous part of West African life. Consequently West Africa had, in turn, become an important part of the wider Muslim civilisation benefitting from all the advantages of the vast cosmopolitan Muslim world:

> From the Indus to Gibraltar, from the Red Sea to Madagascar, from North Africa to the sub-Saharan regions, men and goods circulated … freely … From the twelfth to the sixteenth century, Africa became a crossroads of international trade, exercising an extraordinary attraction on the rest of the world.[10]

Diouf refers to this inter-communication across the Muslim world as 'a global market of ideas and goods.'[11] Indeed there was a continuous stream of scholars, artisans, and traders moving from and into the Muslim parts of West Africa. An important West African Muslim power to emerge at this time was Timbuktu—formerly part of Takrur but now capital of the Mali Empire under the dominion of Mansa Musa (1312–1337). According to the UNESCO *History*, Mali was founded by the Keita, who believed they were descendants of Bilal—the *Muezzin* of the Prophet Muhammad mentioned in the previous chapter—through his son Lawalo, who settled in Manding and founded the city of Kiri or Ki.[12] If this is the case, then Sunjaata, also attributed as the founder of Mali, was in fact the founder of a second Malian kingdom that merged with the first one. This is implied in the UNESCO *History*, and indicates the complexity of

---

9   Ibid., 5.
10 Niane (1984), GHA Vol. IV, 3.
11 Diouf (1998), 5.
12 Niane (1984), GHA Vol. IV, 129.

describing the early history of the Mandingo peoples—a name that later became synonymous with *Muslim* in the transatlantic slave trade.[13] In a famous pilgrimage to Mecca, Mansa Musa demonstrated the power and wealth of his country by inadvertently deflating the price of gold in Cairo as a result of the spending activities of his countrymen who accompanied him on the pilgrimage. He also brought 'back to his country lawyers and descendants of the Prophet Muhammad, as well as a Spanish born Muslim architect, and sent numerous students to North Africa'[14]—again, planting the seeds for future African scholars, some of whom would end up in America as slaves. Some writers have expressed uncertainty about the cause of Mali's sudden prosperity under Mansa Musa's reign.[15] Historical accounts from some of the earliest sources indicate that that wealth may well have come from across the Atlantic. An interesting report by the fourteenth-century Mamluk official Ibn Fadl-Allah al-Umari is worth mentioning, because it suggests that Mansa Musa's predecessor embarked on a voyage to set up a colony in the New World:

> Ibn Amir Hajib continued: 'I asked sultan Musa how the kingdom
> fell to him, and he said: "We belong to a house which hands on
> the kingship by inheritance. The king who was my predecessor
> did not believe that it was impossible to discover the furthest
> limit of the Atlantic Ocean and wished vehemently to do so. So
> he equipped 200 ships filled with men and the same number
> equipped with gold, water, and provision enough to last them for
> years, and said to the man deputed to lead them: "Do not return
> until you reach the end of it or your provision and water give out."
> They departed and a long time passed before anyone came back.
> Then one ship returned and we asked the captain what news they
> brought. He said: "Yes, O Sultan, we travelled for a long time until
> there appeared in the open sea [as it were] a river with a powerful

---

13   Ibid.

14   Diouf (1998), 6.

15   E.g. see Curtin et al. (1978), 110.

current. Mine was the last of those ships. The [other] ships went on ahead but when they reached that place they did not return and no more was seen of them and we do not know what became of them. As for me, I went about at once and did not enter that river." But the sultan disbelieved him.

'Then that sultan got ready 2,000 ships, 1,000 for himself and the men he took with him and 1,000 for water and provisions. He left me to deputize for him and embarked on the Atlantic Ocean with his men. That was the last we saw of him and all those who were with him, and so I became king in my own right.'[16]

Another important Muslim nation of the time was Kanuri, whose Islamic beginnings were almost contemporary with those of Mali's legendary Muslim founder Sunjaata. Mai Dunama Dibbalemi of the Kanuri (1221–1259)[17] completely did away with the pagan ceremonies and legal sanctions, which were still a major feature of the Kanuri people even after their acceptance of Islam.[18] With their base in Kanem, near Lake Chad, the Kanuri ruled at one point a vast territory including Fezzan and maintained control over the trade routes to the Mamluk dynasty of Egypt.[19] The Mamluks—as we have mentioned before—were themselves a dynasty made up of former slaves. Dunama Dibbalemi, according to Diouf, had a school built in Cairo for those of his subjects who were studying there.[20] Other noteworthy Muslim groups included the Hausa and the Borno, who would both play an important role in the emerging transatlantic slave trade from the sixteenth century onwards—but not necessarily as wilful suppliers of slaves. As we go on to relate the stories of some of the Muslim slaves taken to America, in Part 3, a clearer picture

---

16 Al-Umari (1337–1338), *Masaalik al-absaar*, cited in Levtzion and Hopkins (2000), 268-269.

17 This date is from Ibid., 111. Diouf gives a different date: 1210–1248. See Diouf (1998), 6.

18 Curtin et al. (1978), 111.

19 Ibid.

20 Diouf (1998), 6.

of West African Muslim societies and their various nations and groups at the height of the transatlantic trade will emerge.

One of the major impacts of West African Muslim civilisation was the introduction of literacy. We have already given examples of Mansa Musa's, and before him the Kanuri ruler Dunama Dibbalemi's, policies to promote education in their respective kingdoms. Literacy was encouraged among males and females as testified by the statements of Lamine Kebe—a Muslim teacher from Futa Jallon (Guinea) and later, a slave in America. Diouf writes: 'In a continent whose civilizations relied on oral tradition and where no writing system was available, only the Muslims were literate.'[21] Actually the traditional Islamic educational model emphasises both oral transmission and textual authority. As we shall see later, it was in fact this combination of oral and literary transmission of knowledge that differentiated the Muslim slaves from their non-Muslim counterparts, allowing them to challenge the prevalent modes of discourse which otherwise ascribed to American slavery a benevolent function as educator of the black African masses. The importance of Muslim literacy and education is taken up in more detail in the following chapters of this study.

Suffice to say that when the first Portuguese ships made contact with the West African coast in the late fifteenth and early sixteenth centuries, Islam was already an important part of African society, and the Muslim civilisations from the Senegal to the Gulf of Guinea were literate, wealthy, and well connected with other Muslim and African nations. This is not to say that West Africa was wholly or entirely Islamic by the fifteenth century. In fact Islam continued to grow for another 400 years, the popularity of Islam being influenced in various ways by the transatlantic slave trade itself, and then, in the twentieth century, by anti-colonial sentiments.[22] But it is clear that after leaving the *Madajeros* (Spanish Muslims) and the Berbers or Moors behind in

---

21 Ibid.
22 Gomez (1994), 675.

the Iberian peninsula and the Maghreb, the earliest Europeans to make contact with West Africa (who were Portuguese) would have found, to their dismay, many more black Muslims than they would have wished for. Given the recent expulsion of Muslims from Spain in 1492, this Muslim presence in Africa would have posed significant problems for the transatlantic traders. We mentioned in Chapter 4 how papal bulls in the 1450s sought to justify the trade in slaves as a mission to convert the Muslims and pagans into Christians. Notwithstanding this enthusiasm to gain a foothold for Catholicism in the Dark Continent of the 'black Muslims' and African 'savages', there was plenty of consternation and fear about bringing a Muslim people into the New World where they might re-enact the Andalusian experience and convert Native American peoples to Islam. The last thing Spain and Catholicism wanted was another powerful Muslim civilisation to emerge in their newly discovered acquisitions across the Atlantic. In 1501 the Spanish issued a royal decree forbidding any Muslims from entering the New World and specifying that only non-Muslim African slaves should be taken to the Americas. Then, in 1543, the King of Spain ratified another Spanish decree forbidding the movement of Muslims into the New World.[23] Nevertheless, as Gomez points out, it is clear that Muslims (labelled 'Mandingos') were present in Spanish-controlled Florida from 1565 until

---

23 One cannot help but compare this to US President Donald Trump's attempts to impose a modern day ban on Muslims entering America. After various legal battles the US Supreme Court approved a modified version of this ban in June 2017. Omar Jadwat, director of the ACLU's Immigrants' Rights Project, said, 'This ruling will go down in history as one of the Supreme Court's great failures. It repeats the mistakes of the Korematsu decision upholding Japanese-American imprisonment and swallows wholesale government lawyers' flimsy national security excuse for the ban instead of taking seriously the president's own explanation for his action. It is ultimately the people of this country who will determine its character and future. The court failed today, and so the public is needed more than ever. We must make it crystal clear to our elected representatives: If you are not taking actions to rescind and dismantle Trump's Muslim ban, you are not upholding this country's most basic principles of freedom and equality' (https://www.aclu-wa.org/pages/timeline-muslim-ban accessed 26/02/2019).

as late as the latter half of the eighteenth century.[24] Elizabeth Donnan writes of a certain Mr. Percival being instructed to 'begin a trade with the Spaniards for Negroes' to come and work on plantations in South Carolina in 1674.[25] Perhaps the Spanish thought it better to pass off their Muslim slaves to the English colonists at this time. The French and English—not sharing the same historical experience as the Spanish— had, it seems, no qualms whatsoever about bringing Muslim slaves to the New World:

> [...] the French in Louisiana also imported Muslims, as they received slaves from Whydah and Angola, but especially from Senegambia. Gwendolyn Midlo Hall argues that two-thirds of all Africans imported into Louisiana from 1719 to 1743 via the French came from Senegambia, while Rawley estimates that by 1803 some 28,300 slaves had entered Louisiana, many from Senegambia. The Muslim population while unquantifiable must have been significant ... Hall writes: 'The slaves of French Louisiana often kept their African names, many of which were Islamic. Some slaves with French names had Baraca, an Islamic religious title, as a second name.'[26]

It is clear, then, that the import of African Muslim slaves into North America antedates the arrival of the English. It is also clear that the English—like the French before them—had even less reason than their Spanish predecessors not to trade in Muslims. This is further highlighted by the fact that Muslims—or at least Africans from areas of high Muslim concentration—seem to have been actively sought out as slaves. As Gomez states, 'the slave-owning society in Anglophone North America regularly distinguished among various ethnicities within the African

---

24 Ibid., 683.

25 Donnan (1928), 804. See also 804-828.

26 Gomez (1994), 684. Little could they have known that a future president of that same country would bear that same name.

community.'[27] Africans prone to suicide and unruly behaviour, such as the Igbo and Ibibio of southeastern Nigeria, were favoured least of all because they were more difficult to manage and control.[28] Muslims—forbidden to commit suicide by their faith, and taught to accept the decree of God (Allah) with patience (*sabr*)—were far more preferable in this regard. Also, slave owners—particularly in South Carolina, Georgia, and Louisiana—seem to have deliberately sought slaves familiar with rice and indigo cultivation: which meant, in practical terms, Africans from Senegambia, the Gold Coast and Sierra Leone—all areas of high Muslim concentration.[29] Runaway slave adverts confirm, unambiguously, a sizeable Muslim population from these regions; and also indicate that although Muslims are taught to accept the decree of God, they are not obliged to endure the tyranny of men:

> 'two Gambia Negroes, about 5 Feet 6 Inches high, the one his
> Name is Walley [Walli], the other's Bocarrey [Bukhari?]' … In
> 1757[:] 'a Negro man named Mamado' escaped from Rachel
> Fairchild; [1772] … 'A NEGRO FELLOW named HOMADY
> [Amadi, from Ahmed], Has a sulky Look and speaks bad
> English …' In North Carolina in 1808, a one-hundred-dollar
> reward … for the apprehension of Arthur Howe, a white man who
> had taken away a slave named "Mustapha"'[30]

It is interesting to note that these slaves sometimes ran away to live with Native Americans.[31] Perhaps a Spanish fear of an Islamisation of Native Americans was justified, when we consider that some of the Cherokee leaders seem to have had Muslim names and wore Muslim clothes. As we go on to look, in Part 3 at the lives of just three famous Muslim slaves, a

---

27 Ibid.
28 Ibid.
29 Wood (1974), 58-62; Joyner (1985), 14-15; Gomez (1994), 687.
30 Gomez (1994), 687.
31 Ibid., 688.

clearer picture will emerge of the conditions in Africa that would have led to Muslims being enslaved. It should be remembered, however, that Muslims did not willingly sell other Muslims into captivity. In fact no African seems to have sold their people as slaves. But Africans, including Muslims, did sell prisoners of war and Africans who had committed heinous crimes to the Europeans. Also, slave-raiders preyed on enemy tribes and nations to sell them off as slaves and make a quick profit. This was the case with the most famous African Muslim slave—Job Ben Solomon (Ayyub bin Suleiman)—who was abducted whilst on a mission to buy paper for his scholastic pursuits, and to sell slaves (most likely prisoners of war) of his own. It is with his remarkable tale that we begin Part 3.

III

Laam

Orisons of the Slave

This part of the study tells the story of three African Muslim slaves, exploring aspects of their lives and looking at their writings. We begin with the life of Ayyub bin Suleiman, or Job Ben Solomon, narrating his encounter with American slavery and interspersing key events in his life with quotes from the Qur'an and well-known Islamic teachings (Chapter 7). The point in so doing is to try to get a sense of how he may have looked upon the circumstances of his own life at every significant juncture and how he would have drawn upon the qualities of his own education and upbringing, his own culture and religion, his own African, Muslim, spirituality to make sense of, cope with and ultimately overcome the immense challenges he encountered in his life. Seen in this way it is clear that his African–Muslim education was more than enough to allow him not only to resist, but also to overcome the dispossessing and dehumanising forces of American slavery. Chapter 8 goes on to look at the life of 'Abd al-Rahman Ibrahima, also known at the 'Prince of Natchez'. As we narrate his fascinating life story we see glimpses of his African culture, his Islamic training, the strength of his faith, his long suffering forbearance, his wisdom and the hand of Divine 'providence' in delivering him from slavery. We also see some of the dynamics at play in antebellum America itself—the new nation's desire to maintain friendly relations with Morocco; the abolitionists, the

Christian missionaries, the colonists, philanthropists and politicians all trying to manipulate this slave for their own purposes, but all ending up, sometimes unwittingly, in helping him achieve his liberty. And in the midst of all of this, 'Abd al-Rahman's own strategy for achieving not only his own liberty but that of his entire family— one chapter of the Qur'an: the *Surah al-Faatihah* (Chapter 9).

Part 3 concludes with an examination of Salih Bilali, or Ben Ali, an African Muslim slave who became the successful leader of a slave community on Sapelo Island and left many descendants with Islamic retentions. We consider the wider implications and significance of the mysterious document he left behind: the so-called *Ben Ali Diary*— another piece of African-American literature that remains largely ignored to this day.

7

Job Ben Solomon

And make mention (O Muhammad) of Our bondman Job,
when he cried unto his Lord (saying) 'Surely the devil does
afflict me with distress and torment.'

—The Qur'an 38:41[1]

Of all the African Muslims to have ended up as slaves in antebellum America, Ayyub Bin Suleiman—better known as Job Ben Solomon—has attracted the greatest amount of attention. Given the fact that most studies on American slavery have succeeded in ignoring the Muslim presence among slaves in antebellum times, the frequent emergence of writings about Ayyub bin Suleiman is all the more remarkable. He has been described as the 'fortunate slave',[2] and it seems his good fortune has lived on, more than 280 years on, to remind us just how fortunate a slave he was.

The earliest account of Ayyub bin Suleiman was published in 1734—only three years after he was abducted and sold to a Royal African

---

1   The Qur'an (38: 41). Pickthall (trans.) (2008).
2   Grant (1968).

Company (RAC) slave-ship on the Gambia. This account, based—as it claims—on his own words and set down by his friend Thomas Bluett, tells of Ayyub's life in slavery up until his emancipation in England. Bluett played a key role in that emancipation, and accompanied Ayyub on the long voyage from America to England, whence Ayyub would finally make his way back to Africa. We have little reason to doubt Bluett's veracity and his good will towards Ayyub: it seems he was a genuine friend and well-wisher. But Bluett did not accompany Ayyub to Africa and so details of his return home are missing in Bluett's account.

In 1738, however, Francis Moore published his *Travels into the Inland Parts of Africa ... with a Particular Account of Job Ben Solomon.* This work provides us with information of Ayyub's life as a freeman in Africa, making his way back home whilst enjoying the favourable treatment of the same RAC that had enslaved him three years before. Inspired now by the economic advantages an alliance with Ayyub's people seemed to promise, the RAC was keen to ensure that he was treated with all the kindness a man of his rank deserved. Seven years later, in a *New General Collection of Voyages and Travels* volume II, Thomas Astley published a combined version of the previous two accounts of Ayyub's life, including the editor (Thomas Green's) own commentary in the form of footnotes. Francis Moore's account was published yet again, this time in 1759—appearing in the seventeenth volume of a twenty-volume work entitled *The World Displayed, or, A Curious Collection of Voyages and Travels.*

How can this immediate and consistent interest in Ayyub bin Suleiman be explained? For one thing his story is truly remarkable. Austin describes it as 'a romance which has often been told'. And Ayyub was clearly an exceptional individual, though not—as his white acquaintances, well-wishers and friends imagined—because he was a Negro who could read or write, and because he was 'civilised', refined, intelligent and even handsome: there were many more Africans who enjoyed these same qualities (generally thought to be the sole privilege of well-bred white folk). But rather because he showed an aptitude and care for matters beyond his immediate sphere of concern, thinking not only to return to Africa as a freeman, but also making arrangements that would secure the safety of others that might fall into the same predicament as he had, and seeking to acquire knowledge about the places he visited for future use. The timing of his arrival in England also contributed to the popular interest in his life. As Douglas Grant notes, the 'great abolitionist' Thomas Clarkson's observation that he was 'converted to the anti-slavery cause' through reading 'the great authorities of Adanson, Moore, Barbot, Smith, Bosman and others' indicates that 'Job stood in the centre of an impassioned argument [about slavery], both philosophical and moral.[1] Notably, Grant draws attention to the fact that four of the authorities Clarkson mentioned published their travels at more or less the same time Ayyub was in England: 'John Barbot in 1732, William Snelgrave in 1734, John Atkins in 1735, and Francis Moore in 1738'.[2]

> Who were the Noble Savages? Why were the Africans excluded
> from the charity shed upon primitive peoples by the ideal? Could
> Christians enslave their brothers? Were Africans properly to be
> considered men? These were great questions …[3]

England was asking questions of slavery and its part in it, and some of the more eloquent voices against the brutality of slavery—though not necessarily those calling for abolition—sought to inspire others, or were themselves inspired, through personal contact with the likes of Ayyub bin Suleiman or through hearing and recounting the experience of others who had met him. That not all of these anti-slavery voices were voices calling for outright abolition, makes their emphasis on Ayyub bin Suleiman all the more pertinent. Ayyub was also an 'abolitionist' of this kind: there is little doubt that he deplored the brutal treatment of slaves as they were shipped over the Atlantic to an oppressive life of slavery

---

1   Grant (1968), viii.
2   Ibid.
3   Ibid. xi.

in America—he himself had tasted the cruelty of America's peculiar institution and sought, literally, to flee from it:

> Because of Moore's and Bluett's accounts Job became a significant figure in the battle against slavery. The slaves shipped from Africa were an undifferentiated mass. When they were put up for sale, with their naked bodies specially greased and their heads shaven, they could be told apart only by their physical condition, and in their sale and purchase only their condition counted. They were never able to assert their individuality again, except by acts of rebellion, for which they were executed or thrashed back into conformity. The more pliant might become overseers on the plantations or domestic servants, but however favoured they were by their masters, their characters were scrutinized only in their new capacities. The colour of their skins alone reminded their masters, who were entirely ignorant of their language and culture, that they hailed from Africa.[4]

But Ayyub was made a slave whilst himself trading in slaves. Even after his return to Africa Ayyub purchased slaves—though significantly there seems to be no indication that he ever sold slaves again to European traders. Moore also accepted the slave trade and as Grant tells us, 'bargained for slaves at the factories to which he was posted …' But the African practice of slavery, and particularly slavery in Muslim societies, was radically different from that practised by white Christians in the New World (as we have discussed at length in the previous section). For one thing, many Africans, and particularly Muslim Africans—including Ayyub's people—only enslaved prisoners of war. But more than that, Ayyub's countrymen actively sought to restrict the trade in slaves, and his grandfather Ibrahim (*Hibrahim* in Bluett's account), upon founding the town of Bondu (*Bunda*), had passed a law granting protection to anyone who sought refuge in the town from

---

4 Ibid. 143.

being made a slave. As Bluett observed: 'this Privilege is in force there to this Day, and is extended to all in general, that can read and know God, as they express it …'[5] Thus Ayyub's homeland was actually a 'safe-haven for those fleeing from slavery.[6] Given the political atmosphere in England at the time, Ayyub's arrival was thus more than fortuitous for men like Moore, Bluett, and others. Grant writes:

> Job's story figured so prominently in the *Travels* that in the synopsis
> on the title page it was stated that the book included 'a particular
> Account of Job ben Solomon, a *Pholey,* who was in England in the
> Year 1733, and known by the Name of the *African*.[7]

That he was known as the 'African', as declared at the beginning of Moore's work, is significant: for the African Muslims who came after Ayyub, their Islamic manners, morals and literacy would be explained away by denying them their Africanness. In a very real sense, as Austin and others have pointed out (see Chapters 1–5 above), the failure of the majority of modern scholars to consider African Muslim slaves as valid or relevant informants about the African-American experience of slavery, can be seen as an internalisation of this mechanism (hence our emphasis in Chapter 5 on the deep involvement of Africans in Islam from its very inception). Ayyub, however—partly because of his relative distance from America—was acknowledged, in England at least, as a representative of all Africans, and his adherence to Islam contributed in no small way to an emerging English discomfort with the treatment of Negroes as livestock, or worse still, property to be owned and disposed of:

> Job was the first African who could be appreciated as a person.
> As a Muslim, he offered a complete and intelligible contrast to
> the superstitious worshippers of snakes and fetishes who seemed

---

5   Quoted in Austin (1984), 78 where Bluett's entire account is also available.
6   Austin (1997), 53.
7   Grant (1968), 143.

to populate Africa; and as a devout Muslim, who zealously fasted and prayed even in the inclement atmosphere of London and without fellow worshippers to encourage him, he challenged the Christian's lax beliefs. Neither was he ignorant and unlettered. His knowledge may have been circumscribed, but anyone who could write out the whole Koran from memory and discuss its precepts was an unusual guest in an England where illiteracy was commonplace. And mixing in very good English society, he held his own in a way that showed he had been taught to appreciate good breeding, although ignorant of English manners—this 'African Gentleman', Bluett called him. He was altogether different from the impression of the Negro that could be gathered from seeing him as an uprooted slave, or from reading about him in ignorant reports.[8]

Ayyub had made the acquaintance and won the admiration of some of the most respected and influential figures in England at the time. As a member of the Gentleman's Society of Spalding, Ayyub was admitted into an exclusive and prestigious club, which included in its membership Sir Isaac Newton and Alexander Pope.[9] His meetings with Sir Hans Sloane, the Duke of Montague, and the Royal Family were an important feature of his amazing story. Both Bluett and Francis Moore dedicated their accounts of Ayyub's life to the Duke of Montague (the former at Ayyub's own request). Moore described the Duke as Ayyub's friend and protector, writing: 'In the Wilds of Africa your Humanity is praised, and the grateful Arabs pray for you in the Desarts.' If Ayyub had escaped the process of 'de-Africanisation' which all subsequent and contemporary Muslim slaves seemed to have been subjected to, then it seems he had not escaped it entirely: Moore at least should have known better than to imply that Ayyub was an Arab.

---

8   Grant (1968), 143-144.
9   Austin (1997), 56.

Bluett's description of Ayyub as an 'African *Gentleman*' notwith-standing, those who were ill-disposed to abolitionist or anti-slavery sentiments, or those commentators believing in the myth of Negro inferiority even after the abolition of slavery (such as Ulrich B. Phillips), could diminish Ayyub's importance by denying him any representative value as a *black* man or *Negro*:

> Instead of reading his life and his memoir as the history of a representative, intelligent, clearly civilised man trained in Africa, many writers have retold his adventures as the history of an unusual, not quite African individual saved by English generosity. Instead of one of Africa's noblemen, Job was transformed into one of Nature's noblemen. Instead of serving as a contradiction to prevailing theories, Job's obvious civilised and educated traits were overlooked by influential philosopher-scientists of the slave era … who preferred to believe that there was no 'civilisation' in Africa. Further, his as-told-to-Bluett account of the experiences, feelings and observations of an African transported into American slavery has not been considered representative of the experience of thousands of other Africans as discussed in American histories that tend to say there are no records of such matters. His memoirs do not appear in any collection of African American literature.[10]

The rationale employed to de-Africanise Ayyub was also employed by authorities like Kant, Hume, Jefferson, Hegel, and others[11]—lending credibility to the logic which dictated: 'Negroes (i.e. blacks) are stupid: an Intelligent African cannot therefore be a Negro (i.e. black)'. Tragically this same logic has been internalised—consciously or otherwise—by modern American and African-American writers who remain curiously reluctant to make mention of literate African Muslim slaves. Yet these

---

10 Austin (1997), 52.
11 See Judy (1993) Chapter 4, particularly 114-115.

slaves confronted—at the deepest level and in the most direct way—
the myths of a tradition that sought, and in some ways still seeks, to
demonise, de-humanise, or de-legitimise the Other. When an Other like
Ayyub appears, and it is seen that his humanity is undeniable, then his
Otherness—his 'blackness'—must instead be denied. Thus Kant, Hume,
and other celebrated intellects of Europe were unable, like the entire
(post)modern epistemology they helped develop, to escape the very thing
that legitimised their project: in the degradation of the Other they found
an elevation of the Self:

> The Negroes of Africa have by nature no feeling that rises above
> the trifling. Mr Hume challenges anyone to cite a single example
> in which a Negro has shown talents and asserts that among the
> hundreds of thousands of blacks who are transported elsewhere
> from their countries, although many have even been set free, still
> not a single one was ever found who presented anything great in art
> or science or any other praiseworthy quality, even though among
> the whites some continually rise aloft from the lowest rabble, and
> through superior gifts earn respect in the world. So fundamental is
> the difference between these two races of man, and it appears to be
> as great in regard to mental capacities as in colour.[12]

Hume and Kant would have done well to consider Ayyub's story: it is
unlikely that they could have missed knowing of him. Astley's version
of Bluett's and Moore's accounts, in his *New General Collection*, had
allowed Ayyub to become well known outside of England. Grant
observes that J.J. Schwabes' *Allgemeine Histoire der Reisen*, published
in 1747, included Astley's conflation of Moore's and Bluett's writings,
making Ayuub an African of international repute.[13] It is more likely that
faced with talk of his civility and fine qualities, some of the 'greatest

---

12   Kant, *Observations*, 110-11, cited in Judy (1993), 10.
13   Grant (1968), 144.

minds of Europe' decided this was proof enough that Ayyub, and others like him, were not 'Negroes'.

Following his return to Africa, Ayyub would become the centre of an international incident between England and France—bringing mention of his name to French political circles and extending his fame, or perhaps in this case, notoriety, even further. When Ayyub was perceived to be a threat to the French trade in gold and gum on either side of Bondu, they arrested him. His year-long confinement finally ended when the local Muslims enacted a trade boycott, diverting all commerce from the French-dominated Senegal to the English factories on the Gambia.[14] In any case, Ayyub's fame in his own time and in later times was secure:

> Because he had been elected a member of the Gentlemen's Society of Spalding, his name appeared in the list of members given in an appendix to an account of the Society published by John Nichols in 1784, with a biographical, compiled from Moore and Bluett. Nichols later included this account of the Gentlemen's Society in his invaluable collection of Literary Anecdotes of the Eighteenth Century and Job's name again appeared, with a carefully revised biographical note [Literary Anecdotes, 1812. vi. Pt. 1. 90-1].
> Job's name was included by Alexander Chalmers in his General Biographical Dictionary, published in 1816, and his inclusion in the great Biographie Universelle helped equally to ensure that he was not forgotten abroad.[15]

And the remarkable coincidences and happy chances that seem to have directed the course of his endeavours following his initial miserable experience as a slave in colonial Maryland seem to have continued somewhat after his death. When at last, in modern times, it seemed Ayyub would be forgotten for ever and dwindle, like his Muslim

---

14 Austin (1997), 61.
15 Grant (1968), 145.

counterparts, even from the memory of academics and writers—quite by chance, in 1966 or 1967, the first Professor of American Literature at a British University, Douglass Grant, 'feeling a longing for the remote and strange', picked up the seventeenth volume of *The World Displayed; or, A Curious Collection of Voyages and Travels* (1759), and began to 'glance through Francis Moore's "Travels into the Inland Parts of Africa".... I had not read far,' wrote Grant, 'before I came to a chapter with the heading, "The History of Job Ben Solomon" ...'[16] Grant was so enchanted by what he read about 'Job' in Moore's account, that he took to finding and reading all that he could about Ayyub bin Suleiman. By 1968 Grant was able to publish a book-length biography of Ayyub entitled *The Fortunate Slave: An Illustration of African Slavery in the early Eighteenth Century*. A year later, Grant himself passed away.[17, 18]

At about the same time that Grant was researching and writing his biography of Job, Philip D. Curtin managed to include a chapter about 'Ayuba Suleiman Diallo of Bondu' (as he construed Ayyub's name), in his *Africa Remembered* (1967).[19] Austin describes Curtin's work as the first time that 'Job's life was given serious scholarly attention'.[20] Curtin's work is useful in emphasising the African context in Ayyub's story though, as part of a work on Africa, it neglects to consider in any detail the experiences and response of Ayyub to slavery in America. As Austin notes, this has remained a familiar theme in writings about Ayyub:

> Job's full story has seldom been told, and the complete text of his book has seldom been reprinted. Perhaps because it is a proud affirmation of native African culture, religion, and family rather than an unsophisticated tale of the trials faced by a pitiable

---

16 Ibid. iii.

17 Austin (1984), 110 note 11.

18 Curiously it was another incident of international concern involving Ayyub which occurred in 2011 that inspired the current author to finally agree to the publication of this work. See Part 3 below.

19 Curtin (1967), 17.

20 Austin (1984), 73.

black person fleeing, alone, from cruel slaveholders and crushed slaves—the common fare of the once and again popular 'slave narratives'—it has been underplayed where it might count. In addition, it has been overlooked when it might have provided a model, in part at least, for later African and African American memoirs of freedom narratives.[21]

In our own retelling of Ayyub's life, presented below, we shall rely primarily on the version of Bluett's *Memoirs* and Moore's *Travels* provided in Astley's *A New General Collection*, with occasional reference, in comments, to the biography written by Douglas Grant.[22] Consideration of Ronald T. Judy and Gate's respective and interesting observations about the significance of Ayyub's own writing is reserved for the final part of this study. The text given in Astley's *Collection* has been left as intact as possible—including spellings and typography. This is in order to retain a feeling for the context in which the original was written. In commenting on Ayyub's story, we shall attempt, albeit in a small way, to do so from the perspective of a Muslim well-grounded in an Islamic cosmology which sees in every act the Hand of God. Ayyub was a member of a scholarly family, and well versed in the Qur'an. Perhaps we can add something to an understanding of Ayyub's character and personality by attempting to look at his life from his own perspective. We do this with the deliberate aim of departing from the usual treatment of the *Other*, the usual telling of the slave's experience. This is something the firm adherence of Muslim slaves to their religion makes possible in a way which, when looking at their fellow African slaves, is much more difficult.

We begin therefore, as Ayyub himself would have begun, with *In the Name of Allah, the Most Merciful, the Compassionate ...*

---

21 Austin (1997), 52.

22 Other retellings of Ayyub's story are given in Austin (1984), 110 note 11. Though as Austin admits, even his list is only a 'sampling of retellings of Job's life'.

II

And remember our devotee Job: he called his Lord,
'Satan has afflicted me with calamity and torment!'
'Stamp with your foot: here's a cool place to wash, and drink'—
and We restored his family to him, and a like number with
them, as a mercy from Us, and reminder for the rational.
'And take a handful of grass and strike with it,
and do not break your oath.'
We did indeed find him patient, an excellent servant;
For he kept resorting to God.

—The Qur'an (38:41-44)[23]

Thomas Bluett and Francis Moore remain the most important sources
for information about Ayyub. Bluett was an attorney from Kent County
who, according to Grant, had a reputation for intemperance. In 1727
he travelled to England and was ordained as a minister. Returning to
Kent County in 1728 he became a missionary for the Society for the
Propagation of the Gospel. Grant also observes that his congregation
was initially reluctant to accept him, having known him before in his
capacity as an Attorney, but 'they were later reconciled'.[24] Francis Moore
was an important RAC officer during and after Ayyub's captivity and
enslavement. As is implied in Astley's *A New General Collection*, Bluett's
autobiographical sketch of Ayyub's homeland is full of geographical
inaccuracies. Where Bluett did not understand Ayyub's own
explanations, or where he thought it unnecessary to inquire directly
from him, he relied on popular European misconceptions of the African
landscape and therefore makes some clear mistakes (for example about
the location of Bondu and its adjacent river, Fulbe marriage customs,

---

23 The Qur'an (38:41-44). Cleary (trans.) (2004).
24 See Grant (1968), 83 and note 4.

and so forth). Being unfamiliar with Africa, Bluett could only rely on what had been reported before him. Moore's account was all the more important then, in providing a greater and more accurate description of Ayyub's African homeland.

Thomas Green's notes in Astley's edition add a further dimension of criticism to Bluett's and Moore's writings. Green's major objection, it seems, is to a sympathetic treatment of a Muslim or 'Mahommedan' by Christians who should have known better. Where Bluett appears to romanticise Ayyub, particularly as an African Muslim, Green becomes all the more critical. The juxtaposition of streams of agency in this rendition of Ayyub's life are startling and revealing: first we have Ayyub's autobiographical account as understood, interpreted, and made intelligible by an American missionary and friend who was instrumental in securing his emancipation. Second the continuation of Ayyub's story by a RAC officer, an important figure in English slavery operations in Africa and a sympathetic Africanist. Third we have a stubbornly dogmatic editor with strong views about Christianity and 'Mohammedans'— views that are not sympathetic but do attempt, in the fashion of the Orientalist scholar, to be properly objective. Ayyub himself has left us with statements of his own views on the entire matter through his brief writings in Arabic—being almost entirely quotations from the Qur'an found at the beginning of letters addressed to well-wishers and friends in London and elsewhere. As Judy points out, the value of these Arabic writings resides in their ability to escape the processes of agency through their intelligibility as texts in a foreign language. An examination of these writings, reserved for the final part of this study, reveals an Ayyub bin Suleiman who was not simply the passive recipient of favours and kindness from benevolent Englishmen and women that the accounts by Moore and Bluett seem to suggest.

Curtin gives the modern version of Ayyub's name as Ayyuba Suleiman Ibrahima Diallo. Like Ronald T. Judy, we have rendered it in its transliterated Arabic form, Ayyub bin Suleiman (Ayyub the son of

Suleiman), as this is the way Job wrote down his own name in Arabic.[25] Of course Ayyub has been most widely referred to as Job Ben Solomon, this being an English version of his Arabic name, a version which he himself preferred above the slave name Simon which he was originally given.[26] His surname, Diallo, indicates that his family belonged to one of most important divisions of the Fulbe people.[27] Most of Ayyub's family members seem to have been Imams, teachers and scholars. Since, traditionally, teaching Islam was more a religious duty than a profession, the travelling cleric with mercantile interests is a familiar feature of West African Muslim history, and the Diallo family seem to have been a particularly influential clan of such clerics—teaching for spiritual benefit and trading for daily sustenance.

In or around 1680 Ayuub's grandfather, Ibrahim, migrated from the Fulbe state of Futa Toro or Tukulor, in the Senegal Valley, eventually settling in an area west of the Faleme river and slightly south of the Senegal. Here he founded the province of Bondu, owing allegiance to the ruler of Futa Toro, the *satigi* Abu Bakr, who appointed Ibrahim as *Alfa* (learned man, or leader-cleric) of the new land. One of Ibrahim's first acts as Alfa of Bondu was to declare the land a safe haven for anyone fleeing from slavery and injustice.[28]

Following the death of Ibrahim, his son—Ayyub's father—became Alfa. At about the same time, the *satigi* Abu Bakr also died, passing his title to Geladio (Gelazi in Bluett's account). Satigi Geladio sent his son,

---

25 Curtin (1967), 35 note 27; Judy (1993), Chapter 4 and 317 note 47.

26 Curtin (1967), 35 note 27.

27 Ibid. 23 note 3.

28 There is some doubt as to whether Bluett was correct in saying that Ibrahim was the founder of a new town as opposed to a province. The hegemony of Bondu and its allegiance to Futa Toro was contested, and the details are not clear. Ayyub indicates in his writings that he was from Zagha—which may have been the actual town in Bondu, which was founded by his Grandfather. This would reconcile the conflicting accounts, which suggest Gadiaga control of Bondu as pointed out by Curtin. Though Curtin also indicates the possibility that the Sisibe came to Bondu under Tukulor authority. See Curtin (1967), 24-27, 36-37 and note 35; also Bluett Sect. I.

Samba,[29] to Ayyub's father to be educated in the sciences of Islam and the Arabic language. At this time Ayyub was also a student, and so Samba and Ayyub became companions under the same teacher. Following the death of his father, Samba Geladio would become a heroic figure in all Western Sudan, struggling in vain to preserve his claims to the kingship of Futa Toro against the *satigi* Konko Bubu Musa. Eventually his adventures would become the subject of legends and poetry, making him the most celebrated *satigi* of the Denianke dynasty.[30]

Like his princely companion and friend, Ayyub too was destined for leadership and fame, though of a different kind. At the age of 15 he completed his general education and took the office of Imam (probably in Bondu). At about the same time he married the daughter of the Alfa of Bambuk, and two years later they had a son whom he named Abdullah ('the slave of Allah').[31] A few years later he had a second son whom he named Ibrahim, and a third son Samba—named, perhaps, in honour of his friend Samba Geladio. In 1728 Ayyub married a second wife—the daughter of the Alfa of Damga[32] by whom he had a child who, Bluett quite correctly observed, was named after the daughter of the Prophet Muhammad: Fatima. Ayyub's four children and two wives—both daughters of high-ranking men—are a sure sign that by his late twenties or early thirties he was already a man of ample means and a respected member of Bondu society. As an Imam he had benefited from a religious training which would have earned him a reputation for competency in Arabic, memorisation of the Qur'an, leadership, piety, and devotion to

---

29 Bluett writes 'Sambo'.

30 Curtin (1967), 38, note 38.

31 According to Bluett she was the daughter of the *Alfa* of Tombuto or Timbuktu.
    This is presumed to be highly unlikely, considering that Timbuktu was some 600
    miles away from Bondu. Curtin suggests Bambuk. See Curtin (1967), 39 note 40.
    Also Bluett Sect I. Curtin's reasoning for dismissing Timbuktu simply because of its
    distance is questionable. Trade and communication links between various African
    peoples (especially among Muslim co-religionists) is likely to have been stronger than
    has been given credit for in such double-edged logic.

32 Bluett writes *Tomga*. Curtin locates Damga on the southeastern part of Tukulor,
    bordering on Bondu and Gadiaga. See Curtin (1967), 39 note 41, and Bluett Sect I.

worship and the quest for knowledge. As the companion of an African prince whose exploits would become legendary, the son of his teacher, a father, a husband, and an Imam, Ayyub bin Suleiman was well prepared to confront a world radically different from his own—a world and an institution which believed and acted upon the belief that Africans were barely human, let alone civilised. In the person of Ayyub, and men like him, Europe and the 'New World' it was building would meet a 'psycho-intellectual' challenge it still has not been able to reconcile: the formidable Other with an epistemology that could not be deconstructed, and a humanity that could not be stripped of its dignity:

> *It is He Who has Let free the two bodies Of flowing water:*
> *One palatable and sweet,*
> *And the other salt and bitter;*
> *yet has He made a barrier between them.*
> *A partition that is forbidden*
> *To be passed.*[33]

As we have mentioned, Bondu was located close to the Senegal, its eastern borders meeting the Faleme river. The Portuguese had been the first Europeans to arrive here, and they enjoyed a period of dominance of the Senegambia up until the seventeenth century. As the French gradually took control of the Senegal driven by a thirst for gold and gum, the Portuguese—more interested, it seems, in slaves than anything else—turned their attention towards the coastal regions south of the Gambia, creeping steadily towards the Gold Coast where slaves were easier to obtain.[34] Gum was an important commodity for Europe and gold an attractive one. The most accessible supplies of gum were north of the Senegal, but the gum tree also grew in the forests near Bondu. Gold too was near at hand, originating in Bambuk and along the Faleme

---

33 The Qur'an (25: 53). Ali, Abdullah Yusuf, (trans.) (1938).
34 Curtin (1967), 18.

River itself. The French had established a fort at Gadiaga, only a few days walk from Ayyub's homeland; and also at strategic points along the Senegal such as Tambucane (Fort Saint Joseph) and Dramane. The British, also lured by the promise of gold and gum, had meanwhile set up forts along the Gambia, hundreds of miles away from Gadiaga, but nevertheless serving as a respectable trading point into these rich 'inland parts' of Africa:[35]

> The Senegal was an unhandy and expensive river for commerce. Ocean-going ships were usually unable to cross the bar into the river itself, and even smaller craft could only reach Gadiaga in high water (from July to November). Even then, the current was swift and the boats often had to be poled or pulled upstream from the shore. By contrast, tides in the Gambia carried as far as Barrakunda falls in low water, and ocean-going ships could reach points about 120 miles from the mouth in any season. The Senegambian trade was thus highly competitive between the French dominated and the English dominated routes to the interior.[36]

Although the French succeeded in entering Bambuk (in 1725 and 1730), for both the French and the English, the riches of Africa seemed just out of reach—like grapes hanging from a vine just a little too far to be grasped. For Ayyub, this very fact would facilitate both his captivity and his deliverance. In 1730, Ayyub's father Suleiman sent him with two servants to an English ship recently arrived on the Gambia, to sell two slaves (probably enemy *Malinke* captives) and to purchase paper—a cherished commodity for West African scholars. Here, with this juxtaposition between *aalam* and *dunya*, the African Muslim encounter with New World slavery reveals a meaning barely considered; and the story of Job Ben Solomon begins. Slaves were treated as a commodity,

---

35 Ibid. 20.
36 Curtin (1967), 20-21.

and as a commodity they were most important to the development and founding of the New World: this is the theme of the *dunya* ('world')—a word which in Arabic literally means to *reach out for grapes that cannot be grasped,* and by extension refers to *the secular, worldly,* or *mundane.* The founding of the New World was the founding of the secular—that is mundane—world of modernity, built upon a secular epistemology that through the likes of Kant, Hegel, and others, sought to justify the enslavement—i.e. commodification—of the Negro, of the *Other.* Slaves like Ayyub bin Suleiman, in their capacities as Muslim scholars, teachers, and leaders, originated in a tradition that valued the world as *aalam* rather than *dunya.* And, as noted above, the Arabic word *aalam* relates to knowledge (*'ilm*) and scholasticism (*'aalam*), describing the world as an abode of signs—emphasising the spiritual over the temporal or mundane. Ayyub, in selling slaves (not a 'commodity' in Islam) was disposing of prisoners of war and seeking to make a profit, but in buying paper was hoping to gain some spiritual benefit: in his reasons for travelling to the Gambia he was thus going with the intention of seeking benefits in the *dunya* and in the *'aalam.* Thus in accordance with the saying,

> *Actions are but by intention and every man shall have but that which*
> *he intended ...* [37]

Ayyub bin Suleiman would taste the pleasures and the sorrows of both these 'worlds'.

His father had warned him, when he set out for the Gambia, not to cross over the river into the land of the *Malinke,*[38] for they were enemies

---

37 Hadith no. 1 from the *Arbaeen an Nawawiyya.* Op cit. (1998).

38 Bluett writes *Mandingo* (Sect II)—a term which would become synonymous with 'Muslim' in the New World. But as Curtin notes (1967, 39 note 42) the word sometimes referred to 'all of the Mande-speaking peoples, and sometimes more narrowly to the Malinke. Malinke actually lived on both banks of the lower Gambia.' Perhaps the Malinke on the near bank were already Muslims by the 1730s, or at least on friendly terms with Bondu and Futa Toro (?).

of his people and could not be trusted.[39] Perhaps the two slaves he was to sell to the English were themselves *Malinke* who had been captured in a previous encounter. Since Bondu was a self-declared 'safe haven' for those who sought refuge there, we can only assume that Ayyub's two slaves had come to Bondu with hostile intentions, or had been criminals. It is in any case noteworthy, that to sell these 'slaves', Ayyub was instructed by his father to travel several hundred miles to the Gambia, and not to the French operation at Gadiaga which was clearly a safer and more local alternative. If Bondu imposed restrictions on the slave trade—as Ibrahim's declaration upon founding Bondu (as a safe haven) implies— then it seems the further south one travelled, away from the Muslim-controlled lands, the easier it became to trade in them.

Ayyub reached Kau-ur on the Gambia in 1731, having travelled some 200 miles from his homeland. Nearby to Ka-ur, about 110 miles upstream from the mouth of the Gambia, was Joar—where an English ship by the name of *Arabella* had recently arrived. The ship was owned by a London merchant called Mr. Hunt and captained by Mr. Pike, who at the time was in Kau-ur purchasing slaves.[40] For some reason Ayyub and Captain Pike could not come to an amicable arrangement regarding the slaves. Perhaps Ayyub did not like what he saw of their treatment, or Pike did not think the slaves to be of good enough quality, or perhaps the price offered by Pike was too low. As Grant observes, in 1731 the slave markets of the Gambia were well supplied by local wars and hostilities.[41] In any case, Ayyub decided—against the advice of his father—to cross over the river, perhaps with the aim of selling his slaves at Tancrowall some 60 rides downstream and the home of the Portuguese trader Antonio Voss.[42] Moore's description of Voss's house-slaves (quoted in Grant) suggests a better treatment of slaves than what Ayyub may have witnessed at Ka-ur and Joar:

---

39 Bluett Sect II.
40 Curtin (1967), 39 note 43; and Moore's *Travels*, 69.
41 Grant (1968), 66.
42 Grant (1968), 67.

> He [Antonio Voss] is reckon'd to be worth *10.000 l.* Sterling, has got
> a vast Number of House-Slaves, *(viz* Slaves which live with him as
> Servants, a Grandeur much used by the *Portuguese* and *Spaniards)*
> which he keeps for Service and Breed, and are esteemed by him
> almost as much as his own Children ... [43]

Whatever his reasons, Ayyub met up with a friend named Lamine Jay
who knew the Mandingo (*Malinke*) language well, and together they
crossed over the river heading towards Tancrowall. Being mindful,
however, of having opposed his father's advice he sent his two servants
back to Bondu to let him know of his decision.[44]

*What is seen by the young man in a mirror is seen by the greybeard in a
baked brick.*[45]

It is unclear whether or not Ayyub actually met up with Voss and
disposed of his slaves at Tamcrowall, but in any case, he did manage to
sell them, acquiring in the process 'twenty-eight head of cattle'.[46] This was
a pleasurable gain, as the Fulbe were enthusiastic and skilled cattle drivers.
But Ayyub's pleasure would be short-lived. Hoping to cross the river at
Yamina and head back home, the two men stopped over at the house
of an acquaintance of theirs—probably near Damasensa.[47] But, as Grant
observes, it would have been impossible for a stranger driving a large herd
of cattle to go unnoticed in such a deserted country. 'Job could hardly
have expected to return to Cower [Kau-ur] without being observed.'[48]

It was a particularly hot day, and so hanging up their weapons—
Ayyub had in his possession a gold-hilted sword, a gold knife and a

---

43 Moore 49-50; quoted in Grant (1968), 67.
44 Bluett Sect II.
45 Old proverb quoted in Ata-Malik Juvaini, Boyle (trans.) (1997), 347.
46 Grant (1968), 67. The number is from Moore page 69.
47 Ibid. 67-68.
48 Ibid. 68.

quiver of arrows which had been a gift from his old friend Samba—they proceeded to gain some much needed rest.[49] At that point, a passing group of 'Mandingoes' (Malinke?) 'who live upon plunder … and observing him unarmed, rushed in, to the number of seven or eight at once, at a back door, and pinioned Job, before he could get to his arms, together with his interpreter [i.e. Lamine Jay]'.[50]

> *Whatever good, (O man!) happens to thee, is from God,*
> *But whatever evil happens to thee, is from thy (own) soul …* [51]

The enemy proceeded now to shave their heads and beards—something that as an Imam, Ayyub found particularly insulting—though 'the Mandingoes meant no more by it, than to make them appear like Slaves taken in war'.[52] The Mandingoes then carried their prisoners back across the Gambia to Captain Pike, whence they had come. The Captain, finding these two men in good condition, purchased them from their captors: it was the 27th of February 1730. At the earliest opportunity Ayyub protested against his treatment, reminding Captain Pike that he was the same man who had come to him earlier with slaves of his own to sell. 'The Company's factors on the river would not buy any slaves unless they were certain they were entitled to be sold'; but Captain Pike was a separate trader working for the London merchant William Hunt, and, as Grant tells us, 'even the best-intentioned slaver could not have afforded to look too closely at the methods by which his complement was filled'.[53]

The Captain agreed to give Ayyub and his friend an opportunity to redeem themselves for two slaves each:

---

49 Bluett Sect II.
50 Bluett Sect II.
51 The Qur'an (4: 79). Ali, Abdullah Yusuf, (trans.) (1938).
52 Bluett Sect II.
53 Grant (1986), 68-69.

> The Fula [Fulbe] were entirely loyal to each other. They were
> charitable to their people in want; they supported their blind and
> old and lame; they never sold each other into slavery, and made it
> their duty to redeem any of them taken and sold.[54]

And so a messenger was sent off to Bondu, to give Suleiman news of
his son's plight and the opportunity for his rescue. But Bondu was far
away—at least a fortnight's journey from Joar—and Captain Pike only
allowed four days for the despatch and the return of this messenger.
Finally, on the first day of March 1730, the *Arabella* was loaded with
its cargo of slaves and other merchandise; and on this day Ayyub bin
Suleiman and Lamine Jay became 'Negroes'.[55]

Bluett's account is silent about the details of this transformation. But
the preparation and seasoning of slaves is a process well documented
in other sources. They would have been stripped of all their clothing,
branded, and then shackled in pairs. The women in shame would often
squat to hide their nakedness, but for Muslims—male as well as female—
who were taught to cover their bodies, this humiliation must have been
particularly unbearable:

> If the market was good a captain would load slaves until simple
> prudence told him to stop. They would be compelled to lie head
> to foot and side by side, so close that they could hardly turn over,
> and if a supplementary platform was inserted between decks in
> order to take more rows, they might not even have room enough
> to sit up straight. A bucket in the corner was the only receptacle
> for slops. Even in fine weather, when the air-ports could be left
> wide open at night, the ventilation must have been poor, but in
> bad weather, when the slaves could not be brought up on deck and
> most of them were sick and the air-ports had to be battened down,

---

54 Grant (1968), 69 quoting from Moore (1744), 32-3 and Mollien (1820), 65.
55 Bluett Sect II.

the conditions below often passed belief. The stink and mess were hardly to be borne, the heat generated by so many bodies packed tight into a small space was intense, and the air was foul enough to extinguish a light.[56]

On the 11th of April the *Arabella* passed through James Fort on the Gambia—stopping only to pick up more slaves—before slipping out a few days later, into the Atlantic, with Ayyub and Lamine among its black cargo ... [57]

> *Or do you suppose you will enter paradise without there having happened to you the likes of what happened to those who passed away before you?*
>
> *Misery and distress befell them, and they were so shaken that the messenger and those who believed with him said,*
>
> *'When will God's help come?'*
>
> *Ah, but the help of God is near!*[58]

After surviving the horrors of this so-called 'Middle Passage', Ayyub found himself in the slave market of Annapolis in colonial Maryland. Here a certain Vachell Denton, also in the employ of the London merchant Mr. Hunt, took charge of the slaves from Captain Pike. Mr. Denton sold Ayyub to a Mr. Tolsey who owned a tobacco plantation on Kent Island, Chesapeake Bay.

Ayyub was not accustomed to the labour and toil of plantation work, and being a man of learning and education from an influential family, the harsh treatment meted out to him and (no doubt) other slaves was intolerable. Finally Ayyub began to weaken and grow ill, until his new

---

56 Grant (1986), 73.

57 See the entry in Moore's journal page 69, quoted in Grant (1986), 40.

58 The Qur'an (2:214). Cleary, (trans.) (2004).

master decided to give him easier work. He was put now in charge of Mr. Tolsey's cattle—something in which he no doubt excelled, being a Fulbe and owner of cattle himself. In this change of daily tasks perhaps Ayyub found some small comfort, but he missed his homeland, his wives, and his children. The language here was alien to him and the people strange and ill-mannered towards Africans. What other horrors he might have witnessed we cannot know, but it is clear that Ayyub, like all slaves, was in no way happy with his lot. News reached him, from other slaves arriving from the Gambia, that his old friend, the *satigi* Samba, had gone to war against the Mandingoes in order to punish them for his abduction, and also that his father had sent slaves to redeem him from Captain Pike, but that they had arrived just after the *Arabella* had sailed away.[59]

Nothing in his experience had succeeded in shaking his character or breaking his resolve. The Fulbe were a proud lot, and as a Muslim and a young Imam, Ayyub sought help and assistance against his situation from Allah. He was in the habit, says Bluett, of withdrawing into the woods to pray, but a white boy, who frequently watched him, began teasing him and disturbing his meditations.[60] Prayer was the only solace he enjoyed in this cruel and unfamiliar land; he spoke no English and had no friends to turn to. If now even his prayers were not inviolable, then he would have no more of it, and seek alternate means: he fled off into the woods, thinking perhaps that he had no more to lose by doing a desperate thing …

He headed eastwards, in the direction of Africa, travelling for 30 or 40 miles until he arrived in modern day Kent County, Delaware. At the time, this area was claimed by Pennsylvania and Maryland, drawing Bluett to comment that 'it is properly a part of Maryland'. Pennsylvanian law stipulated that any slave found away from his master's house without permission should be flogged with ten lashes, and if his master was not known, should be kept in gaol until he could

---

59 Bluett Sect II.
60 Bluett Sect II.

be identified.[61] And so, before long, Ayyub was spotted and the decree of the law passed over him.

Bluett notes that it was the month of June 1731, and he was attending court in Kent County, when he heard of a peculiar slave being kept in gaol; who spoke no English, but prayed in a strange fashion and could write in an unintelligible tongue:

(I) went with several gentlemen to the goalers [*sic*] house, being a tavern, and desired to see him. He was brought into the tavern to us, but could not speak one word of English. Upon our talking and making signs to him, he wrote a line or two before us, and when he read it, pronounced the words Allah and Mahommed; by which, and his refusing a glass of wine we offered him, we perceived he was a Mahometan, but could not imagine of what country he was, or how he got thither; for by his affable carriage, and the easy composure of his countenance, we could perceive he was no common slave.

When Job had been some time confined, an old Negroe man, who lived in that neighbourhood, and could speak the Wolof language,[62] which Job also understood, went to him, and conversed with him. By this Negroe the keeper [i.e. the gaoler] was informed to whom Job belonged, and what was the cause of his leaving his master. The keeper thereupon wrote to his master, who soon after fetched him home, and was much kinder to him than before; allowing him a place to pray in, and some other conveniences, in order to make his slavery as easy as possible.[63]

It is to Ayyub's credit, that although, after his return to Mr. Tolsey, his circumstances were improved somewhat, he was not content to remain

---

61 Curtin (1967), 42 note 49.

62 Curtin notes that the Wolof language was closely related to Ayyub's native Pular. See Curtin (1967) 42 note 51.

63 Bluett Sect II.

a slave. In later times, commentators like Ulrich B. Phillips and Stanley Elkins would try—with very different reasoning—to portray the slave as resigned to his fate; they would have done well to consider the story of Ayyub.

> *We will certainly test you*
> *Until We know those of you who strive*
> *and those who are constant;*
> *We will certainly bring out the facts about you.*[64]

Recognised now as an 'unusual' Negro, who could read and write—albeit in a foreign language—Ayyub was given access to paper and a pen. He took now to composing a letter to his father, telling him of his story and explaining his circumstances. This letter he had sent to Mr. Denton—the same man who had sold him to Mr. Tolsey (his 'master')—requesting that it might be given to Captain Pike and then, upon his reaching the Gambia, to some countryman in Joar, by which means it might eventually come to his father in Bondu. In other words, Ayyub was seeking to use the very route by which he had been brought into slavery to establish a connection back to his homeland and his people. For scholars like Gates,[65] this letter was the beginning of Afro-American literature: it was a letter in Arabic, and it began:

> *'In the name of Allah, the Most Merciful, the Most Kind.'*

By the time Vachell Denton received the letter, however, Captain Pike had already set sail for England, and so he sent instead a message to Mr. Hunt—the London merchant who employed Captain Pike—with instructions that the enclosed letter was meant for the Captain, who had been asked to take it back with him to Africa. But the letter arrived too

---

64 The Qur'an (47:31). Cleary, (trans.) (2004).
65 See Judy (1993), 149.

late in London for Mr. Hunt to pass it on to Captain Pike. And so it seemed Ayyub's attempt had ended in failure.

> *Remember how the Unbelievers plotted against thee, to keep thee in bonds, or slay thee, or get thee out (of thy home). They plot and plan, and God too plans; but the best of planners is God.*[66]

Mr. Hunt decided to keep the letter until a suitable opportunity could be found to send it on its way. Obviously fascinated by its mystery—compounded by the fact that it was written in Arabic by a Negro slave—he had occasion to show Ayyub's letter to his friend James Oglethorpe—the then director of the RAC, Member of Parliament and future founder of the colony of Georgia. Mr. Oglethorpe, noted for his philanthropy, arranged for the letter to be translated by John Gagnier, the Laudian Professor of Arabic at Oxford.[67]

> *[…] 'Ye chiefs! Here is delivered to me—a letter worthy of respect. It is from Solomon, and is (as follows): "In the name of God, most Gracious, Most Merciful; Be ye not arrogant against me […] "'*[68]

The contents of the letter, now intelligible in translation, revealed the author's erudition, eloquence and noble character in a way which impressed Oglethorpe, so much so that he decided to secure Ayyub's release. This was in June 1732:

> [Ogelthorpe] … took compassion on Job, and gave his bond to Mr. Hunt for the payment of a certain sum,[[69]] upon the delivery of Job here in England. Mr Hunt upon this sent to Mr Denton who purchased him again of his master for the same money which Mr

---

66 The Qur'an (8:30). Ali, Abdullah Yusuf, (trans.) (1938).

67 Grant (1968), 85.

68 The Qur'an (27:29–31). Ali, Abdullah Yusuf, (trans.) (1938).

69 This being £45—Ayyub's purchase price. See Grant (1986), 85.

Denton had formerly received for him; his master being very willing to part with him, as finding him no ways fit for his business.[70]

Winter was approaching fast by the time Ayyub was taken back by Vachell Denton. The rivers were frozen over, and on account of the ice, no ships were available for passage to England. Like the last time he met Vachell Denton, Ayyub was still a slave, and in the custody of Denton's employer, Mr. Hunt. But like the letter he had sent on before him, he was at the first stage of a journey back home. All he could do was wait, and be content.

> *Follow thou the inspiration sent unto thee, and be patient and constant, till God do decide: for He is the best to decide.*[71]

Whilst living with Mr. Denton, Ayyub had the opportunity of meeting a certain Reverend Mr. Henderson, whom Bluett describes as 'a gentleman of great learning, minister of Annapolis, and commissary to the Bishop of London'.[72] Henderson was well impressed by Ayyub and portrayed him as a pious man of great learning; as were other friends and acquaintances of Mr. Denton. Bluett also, it seems, had occasion to meet Ayyub often during this time. Several months later, the weather having improved, a ship was made ready for England. It was March 1733:

> [Ayyub] set sail in the *William*, Captain George Uriel Commander; in which ship I was also a passenger. The character which the Captain and I had of him at Annapolis, induced us to teach him as much of the English language as we could, he being then able to speak but few words of it and those hardly intelligible. This we set about as soon as we were out at sea, and in about a fort-night's time taught him all his letters, and to spell almost any single syllable,

---

70 Bluett Sect II.
71 The Qur'an (10: 109). Ali, Abdullah Yusuf, (trans.) (1938).
72 Bluett Sect II.

when distinctly pronounced to him; but Job and myself falling sick, we were hindered from making any greater progress at that time. However, by the time that we arrived in England, which was the latter end of April, 1733, he had learned so much of our language, that he was able to understand most of what we said in common conversation; and we that were used to his manner of speaking could make shift to understand him tolerably well.[73]

Ayyub's education during this voyage, was it seems, a two-way process. Ayyub was meticulous in practising his faith, and Bluett and the Captain were eager observers. As Bluett continues his account, he refers now to Job's co-religionists as 'Mussulman' where before he had called him a '*Mahommetan*'—a term offensive to Muslims because it implies the worship of Muhammad, rather than God:

During the voyage he was very constant in his devotions; which he never omitted, on any pretence, notwithstanding we had exceeding bad weather all the time we were at sea. We often permitted him to kill our fresh stock, that he might eat of it himself; for he eats no flesh, unless he has killed the animal with his own hands, or knows that it has been killed by some Mussulman. He has no scruple about fish; but won't touch a bit of pork, it being expressly forbidden by their law. By his good nature and affability he gained the good will of all the sailors, who (not to mention other kind offices) all the way up the channel showed him the head lands and remarkable places; the names of which Job wrote down carefully, together with the accounts that were given him about them. His reason for so doing, he told me, was that if he met with an Englishman in his country, he might by these marks be able to convince him that he had been in England.[74]

---

73 Ibid.
74 Ibid.

Upon arrival in England, Ayyub was faced with yet another setback: James Ogelthorpe had retired from the RAC and had left England for Georgia. Grant writes: 'The reasons for Ogelthorpe's disassociating himself from the Company are not at all clear, but in addition to the very heavy duties he had voluntarily taken upon himself when he had become one of the trustees of the new colony of Georgia, he may have had scruples about being active in any business concerned with slavery.'[75] Indeed, slavery was initially outlawed in Georgia as a result of Ogelthorpe's opposition. The absence of Ogelthorpe meant that Ayyub was still owned by Mr. Hunt, who consequently arranged for him to be taken to residence at Limehouse. Thomas Bluett, meanwhile, went off to visit friends in the country: Ayyub was now alone once more, still a slave, and in another, and equally alien, land. Grant observes that it was a precarious time for black people in England. Attempts had been made, with the encouragement of some Christians like the Quakers, to baptise slaves against the wishes of their owners and thus emancipate them from both the cruelty of slavery and the tyranny of idolatry. But in 1729 concerned slave owners, planters, and merchants had succeeded in gaining a legal ruling which held that:

> a slave by coming from the West Indes to Great Britain or Ireland,
> either with or without his master, doth not become free, and that
> his master's property or right in him is not therefore determined
> or varied, and that Baptism doth not bestow freedom on him nor
> make any alteration in his temporal condition in these Kingdoms;
> we are also of [the] opinion that the Master may legally compel
> him to return again to the Plantations.[76]

As a consequence of this ruling, black men were often abducted in the streets—whether they were runaways or not—and sold off to the West Indies as slaves. Thomas Clarkson, himself to be influenced by Ayyub's

---

75   Grant (1986), 87.

76   Cited in Grant (1986), 88 from a quote in Dorothy George, *London Life in the Eighteenth Century*, 1930.

story, would write in 1808 about how this ruling had made England as dangerous a place for the black man as America:

> In a little time slaves absconding were advertised in the London papers as runaways, and rewards offered for the apprehension of them, in the same brutal manner as we find them advertised in the land of slavery. They were advertised also ... to be sold by auction, sometimes by themselves, and at others with horses, chaises, and harness. They were seized also by their masters, or by persons employed by them, in the very streets, and dragged from thence to the ships; and so unprotected now were these poor slaves, that persons in nowise concerned with them began to institute a trade in their persons, making arrangements with captains of ships going to the West Indies to put them on board at a certain price.[77]

In line with this slave trade direct from England, Mr. Hunt, it seems, was approached by people offering to buy Ayyub from him for their own purposes. But Hunt had already contacted the RAC, and in the terms of the original agreement with Ogelthorpe, offered to sell Ayyub to them for £45. The RAC, following the advice of its new Deputy-Governor, Charles Hayes, agreed to purchase Ayyub, making their intentions very clear: 'the said Negro understands and writes Arabick and may be of service to the Company on giving him his freedom and sending him to Gambia, which is his native country ...'[78] Fortunately for Ayyub, his friend Thomas Bluett came to see him at Limehouse, and when Ayyub told him of his situation, he acted immediately: taking Ayyub with him to Cheshunt. Here in the company of his only real friend in England, Ayyub was to make his acquaintance with some of the most respectable and notable Englishmen and women of the time. In this company he would excel, and demonstrate the learning and skill he had acquired in Africa:

---

77 Thomas Clarkson, *The History of the...Abolition of the Slave-Trade* cited in Grant (1986), 88.

78 Public Records Office T. 70/93, 243.

After I had visited my friends in the country, I went up on purpose to see Job. He was very sorrowful, and told me, that Mr. Hunt had been applied to by some persons to sell him, who pretended they would send him home; but he feared they would either sell him again as a slave, or if they sent him home would expect an unreasonable ransom for him. I took him to London with me and waited on Mr. Hunt, to desire leave to carry him to Cheshunt in Hartfordshire; which Mr. Hunt complied with. He told me he had been applied to, as Job had suggested, but did not intend to part with him without his own consent; but as Mr. Ogelthorpe was out of England, if any of Job's friends would pay the money, he would accept of it, provided they would undertake to send him home safely to his own country. I also obtained his promise that he would not dispose of him till he heard farther from me.

Job, while he was at Cheshunt, had the honour to be sent for by most of the gentry of that place, who were mightily pleased with his company, and concerned for his misfortunes. They made him several handsome presents, and proposed that a subscription should be made for the payment of the money to Mr. Hunt. The night before we set out for London from Cheshunt, a footman belonging to Samuel Holden, Esq.; brought a letter to Job, which was, I think, directed to Sir Byby Lake [deputy governor of the Royal African Company]. The letter was delivered at the African House [RAC headquarters in London]; upon which the House was pleased to order that Mr. Hunt should bring in a bill of the whole charges which he had been at about Job, and be there paid; which was accordingly done, and the sum amounted to fifty-nine pounds, six shillings, and eleven pence half-penny. This sum being paid, Mr. Ogelthorpe's bond was delivered up to the Company.[79]

---

79 Bluett Sect II.

Although no longer in the possession of Mr. Hunt, Ayyub was still not free. Indeed Bluett was wholly dissatisfied with the situation, thinking, as did Ayyub, that he had merely switched owners, but remained still a slave. In the meantime, Ayyub's circle of friends had increased. They admired him for many different reasons: some for his appearance, others for his intelligence, his manners, his wit, and for his piety. Whilst at Cheshunt, it seems, Ayyub not only prayed regularly—as he had done throughout his ordeal—but also observed the fast of Ramadhan, which as an Imam, he would have known was not required of someone in his position as a traveller and slave in a strange (and hostile) land. As Bluett's account testifies, his hosts observed his behaviour with great enthusiasm and curiosity, asking him many questions and enjoying the novelty of this black man, who, for some at least, was a 'noble savage', and for others, like Bluett, an 'African gentleman' different in appearance from other Negroes:

> Job was about five feet ten inches high, strait limbed, and naturally of a good constitution; although the religious abstinence which he observed, and his fatigues he lately underwent, made him appear something lean and weakly. His countenance was exceeding pleasant, yet grave and composed; his hair long, black, and curled, being very different from that of the Negroes commonly brought from Africa.
>
> His natural parts were remarkably good; and I believe most of the gentleman that conversed with him frequently, will remember many instances of his ingenuity. On all occasions he discovered a solid judgement, a ready memory, and a clear head. And, notwithstanding the prejudices which it was natural for him to have in favour of his own religious principles, it was very observable with how much temper and impartiality he would reason in conversation upon any question of that kind, while at the same time he would frame such replies, as were calculated at once to support his own opinion, and to oblige or please his opponent.

In his reasoning there appeared nothing trifling, nothing hypocritical or over-strained; but on the contrary, strong sense, joined with an innocent simplicity, a strict regard to truth and a hearty desire to find it. Tho' it was a considerable disadvantage to him in company, that he was not sufficient master of our language; yet those who were used to his way, by making proper allowances, always found themselves agreeably entertained by him.

The acute of his genius appeared upon many occasions. He very readily conceived the mechanism and use of most of the ordinary instruments which were showed to him here; particularly upon seeing a plow, a grist mill, and a clock taken to pieces, he was able to put them together again himself without any further direction.

His memory was extraordinary; for when he was fifteen years old he could say the whole Alcoran by heart, and while he was here in England he wrote three copies of it without assistance of any other copy, and without so much as looking to one of those three when he wrote the others. He would often laugh at me when he heard me say I had forgot any thing, and told me he hardly ever forgot any thing in his life, and wondered that any body should.

In his natural Temper there appeared a happy Mixture of the Grave and Chearful, a gentle Mildness, guarded by a proper Warmth, and a kind and compassionate Disposition towards all that were in Distress. In conversation he was commonly very pleasant; and would every now and then divert the company with some witty turn, or pretty story, but never to the prejudice of religion, or good manners. I could perceive, by several slight occurrences, that notwithstanding his usual mildness he had courage enough, when there was occasion for it ...[80]

Ayyub's competency as Imam, and his abilities as a theologian, are indicated by a particular incident related by Bluett, where Ayyub managed

---

[80] Bluett Sect IV.

to turn an ordinarily mundane event into a lesson on *tawhid*—or the oneness and unicity of God—the principal doctrinal difference between the trinitarianism of Christianity and the monotheism of Islam. Ayyub was also clearly a scholar, and took enthusiastically to a study of the Bible, to see if there really was any scriptural authority for the Christian belief in the trinity. As Bluett's account indicates, Ayyub's integrity and sophistication, along with his moral uprightness and his explanations of Islam, could not be reconciled with the usual Orientalist perception of that religion as *Other*. That is the perception of Islam as sensual and morally deficient. Bluett, being a preacher himself, concluded that Ayyub's interpretation of Islam was different, and obviously superior, to that of the Turk: in other words, consciously or otherwise, he applied the same device that allowed and allows for the possibility of the *noble savage*. If the *Other* becomes unintelligible by reason of his *sameness*—that is, his lack of *Otherness*, his intelligibility to us as an example for the *Self*—then to the extent of his intelligibility, his *Otherness* must be denied whilst at the same time further exaggerating the grossness of the *Other*. We cannot blame Bluett too harshly for doing this: it is the only way—without self-effacement—for us to feel capable of acknowledging the very thing, which by denying, had allowed us to preserve our sense of self-worth in spite of the evidence of our actions. Bluett writes:

> Job's aversion to pictures of all sorts was exceeding great; insomuch, that it was with great difficulty that he could be brought to sit for his own. We assured him that we never worshipped any picture, and that we wanted his for no other end but to keep us in mind of him. He at last consented to have it drawn; which was done by Mr. Hoare. When the face was finished, Mr. Hoare asked what dress would be most proper to draw him in; and upon Job's desiring to be drawn in his own country dress, told him he could not draw it, unless he had seen it, or had it described to him by one who had: upon which Job answered, if you can't draw a dress you never saw, why do some of you painters presume

to draw God, whom no one ever saw? I might mention several
more of his smart repartees in company, which showed him to be
a man with humour, as well as good sense: but that I may not be
tedious, what I have said shall suffice …

As to his religion, 'tis known he was a Mahometan [Muslim],
but more moderate in his sentiments than most of that religion are.
He did not believe a sensual paradise, nor many other ridiculous
and vain traditions, which pass current among the generality of the
Turks. He was very constant in his devotion of God; but said, he
never prayed to Mahommed, nor did he think it lawful to address
any but God himself in prayer. He was so fixed in the belief on
one God, that it was not possible, at least during the time he was
here, to give him any notion of the Trinity; so that having had a
New Testament given him in his own language, when he read it,
he told me he had perused it with a great deal of care, but could
not find one word in it of three Gods, as some people talk: I did
not care to puzzle him, and therefore answered in general, that the
English believed only in one God. He showed upon all occasions
a singular veneration for the name of God, and never pronounced
the word Allah without a peculiar accent, and a remarkable pause:
and indeed his notions of God, Providence, and a future state, were
in main very just and reasonable.[81]

The gift of a New Testament in Arabic, mentioned by Bluett, was
produced by the Society for the Promotion of Christian Knowledge in
1726.[82] The man who presented it to Ayyub was George Sale, a learned
Orientalist and member of the society. According to Grant, Sale 'wrote
to the Society in June requesting a New Testament and Psalter and a
Catechetical Instructions in Arabic, which had all been prepared for and
issued by the Society, for the use of the "Poor Mahometan Black redeemed

---

81 Bluett Sect IV.
82 Grant (1968), 97.

by order of Mr. Ogelthorpe" ...'[83] At the time, Sale was completing a translation of the Qur'an which was to be his greatest work. For all his praise as a scholar—Grant describes him as 'one of the most remarkable scholars of his age'[84]—Sale was finding the task difficult, and although after his initial studies in Law he had taken to Arabic, his translation of the Qur'an was from a Latin version produced by Maracci in 1689. Maracci, who was Confessor to Pope Innocent XI, dedicated his work to the Holy Roman Emperor Leopold I; introducing it with an entire volume entitled 'Refutation of the Qur'an'.[85]

Maracci's version amounted to a garbled piece of work, with selected passages taken, it seems, at random from Arabic commentators in a manner designed to please the Pope as much as possible. The fact that Sale, despite his pretensions to a command of the Arabic, almost reproduced Maracci word for word, suggests that the presence of Ayyub bin Suleiman, an Imam and Arabic speaker, would have been invaluable to him. It is likely that at least one of the three Qur'ans Ayyub wrote down from memory were for his benefit. Sale was not the only intellectual to actively seek out Ayyub. Grant writes:

> Other figures in the world of intellectual London besides George
> Sale had hurried to make Job's acquaintance on his arrival, and
> among them was Sir Hans Sloane, physician to Queen Caroline,
> and the greatest collector of 'rarities' in his age ...
> Sir Hans could have learnt from Ogelthorpe of Job's strange
> history, but he would have looked forward to his coming out of
> self-interest, as well as curiosity. The range of his collection, which
> were housed at this time in Bloomsbury, was extraordinary: mineral
> specimens, precious stones, birds and butterflies from both Indies
> and elsewhere, mechanical contrivances, Egyptian mummies,
> Roman antiquities, miscellaneous curiosities, and medals and

---

[83] Grant (1968), 97.
[84] Ibid.
[85] Ibid.

books—42,000 books and manuscripts, all superbly bound. Among the medals and manuscripts were many in Arabic and these, Sir Hans had hoped Job would be able to translate.

Sir Hans was not disappointed; at least he was satisfied with Job's efforts and impressed by his learning. A year after Job's return to Africa he told a correspondent that he had some of his Arabic coins 'interpreted by a native of the inward parts of Africa, a black Mahometan priest who had great knowledge of the Ancient as well as modern Arabick.' But there were other matters in which Job might also be helpful, and Sir Hans foresaw that he could make a useful correspondent on his return home, and an agent for forwarding curiosities.[86]

It is unlikely that Ayyub allowed himself simply to be exploited by well-intentioned intellectuals like Sloane. Whether he realised it or not, Ayyub probably found much of interest in Sloane's collections for his own intellectual endeavours. Ayyub impressed many of Sloane's acquaintances, so much so that Maurice Johnson and William Bogdani, the Clerk of the Ordnance at the Tower of London, proposed his election into the Gentleman's Society of Spalding (founded in 1710). This remains an extraordinary testament to Ayyub's strength of character and his personal attributes—other members connected to the society included Alexander Pope and Sir Isaac Newton; but Ayyub bin Suleiman, or rather—according to the minutes of the Society for 6th June 1734 (the date of his election)—the 'learned and worthy Job Jalla', was a Negro, and a former slave.

In any case, perhaps more sincere in his friendship towards Ayyub was Nathaniel Brassey, one of Bluett's friends, and an important figure in the City. Brassey was a banker and Member of Parliament who opened the subscription, and made up the shortfall, which ultimately resulted in Ayyub's full redemption (see below). Brassey also paid for the clothes, prepared in the Fulbe style, which Ayyub wore for his audience with the

---

[86] Grant (1968), 99-100.

King and Queen. Following his return to Africa, Ayyub would write a letter to Nathaniel Brassey thanking him for his concern. The letter is discussed in the final part of this study.

It is to Bluett's credit that he helped Ayyub secure complete independence from the RAC by soliciting the help of Nathaniel Brassey, and to the latter for ensuring that the attempt was not in vain. Before finishing the story of Ayyub's adventures in England, we should point out that two of the subscribers to Ayyub's fund were themselves African Muslims: the envoys of the Bey of Tunis who, notes Grant, had arrived at the Court of St. James in October 1733. Grant also notes that Ayyub went to call upon them on a Friday, although he was very busy.[87] Perhaps Ayyub, being an Imam, conducted the Friday congregational prayer *Salatul-jumu'ah* with these diplomats.

Bluett continues Ayyub's story after the RAC purchased him from Mr. Hunt:

> Job's fears were now over, with respect to his being sold again as
> a slave; yet he could not be persuaded but that he must pay an
> extravagant ransom, when he got home. I confess, I doubted much
> of the success of a subscription, the sum being great, and Job's
> acquaintance in England being so small; therefore to ease Job's
> mind, I spoke to a gentleman about the affair, who has all along
> been Job's friend in a very remarkable manner. This gentleman was
> so far from discouraging the thing, that he began the subscription
> himself with a handsome sum, and promised his further assistance
> at a dead lift. Not to be tedious: several friends, both in London
> and in the country, gave in their charitable contributions very
> readily; yet the sum was so large, that the subscription was about
> twenty pounds short of it; but that generous and worthy gentleman
> before mentioned, was pleased to make up the defect, and the
> whole sum was completed.

---

87 Grant (1968), 103-104.

I went (being desired) to propose the matter to the African
Company; who, after having heard what I had to say, showed me
the orders that the House had made; which were, that Job should
be accommodated at the African House at the Company's expence,
till one of the Company's ships should go to Gambia, in which
he should be sent back to his friends without any ransom. The
Company then asked me, if they could do any thing more to make
Job easy; and upon my desire, they ordered, that Mr. Ogelthorpe's
bond should be cancelled, which was presently done, and that Job
should have his freedom in form, which he received handsomely
engrossed, with the Company's seal affixed; after which the full sum
of the whole charge (viz. Fifty-nine pounds, six shillings, and eleven
pence half-penny) was paid in to their clerk, as was before proposed.

Job's mind being now perfectly easy, and being himself more
known, he went chearfully among his friends to several places,
both in town and country. One day being at Sir Hans Sloane's he
expressed his great desire to see the Royal Family. Sir Hans promised
to get him introduced, when he had clothes proper to go in. Job
knew how kind a friend he had to apply upon occasion; and he was
soon cloathed in a rich silk dress, made up after his own country
fashion, and introduced to their Majesties, and the rest of the Royal
Family. Her Majesty was pleased to present him with a rich gold
watch; and the same day he had the honour to dine with his Grace
the Duke of Montague, and some others of the nobility, who were
pleased to make him a handsome present after dinner. His Grace,
after that, was pleased to take Job often into the country with him
and show him the tools that are necessary for tilling the ground,
both in gardens and fields, and made his servants show him how to
use them; and afterwards his Grace furnished Job with all sorts of
instruments, and several other rich presents, which he ordered to be
carefully done up in chests, and put on board for his use. 'Tis not
possible for me to recollect the many favours he received from his
Grace, and several other noblemen and gentlemen, who showed a

singular generosity towards him; only, I may say in general, that the goods which were given him, and which he carried over with him, were upwards of 500 pounds; besides which, he was well furnished with money, in case any accident should oblige him to go on shore, or occasion particular charges at sea. About the latter end of July last [1734] he embarked on board one of the African Company's ships, bound for Gambia; where we hope he is safely arrived, to the great joy of his friends, and the honour of the English nation.[88]

One would imagine that after all his adventures Ayyub would have been content to merely set off on a ship to Africa, waving all his misfortunes goodbye. But it is a testament to his character that before leaving he did not forget his friend Lamine Jay, securing from the Duke of Montague a promise that he would find out where Jay was in Maryland and arrange for his release and return to Africa. A promise that, it seems, did lead to the emancipation and return of Lamine Jay. Moreover, Ayyub persuaded the RAC to agree to allow any Muslim bought as a slave by the Company in Africa to redeem himself in exchange for two other slaves. Grant observes that 'the Company's rather surprising agreement to this request was not merely nominal and intended to placate Job, backed up as he now was by powerful friends, but they sent instructions to their agents in the Gambia that this arrangement should be put into effect'.[89]

Ayyub bin Suleiman was an Imam with political connections in a land rich in gold and gum. Up until now, the French had dominated this trade, but the English, with their posts on the Gambia, sought desperately to divert that monopoly. Bluett, in the concluding part of his account, reveals the benefits of befriending Ayyub:

Considering the singular Obligations he is under to the English, [Job] may possibly, in good time, be of considerable service to

---

88   This is where Bluett's Sect II ends.
89   Grant (1968), 108.

us also; and that we have reason to hope this from the repeated
Assurances we had from Job, that he would, upon all occasions, use
his best Endeavours to promote the English Trade before any other.[90]

Thus the RAC hoped to be recompensed for its investment in Ayyub
with a trade arrangement with Bondu. The remaining chapters of
Ayyub's story were told by Francis Moore, who at the time was in James
Fort on the Gambia. In the following section, by way of concluding
Ayyub's story, we have selected only a few pieces from Moore's *Travels*
which speak of Ayyub.

III

It was the 8th of August 1734, and Ayyub was on his way home in the
RAC ship, the *Dolphin*. The ship arrived at James Fort at around noon,
saluting with nine guns and receiving a nine-gun salute in return. Francis
Moore came out from the Fort to meet the crew and its passengers ...

From Moore's *Travels into the Inland Parts of Africa* (1738):

[After the salute, there] came on shore the captain, four writers,
one apprentice to the Company, and one black man, by name Job
Ben Solomon, a Pholey of Bundo in Foota [i.e. Futa Toro] [...]
    After he had continued in England about fourteen months,
he wanted much to return to his native country, which is Bundo
[...] of which place his father was high-Priest, and to whom he
sent letters from England. Upon his setting out from England
he received a good many noble presents from her most Gracious
Majesty Queen Caroline, his Highness the Duke of Cumberland,
his Grace the Duke of Montague, the Earl of Pembroke, several
ladies of quality, Mr. Holden, and the Royal African Company,
who have ordered their agents to show him the greatest respect.

---

90 See Austin (1997), 58.

Job Ben Solomon having a mind to go up to Cower [Ka-ur] to talk with some of his countrymen, went along with me. […] On the 26th we arrived at the Creek of Damasensa, and having some old acquaintances at the town of Damasensa, Job and I went up in the yawl; in the way going up a very narrow place for about half a mile, we saw several monkeys of a beautiful blue and red, which the natives tell me never set their feet on the ground, but live entirely amongst the trees, leaping from one to another at so great distances, as any one, were they not to see it, would think improbable.

In the evening, as my friend Job and I were sitting under a great tree at Damasensa, there came by us six or seven of the very people who robbed and made a slave of Job, about thirty miles from hence, about three years ago; Job tho' a very even-tempered man at other times, could not contain himself when he saw them, but fell into a most terrible passion, and was for killing them with his broad sword and pistols, which he always took care to have about him. I had much ado to dissuade him from falling upon the six men; but at last, by representing to him the ill consequences that would infallibly attend such a rash action, and the impossibility of mine or his own escaping alive, if he should attempt it, I made him lay aside the thoughts of it, and persuaded him to sit down and pretend not to know them, but ask them questions about himself; which he accordingly did, and they answered nothing but the truth. At last he asked them how the king their master did; they told him he was dead, and by further enquiry we found, that amongst the goods for which he sold Job to Captain Pyke there was a pistol, which the king used commonly to wear slung about his neck with a string; and as they never carry arms without being loaded, one day this accidentally went off, and the ball's lodging in his throat, he died presently. At the closing of this story Job was very much transported, that he immediately fell on his knees, and returned thanks to Mahomet [this is clearly a mistake by Moore, as Job explained to Bluett, it was inconceivable for a Muslim to pray

to anyone except God] for making this man die by the very goods
for which he sold him into slavery; and then turning to me, he
said, 'Mr. Moore, you see now God Almighty was displeased at this
man's making me a slave, and therefore made him die by the very
pistol for which he sold me; yet I ought to forgive him, says he,
because had I not been sold, I should neither have known any thing
of the English tongue, nor have had any of the fine, useful and
valuable things I now carry over, nor have known that in the world
there is such a place as England, nor such noble, good generous
people as Queen Caroline, Prince William, the Duke of Montague,
the Earl of Pembroke, Mr. Holden, Mr. Ogelthorpe, and the Royal
African Company.'

On the 1st of September we arrived at Joar, the freshes being
very strong against us. I immediately took an inventory of the
company's effects, and gave receipts to Mr. Gill for the same. After
which we unloaded the sloop, and then I sent her to Yanimarew
for a load of corn for James Fort, where we stayed till the 25th, and
then came back to Joar, during which time I made some trade with
the merchants, though at a pretty price.

On Job's first arrival here, he desired I would send a messenger
up to his own country to acquaint his friends of his arrival. I spoke
to one of the blacks which we usually employ upon these occasions
to procure me a messenger, who brought me a Pholey, who knew
the High Priest his father [i.e. Suleiman], and Job himself, and
expressed great joy at seeing him in safety returned from slavery,
he being the only man (except one) that was ever known to come
back to this country, after having been once carried a slave out of
it by white men. Job gave him the message himself, and desired his
father should not come down to him, for it was too far for him to
travel; and that it was fit for the young to go to the old, and not
for the old to come to the young. He also sent some presents by
him to his wives, and desired him to bring his little one, which
was his best beloved, down to him. After the messenger was gone,

Job went frequently along with me to Cower [Ka-ur], and several other places about the country; he spoke always very handsome English, and what he said, took away a great deal of the horror of the Pholeys for the state of slavery amongst the English; for they being generally imagined, that all who were once sold for slaves, were generally either eaten or murdered, since none ever returned. His description of the English gave them also a great notion of the power of England and a veneration for those who traded amongst them [Job was clearly paying back the RAC and his English friends for their good conduct towards him, by advocating trade with the English]. He sold some of the presents he brought with him from England for trading-goods, with which he bought a woman-slave and two horses, which were useful to him there, and which, he designed to carry with him to Bundo, whenever he should set out thither. He used to give his country people a good deal of writing-paper, which is a very useful commodity amongst them, and of which the Company had presented him with several reams. He used to pray frequently, and behaved himself with great mildness and affability to all, so that he was very popular and well-beloved. The messenger not being thought to return soon, Job desired to go down to James Fort to take care of his goods, I promising to send him word when the messenger came back, and also to send some other messengers, for fear the first should miscarry.

On the 26th I sent down the Fame sloop to James Fort, and Job going along with her, I gave the master orders to show him all respect he could.

[…] On the 14th[91] a messenger, whom I had sent to Job's country, returned hither with letters, and advice that Job's father died before he got thither, but that he had lived to receive the letters sent by Job from England, which brought him the welcome news of his son's being redeemed out of slavery, and the figure he

---

91 Curtin gives the date as 14th February 1735(?). See Curtin (1967), 58.

made in England. That one of Job's wives was married to another man; but that as soon as the husband heard of Job's arrival here, he thought it advisable to abscond: that since Job's absence from this country, there had been such a dreadful war, that there is not so much as one cow left in it, tho' when Job was there it was a very noted country for numerous herds of large cattle. With this messenger came a good many of Job's old acquaintances, whom he was exceeding glad to see; but notwithstanding the joy he had to see his friends, he wept grievously for his father's death, and the misfortunes of his country. He forgave his wife, and the man that had taken her; for says he, Mr. Moore, she could not help thinking I was dead, for I was gone to a land whence no Pholey every yet returned; therefore she is not to be blamed, nor the man neither. For three or four days he held a conversation with his friends without any interruption, unless to sleep or eat.

[…] On the 8th [April 1735], having delivered up the company's effects to Mr. James Conner and taken proper discharges for the same, I embarked on board the Company's sloop James, to which Mr. Hull accompanied me, and parted with me in a very friendly manner. Job likewise came down with me to the sloop, and parted with me with tears in his eyes, at the same time giving me letters for his Grace the duke of Montague, the Royal African Company, Mr. Ogelthorpe, and several other gentlemen in England, telling me to give his love and duty to them, and to acquaint them, that as he designs to learn to write the English tongue, he will, when he is master of it, send them long epistles, and full accounts of what shall happen to him hereafter; desiring me, that as I had lived with him almost ever since he came here, I would let his Grace and other gentlemen know what he had done, and that he was the next day going with Mr. Hull up to Yanimarew, from whence he would accompany him to the gum forest, and make so good an understanding between the Company and his country people, that the English nation should reap the benefit of the gum trade; saying at last, that he would spend his days endeavouring to do good for the English, by whom he head received such innumerable favours.[92]

And make mention of Our bondman Job, when he cried
unto his Lord (saying): Lo! The devil doth afflict me
with distress and torment.

(And it was said unto him): Strike the ground with thy foot.
This (spring) is a cool bath and a refreshing drink.

And we bestowed on him (again) his household and
therewith the like thereof, a mercy from Us, and a
memorial for men of understanding …

Lo! We found him steadfast, how excellent a slave!
Lo! He was ever turning in repentance (to his Lord).

—Qur'an (38:41-44)[93]

---

92 Moore's *Travels* (1738), (145-148, 158-159, 171-172)
93 The Quran. Pickthall (trans.) (reprint 2008).

8

'Abd al-Rahman Ibrahima

And when My servants ask thee about Me—
behold I am near; I respond to the call of him
who calls, whenever he calls unto Me [...]

—The Qur'an 2:186

In an essay entitled *The Mask of Obedience*, Bertram Wyatt-Brown begins with the story of two slaves sold to a 'dirt-farmer of Spanish Natchez' in August 1788:

> One of the slaves was named Samba, 'second son', in the fullah
> language of his native [...] Futa Jallon [in present day Guinea].
> The other captive had a much more unusual name and finer
> pedigree: 'Abd al-Rahman Ibrahima. He was the son of Sori, the
> alimami, or theocratic ruler, of the Fulani [Fulbe] tribal group [...]
> that traded with distant Timbuktu, where Ibrahima had received
> Islamic training.[1]

---

[1] Bertram Wyatt-Brown, 'The Mask of Obedience: Male Slave Psychology in the Old South', *Society and Culture in the Slave South*, J. William Harris, (ed.), (1992), 128-9.

Wyatt-Brown goes on to describe how, unlike Samba, 'Abd al-Rahman attempted to escape from his master and to resist the humiliation of slavery—though he finally resigned himself to his lot out of a kind of 'Islamic fatalism'[2] and a tribal 'honour-guilt' ethic—forcing upon himself a 'mask of obedience' in a ritualised surrender to his master's wife.[3] After weeks of hiding out in the woods, Ibrahima returned to his master's house to find his wife there alone: 'But rather than recoil in terror, she smiled [...] and offered her hand in greeting. Ibrahima took it, then knelt on the floor and placed her foot on his neck.'[4] The version of events as told by Wyatt-Brown is interesting, since he omits to mention the background of Samba—'Abd al-Rahman's companion—who was in fact a member of 'Abd al-Rahman's personal guard in the Futa Jallon army and who stood firm with him when they were ambushed by enemies (see below). Furthermore, in mentioning 'Abd al-Rahman's Islamic training in 'faraway Timbuktu' (note the emphasis on distance, as if 'Abd al-Rahman's literacy was an exception to the general rule) whilst remaining silent about his companion's, there is an implication that Samba was not educated. And yet this assumption cannot be derived from the facts before us. Moreover he distinguishes between the names of the two slaves by emphasising that 'Samba' was a name from the Fullah language—the Futa Jallon vernacular—whereas 'Abd al-Rahman Ibrahima was 'a much more unusual name'.

In fact both men were Fulbe, like Ayyub bin Suleiman, and both Muslim. According to his own account, 'Abd al-Rahman was actually born in the fabled city of Timbuktu—the ancient home of Mansa Musa, and a great centre of Islamic learning and civilisation. In the 1720s his father—the *Almaamy* Ibrahima Yoro Pate Sori—described as 'one of the most important leaders in Guinean history',[5] together

---

2   Ibid. 129: 'Since suicide was a serious violation of the Koran, he was left to assume that Allah had intended his predicament.'

3   Ibid.

4   Ibid. 129-123.

5   Gomez (1994), 691.

with Karomoko Alfa, launched a series of campaigns of liberation and conquest, probably against the same pagan enemies from which Ayyub's abductors derived.[6]

The campaigns were successful, and as a result Fulbe control expanded, so much so that in approximately 1767,[7] when 'Abd al-Rahman was five years old, his father settled in Timbo as king of Futa Jallon. Following the traditional Islamic model, at the age of seven, 'Abd al-Rahman was sent back to Timbuktu to pursue his studies in earnest. Later he was sent to Jenne in Massina—some thousand miles away to the north east, but closer than Timbuktu. Jenne had been a seat of Islamic learning since the eighth century, and was also probably the original home of 'Abd al-Rahman's Fulbe ancestors.[8]

Contrary to the implication in Wyatt-Brown's article, it is highly likely that Samba also received an extensive education. Even if he did not travel in his early childhood as much as 'Abd al-Rahman, though there is no reason why he shouldn't have, other centres of learning were closer to home. We know that part of 'Abd al-Rahman's education was in his 'native' Timbo, in Futa Jallon itself; and, as Austin notes, many European visitors observed—with some surprise given the usual perception of Africa and the poor state of literacy back home—that in Futa Jallon '… there are schools in every town, the majority of the people are able to read, and many possess books of law and divinity'.[9] Moreover, according to at least one modern historian, 'at the beginning of the nineteenth century, 60 percent of the population of the Futa Jallon and Bundu could read and write Arabic script …'[10]

The need, felt probably quite unconsciously by writers such as Wyatt-Brown, to distinguish the obviously literate, sophisticated, and

---

6   See Chapter 7.

7   Austin states that 'Abdul Rahahman' was born in 1762. From his own account we
    know 'Abd-al-Rahman was five years old when his father moved to Timbo. See Austin
    (1984), 124.

8   For Jenne, see J. Spencer Trimingham, *Islam in West Africa*, (Oxford: 1959), 31.

9   See Austin (1984), 248 note 38.

10 Suret-Canale and Barry, quoted in Austin (1984), 248 note 38.

articulate slaves from their companions whose biographies were never made known and whose backgrounds were never revealed has its origins in antebellum slavery itself. 'Abd al-Rahman's encounter with that institution, an encounter which consumed the better part of his life, particularly exposes the mechanisms behind this phenomenon. Struck by the learning and intelligence of certain Muslim slaves (which is not to say that there were not non-Muslim slaves equally learned), the slave masters and American public in general felt at a loss to reconcile their backgrounds with the usual nonsense about 'black savages' being salvaged by the institution of slavery, and as Ulrich B. Phillips would argue, receiving the 'glorious stamp of civilisation'.[11] Since these Muslim slaves—like 'Abd al-Rahman—were living evidence against the supposed backwardness of the 'Negro race' they had to be portrayed as somehow different to their countrymen. 'Abd al-Rahman, with his Arabic name and royal background, was portrayed as a Moorish prince and his education was therefore explained away as an 'Arab' education, not an 'African' one.[12] Like most Muslim slaves 'Abd al-Rahman was exposed to the phenomenon of 'de-Africanisation', and to some extent played along with it entirely. As late as 1968 James Register produced a book based on 'Abd al-Rahman entitled *Jallon: Arabic Prince of Old Natchez*, which one commentator at least has described as a 'racist life story with possible folkloric value'.[13] Cyrus Griffin, who wrote a series of articles about 'Abd al-Rahman (or 'Prince' as he was known) in 1828, described him thus:

> Prince is a Moor. Of this however, his present appearance suggests a doubt. The objection is that 'he is too dark for a Moor and his hair is short and curly'. It is true such is his appearance; but it was materially different on his arrival in this country [...] It is true that his lips are thicker than are usually

---

11 Quoted in Davis (1982), 3.
12 Austin (1997), 69.
13 Ibid. 68.

those of the Moor; but the animal frame is not that of any Negro we have ever seen. And if the facial angle be an infallible criterion the point is established, his being equal and perhaps greater, than most of the whites.[14]

As Sylviane Diouf rightly states, 'Clearly it was of great importance to deny any trace of Africanness to the "outstanding" slaves …'[15] and this trend has continued—perhaps unconsciously—right into the present day. What was outstanding about 'Abd al-Rahman, apart from his royal heritage, the fact that he could speak five languages and write in Arabic (the equivalent of an Englishman of the time being learned in Latin); apart from the fact that he was something of a war hero in his native lands and carried himself with a dignified bearing even as a slave; aside from the fact that he was in his mid-twenties, married and a father when he was captured as a prisoner of war and sold into slavery; is that through his entire 40 years as a slave he never forgot his African heritage—especially his education and faith.

West Africa has long been a centre of Islamic education, and at least some of the people residing in that wide geographic region have managed to preserve the traditional Islamic learning methods which Ayyub bin Suleiman, 'Abd al-Rahman Ibrahima, Bilali Muhammad (Ben Ali), and the other slaves we know about benefitted from. A traditional Islamic education would have involved, depending upon the level attained by the student and the 'profession' he had in mind, the study of such disciplines as *'ilm-ut-tajweed* (Qur'anic recitation), *sunnah/ahadith* (the critical examination of traditions concerning the life of the Prophet Muhammad and his companions), *tafsir* (Qur'anic commentary), *nahw* (grammar), *mantiq* (logic), *balaagha* (rhetoric), *adab* (belles-lettres), *kalaam* (scholastic theology), and *fiqh* (law and

---

14 Cyrus, Griffin, 'Prince the Moor', *Southern Galaxy*, June 5 1828, quoted in Diouf (1998), 94; and Austin (1984), Document III, 139.
15 Diouf (1998), 94.

jurisprudence) among others.[16] Each of these sciences would be taught from a specific set text—the text would have to be memorised along with its commentaries and repeatedly written on a slate board. Finally the student would be tested for his memorisation and understanding of the text. Like his teacher before him, the student—if he passed to his teacher's satisfaction—would then be given *ijaza* or permission to make use of this text and teach it to others in the appropriate way. Thus each graduate could trace a line of teachers right back to the original 'master' or author of the text (or to God, in the case of the Qur'an, via the Prophet Muhammad who received it—according to the teachings of Islam—from the angel Gabriel, who in turn received it from Allah). These chains of transmission, *silsilah* or *sanad*, are still extant to this day—particularly in parts of West Africa and amongst Sufi orders throughout the world—highlighting the continuity of the Islamic tradition. 'Abd al-Rahman's uncle himself appears to have been initiated into the Sufi order of the Qadariyya, and it is possible, though by no means certain, that 'Abd al-Rahman too would have been educated within that same branch.[17]

In any case, the strength of his early education was to shine through many years later and in a foreign land: when 'Abd al-Rahman was liberated at the age of 65 in the most extraordinary of circumstances, and began a long tour of the United States—meeting as he did many influential figures of the time (including President John Quincy Adams, whom he described as 'the best piece of furniture in the White House'[18])—he was still able to write in Arabic and accurately copied verses of the Qur'an from memory. Not only had he survived the shock of capture, being stripped naked, branded, transported in various ships for almost half a year, and then 40

---

16 See for example Cook, Bradley J. (ed.), *Classical Foundations of Islamic Educational Thought: A Compendium of Parallel English-Arabic Texts*, Brigham Young University Press (2010), xx. See also Danner, Mary Ann K., (trans.), *The Key to Salvation: A Sufi Manual of Invocation*, (Cambridge: 1996), 2.

17 See Austin's comments to an account by Cyrus Griffin (1827) quoted in Austin (1984) at 245 note 21.

18 Austin (1998), 12.

years of slavery in Natchez Mississippi—he had retained his identity and at least a fair portion of his education.

It is interesting that neither Stanley Elkins—who theorised that the shock and detachment process of being made a slave and the closed system of slavery itself effectively destroyed the personality and humanity of the Negro; nor Ulrich B. Phillips—who found the slaves docile and lacking in the niceties of civilisation; took 'Abd al-Rahman's story into consideration.[19] Of course they may have decided to believe the nonsense that 'Abd al-Rahman was a 'Moor' and not a genuine African, or they may have thought him to be an exception to the general rule. What is tragic, however, is that with the exception of Terry Alford's meticulously investigated and excellent biography (published in 1977),[20] 'Abd al-Rahman's Muslim roots and his full story has rarely been taken into account in modern writing.[21] Where he is mentioned—such as in Wyatt-Brown's essay—his full story is not repeated: if it were, Wyatt-Brown's argument that 'Abd al-Rahman resigned completely to his fate as a slave and put on a 'mask of obedience' would not be possible. As his story shows, Ibrahima in fact attempted, on the contrary, to make it blatantly obvious that he was not a docile, childish savage, who deserved to be enslaved by enlightened Christian masters. The way he did this, ultimately, was in his writings. Like Ayyub bin Suleiman (Job Ben Solomon), he wrote almost entirely from the Qur'an. But unlike Ayyub bin Suleiman, 'Abd al-Rahman wrote almost exclusively only one part of the Qur'an: the *Surah al-Faatihah*— or the Chapter of 'Opening'. We shall consider the meaning of the *al-Faatihah* and the reason why 'Abd al-Rahman, and other slaves, may have written it in the next chapter. The following section is concerned with summarising 'Abd al-Rahman's life; though in the course of so doing, we shall necessarily mention a few points concerning this most eloquent and sophisticated mode of resisting both the institution of antebellum

---

19 Elkins (1969).

20 Alford (1977).

21 In 2006 an award-winning movie based on Alford's book was produced for PBS by Unity Productions.

slavery and the missionary zeal of the men whose motivation in helping 'Abd al-Rahman lay in the desire to turn him into the 'chief pioneer of civilisation to the unenlightened—that, armed with the Bible, he may be the foremost of that band of pilgrims who shall roll back the mighty waves of darkness and superstition, and plant the cross of the Redeemer upon the furthermost mountains of Kong!'[22]

II

In May 1828 *The African Repository* published an oral account of 'Abd al-Rahman's life, which he had dictated to Ralph R. Gurley, the then secretary of the American Colonisation Society (ACS). The ACS was committed to sending free blacks to Liberia, where, it was hoped, they would spread the good news of the Gospel and help to colonise the 'dark continent' with the light of ('white') American values and civilisation. Austin says that Gurley was very much impressed by 'Abd al-Rahman when he met him in Washington, D.C., and asked him to write an autobiography in Arabic. This manuscript remains to be discovered, but for the benefit of his non-Arabic speaking audience, he gave a short, oral, telling of his life. Gurley explained:

> At our request, Prince has written a concise history of himself, and
> we have penned a translation of it from his lips. The only liberty
> we have taken, is to correct those grammatical inaccuracies which
> resulted from his imperfect knowledge of our language.[23]

Before meeting Gurley, 'Abd al-Rahman had much occasion to talk to the failed attorney, but successful editor of the *Natchez Southern Galaxy*: Cyrus Griffin. Griffin and his rival in trade, Andrew Marschalk, would eventually become involved in a war of words and newspaper articles

---

22 Cyrus Griffin (1827), full text in Austin (1984), document II, at 134.

23 *The African Repository*, May 1828, 77-81. Quoted in Austin (1997), 80.

concerning the wisdom of having a 'Negro/Moor', Prince or otherwise, travelling up and down the country dining with political leaders and black agitators. Ironically, Marschalk, as we shall see, had been instrumental in 'Abd al-Rahman's release, but finally tried to distance himself from the actions in a series of articles where he asserted that 'Abd al-Rahman's movements and the toasts he received in Boston were attempts by President John Quincy Adams's spokesmen at 'actually exciting the slaves to revolt, by the same species of arguments which produced the massacre of St. Domingo [in 1804].'[24] From Natchez to New Orleans, newspapers took sides in the debate between pro-Jackson supporters and Adams supporters, reprinting Marschalk's articles and discussing 'Abd al-Rahman.[25] 'At least one broadside for the Democrats,' writes Austin, 'offered an argument for voting the Jackson ticket that included references to 'Abd al-Rahman.'[26]

But 'Abd al-Rahman was an old man when all this fuss and attention converged upon him. His beginnings and his end, however, were in Africa. This is what Gurley claimed to take down from his own mouth about his life, and what was printed in the *African Repository*:

'Abduhl Ar-Rahman's History

[*The African Repository*, American Colonisation Society, May 1828]

I was born in the city of Tombuctoo. My father had been living in Tombuctoo, but removed to be King in Teembo, in Foota Jallo. His name was Almam Abrahim. I was five years old when my father carried me from Tombuctoo. I lived in Teembo, mostly, until I was twenty-one, and followed the horsemen. I was made Captain when I was twenty-one—after they put me to that, and found I had a very good head, at twenty-six, they sent me to fight the Hebohs [probably 'Hebos', pagan enemies of the Fulbe] because they destroyed the

---

24 See Austin, (1997), 78.
25 Ibid.
26 Ibid.

vessels that came to the coast, and prevented our trade. When we
fought, I defeated them. But they went back one hundred miles
into the country, and hid themselves in the mountain. We could
not see them, and did not expect there was any enemy. When we
got there, we dismounted and led our horses, until we were half
way up the mountain. Then they fired upon us. We saw smoke, we
heard guns, we saw the people drop down. I told every one to run
until we reached the top of the hill, then to wait for each other until
all came there, and we would fight them. After I had arrived at the
summit, I could see no one except my guard. They followed us, and
we ran and fought. I saw this would not do. I told everyone to run
who wished to do so. Every one who wished to run, fled. I said I
will not run for an African ['Abd al-Rahman probably said '*kaafir*'
i.e. unbeliever, as noted by Austin[27]]. I got down from my horse
and sat down. One came behind and shot me in the shoulder. One
came before and pointed his gun to shoot me, but seeing my clothes,
(ornamented with gold), he cried out, that! the King. Then every one
turned down their guns, and came and took me. When they came
to take me, I had a sword under me, but they did not see it. The first
one that came, I sprang forward and killed. Then one came behind
and knocked me down with a gun, and I fainted. They carried me
to a pond of water, and dipped me in; after I came to myself they
bound me. They pulled off my shoes, and made me go barefoot one
hundred miles and led my horse before me. After they took me to
their own country, they kept me one week. As soon as my people got
home, my father missed me. He raised a troop and came after me;
and as soon as the Hebohs knew he was coming, they carried me to
the Mandingo country, on the Gambia. They sold me directly, with
fifty others [one of whom was Samba, mentioned in Wyatt-Brown's
articles above] to an English ship ... [28]

---

27 See Austin (1997), 81.
28 *The African Repository*, May 1828, (77-81), reproduced in Austin (1997), 80-81.

Following this sale, like all the slaves before and after him, 'Abd al-Rahman and his men were stripped, branded, shackled in chains, and stuffed into the tightly packed cargo-hold of a slave ship. 'Abd al-Rahman does not recount the horrors of the especially long and harsh voyage to the New World—or else people like Gurley, Griffin, and others have chosen to omit them from their various versions of his words. Nevertheless, 'Abd al-Rahman does detail with accuracy the various places he was taken, and Terry Alford retracing his journey uncovered the extent of his suffering in his 1977 biography.[29] Stanley Elkins— recounting the usual suffering of slaves through the 'Middle Passage' (the transatlantic crossing)—thought no human, African or otherwise, capable of retaining his humanity through such an ordeal (especially when combined with the closed system of plantation life). But 'Abd al-Rahman's experience was even worse than the usual horrors of that journey, and yet he survived and returned to Africa 40 years later. The horrors were real, but Elkins had underestimated the power of humanity in these 'Negroes', the strength of their traditions and education, and the significance of their complete reliance upon God in the face of those horrors. 'For half a year,' explains Austin, 'Abd al-Rahman 'was almost completely shipbound.'

> He rode the Gambia for a week; suffered the three-thousand mile,
> six week sail across the Atlantic to Dominica in the Caribbean;
> and then had to undergo another 2,200 miles and six more weeks'
> passage across the Caribbean to the Mississippi River. There he
> remained shipbound for another week before landing in Spanish
> New Orleans, a city then only two-thirds the size of Timbo. His
> waterborne ordeal was not yet over. After a month's stay there, he
> was finally carried three hundred miles upriver, and in another
> thirty days he had arrived at what was to be his home away from
> home, Natchez.

---

29 Alford (1977).

It is a wonder anyone survived such a journey. But ['Abd]
ar-Rahman had been a warrior; survive he did. Ill, weak, and
wrapped with rope, he was sold, shorn of his long hair, and
named—by his purchaser, Thomas Foster—'Prince' because of
his still proud ways and attempts to tell of his African position
through a Mandingo translator.[30]

'Abd al-Rahman Ibrahima, only twenty-six, a prince, a commander of
men and armies, a Fulbe, and a Muslim whose name literally means
'slave of the All-Merciful [God]', could not bear to be the slave of another
man. But he was weak and feeble after his ordeal, and so did as he was
told: he laboured in the field for his 'master', endured whippings and
beatings, and ignored the treatment meted out to his fellow countrymen
and women, and himself; as if they were animals, or mere things to be
possessed. Finally, when some of his strength returned, he fled, like Ayyub
bin Suleiman so many years earlier, into the woods. But unlike Ayyub,
he did not go far: for weeks he hid and searched and planned, but no
one else had dared to act as bravely as he, there were no fellow fugitives
to ally with, no men to muster into a force of resistance. He turned
therefore back to Thomas Foster's plantation, and entered the house. As
Wyatt-Brown relates, Foster himself was away and only his wife, Sarah,
was present. And this is when, as mentioned above, she offered her hand
to him in greeting, and 'Abd al-Rahman took it, then knelt on the floor
and placed her foot on his own neck.[31] Wyatt-Brown is correct in saying
that this is a significant act. Sarah attributed his actions to the 'power
of [her] smile and [her] touch';[32] but it was neither of these that had
brought him back to the house in the first place. 'Abd al-Rahman came
back of his own free will—he could have continued, like Ayyub had

---

30 Austin (1997), 70-71.
31 Alford (1977), 45-47, quoted in Wyatt-Brown (1992), 130. Also see Steve Power, *The
    Memento: Old and New Natchez 1700–1897*, (1897), 13-14 (reprinted by Myrtle Bank
    Publishers, 1984).
32 See Austin (1984), 127; and Alford (1977), 42-48.

done, into another town, or state—he was an accomplished soldier, and a commander, whilst Ayyub had been a cleric and a merchant. He came back, and himself placed Sarah's foot over his neck—this was a wilful act of surrender: she was, after all, in the common white perception of Negroes at the time, wholly vulnerable to this 'savage' newly arrived from Africa. In doing this, 'Abd al-Rahman was declaring his civility, acknowledging the circumstances in which Allah had placed him, and declaring that he had *chosen* to accept the authority of Sarah and her husband over him. Previously he had been sold to them. But now, he had come to them of his own accord; and as easily as he had come, he could leave again—even if that meant escaping into the unknown.

'Abd al-Rahman excelled himself on the plantation: a man used to leading, he became, in effect, an overseer of the other slaves.[33] Many of these were, no doubt, pagans among whom were men from nations and tribes that were enemies of Futa Jallon. His obvious disdain and sense of superiority over these men did not go unnoticed, and would later be used to reinforce the notion that 'Abd al-Rahman was a Moor, rather than a Negro. Even as a slave 'Abd al-Rahman was notably dignified, honest and hardworking. Later, Cyrus Griffin would write:

> Prince has been the property of Col. James F. [this is a mistake,
> as his owner was Thomas Foster[34]] of this place, during his whole
> captivity. During that time, Col. F. states that he has never known
> him intoxicated, (he makes no use of ardent spirits) —never
> detected him in dishonesty or falsehood—nor has he known him
> guilty of a mean action; and though born and raised in affluence,
> he has submitted to his fate without a murmur, and has been an
> industrious and faithful servant.[35]

---

33 Austin (1997), 127.
34 See Austin (1984) note 12 at 244.
35 Cyrus Griffin, *Natchez Southern Galaxy*, December 13th 1827, reproduced in Austin (1984), 134-136.

Eventually, after 30 years as a hardworking and able slave,[36] 'Abd al-Rahman's efforts were acknowledged, and he was given a small plot upon which to grow his own food. In 1794 or 1795 he had married an American-born slave and a Baptist by the name of Isabella. Austin describes this marriage to an 'American-born, and dark-skinned, Baptist' as a 'contradiction of his supposed religious and racial stance';[37] but 'Abd al-Rahman would have known that marriage to a Christian or Jew ('the People of the Book') was perfectly legal according to the Qur'an, and as mentioned earlier, his apparent disdain for certain other slaves was due to their enmity with the Fulbe, not due to their racial origins. In any case, his marriage to Isabella was a truly successful one, and soon 'Abd al-Rahman was the father of four sons, and later, the grandfather of eight children.

Perhaps he would have passed away anonymously, leaving his Afro-American children and their descendants to a future American milieu that would hardly acknowledge any such thing as an African civilisation, let alone an African Muslim one. But in or around 1807, fate was kind to him, and Allah's mercy (*rahma*) descended on his slave (*'Abd al-Rahman*), in the form of an old acquaintance by the name of Dr. Cox:

His Interview With Dr. Cox

[*The African Repository*, American Colonisation Society, May 1828]

Dr. Cox was a surgeon on board a ship. He went ashore in Africa, and got lost. When he returned, he found the vessel gone. He sent out to travel, and came into my country, Foota Jallo—our people saw him, and ran and told my father, that they saw a white man. My father told them to bring the white man here, that he might see him. They brought Dr. Cox, and my father asked him whither he was going. He said he knew not where to go, that the ship left him, and that he had a bad sore leg. My father inquired what was

---

36 The 'thirty-years' is a guess based on 'Abd-al-Rahman's comments quoted below.
37 Austin (1997), 71.

the matter with his leg. He said he had wounded it in travelling.
My father told him he had better go no farther, but stay with him,
and he would get a woman to cure his leg. He was soon cured.
My father told him to stay as long as he chose. He remained six
months.[38] One day my father asked him, if he wished to go back to
his own country. He said yes. My father said, what makes you desire
to go back—you are treated well here? He answered, that his father
and mother would be anxious, when the vessel returned without
him, thinking he might be dead. My father told him, whenever you
wish to go, I will send a guard to accompany you to the ship. Then
fifteen men were sent with him by my father for a guard, and he
gave him gold to pay his passage home. My father told the guard,
that if a vessel was there, to leave the Doctor, but not to go on board
the ship;[39] and if there was no vessel, to bring the doctor back.[40]
They waited some time, and then found the same vessel in which
he came, and in that he took his passage. After that I was taken
prisoner, and sent to Natchez. When I had been there sixteen years,
Dr. Cox removed to Natchez, and one day I met him in the street.
I said to a man who came with me from Africa, Sambo [*Samba*],
that man rides like a white man I saw in my country. See when he
comes by; if he opens but one eye, that is the same man. When he
came up, hating to stop him without reason, I said master, you want
to buy some potatoes? He asked, what potatoes have you? While he

---

38 The same amount of time 'Abd-al-Rahman was shipbound and in transit from Africa
to Mississippi.

39 This was most likely for fear that they would be taken captive and sold off as slaves,
despite the fact they were helping Dr. Cox. This prudence on the part of 'Abd-al-
Rahman's father, Sori Ibrahim, not only shows his wisdom, but the reputation for
treachery which European traders dealing on the coast seem to have had.

40 A useful comparison can be made between this episode and the story of Ayyub bin
Suleiman. Whereas the RAC assisted his return, and also lavished him with gifts, they
did so for commercial reasons. Dr. Cox had wandered into Futa Jallon by chance, but
the Fulbe hospitality and their giving him gold as well as a guard to escort him safely
to the Gambia, for no 'worldly' benefit to themselves, indicates a level of civilisation
and humanity unequalled by those who considered the Negro to be savage.

looked at the potatoes, I observed him carefully and knew him, but he did not know me. He said boy, where did you come from? I said from Col. F's [actually Mr. Foster's]. He said, he did not raise you. Then he said, you came from Teembo? I answered, yes sir. He said, your name Abduhl Ar-Rahman? I said, yes, sir. Then springing from his horse, he embraced me, and inquired how I came to this country? Then he said, dash down your potatoes and come to my house. I said I could not, but must take the potatoes home. He rode quickly, and called a Negro woman to take the potatoes from my head. Then he sent for Gov. W. to come and see me. When Gov. W. came, Dr. Cox said, I have been to this boy's father's house, and they treated me as kindly as my own parents. He told the Gov. if any money would purchase me, but my master was unwilling to sell me. He offered large sums for me, but they were refused. Then he said to master, if you cannot part with him, use him well. After Dr. Cox died, his son offered a great price for me.

Dr. Cox's and later, his son's attempts at helping 'Abd al-Rahman did not go unnoticed. Although both father and son failed to persuade Thomas Foster to give him up, news of 'Abd al-Rahman's royal heritage, and the hospitality his people showed to a white man in distress, spread quickly in Natchez. Foster relieved the ageing Prince of his more strenuous duties, assigning him instead to the care of his horses and cattle. A newspaper editor, Andrew Marschalk, became interested in 'Abd al-Rahman's story and invited him several times to talk about Africa, his life and the customs of his people. Marschalk suggested that 'Abd al-Rahman might write a letter to his folks, which through the State Department's consul in Tunisia, might be delivered to his father. In 1826 'Abd al-Rahman, now in his sixties, took up a pen for what was probably the first time since leaving Africa, and wrote a letter to his father in Arabic. The letter sparked off a series of lengthy exchanges between the United States and Morocco—the first nation to recognise the independence of the United States. The Moroccans, of course, would have recognised 'Abd al-Rahman's black African—rather than (Arab) 'Moorish', origins. But as Muslims they also recognised a duty to assist a fellow Muslim. Two years later, Henry Clay—the then Secretary of State—wrote to Marschalk saying that the United States would pay the price for freeing the 'Moor', and his transportation to Washington, D.C.

Thomas Foster agreed to this, on condition that he be returned to Africa and 'not permitted to enjoy his liberty in this country'. The interest of the State Department was clearly motivated by the desire to gain a 'favourable impression' with Morocco, and founded on the erroneous belief that 'Abd al-Rahman was a Moor. A belief, which articles by Cyrus Griffin (and others), as we have mentioned, perpetuated.

From the Department of State

Washington, 12th Jan. 1828

Andrew Marschalk, Esq. Natchez:

Sir, —Your letters, both of the 13th ultimo, and the 20th of August last, have been received. The President is obliged by your attention, to the subject of the Moorish Slave, now in the possession of Mr. Thomas Foster. The object of the President, being to restore Prince, the slave mentioned to his family and country, for the purpose of making favourable impressions, in behalf of the United States, there is no difficulty in acceding to the conditions prescribed by Mr. Foster, which I understand to be, that Prince shall not be permitted to enjoy his liberty in this country, but be sent to his own, free from expense to Mr. Foster, who is pleased to ask nothing for the manumission of Prince of those conditions.

I have, therefore, to request that you will complete the humane agency, which you have so kindly undertaken, by calling upon Mr. Foster, assuring him that the above conditions shall be complied with, and receiving the custody of Prince from him. You will then be pleased to send Prince to this city, either by River or by the see

[sic], as you may determine to be most convenient, for the purpose of his being transported to his native country. In order to defray the expenses of decently, but plainly clothing him, if it should be necessary, and those incident to his voyage and journey to this place, you are authorised to draw upon me, at sight, for a sum not exceeding two hundred dollars, and I have to request, that you will have the goodness to render an account of the disbursements you may make under this authority.

I am, with great respect, your obedient serv't.

(signed) H. Clay[41]

'Abd al-Rahman was not as happy at the news as one might expect. He loved Isabella dearly and did not want to leave without her. But Isabella, it seems, was a valuable slave, 'the plantation's obstetrick practitioner and doctress';[42] and Foster did not wish to lose her. Finally, however, he agreed that she could be purchased for $200. Within a day, local citizens—who had been following 'Abd al-Rahman's story both in Cyrus Griffin's and in Marschalk's respective newspapers, ever since his meeting with the now deceased Dr. Cox—managed to raise $293 by subscription within twenty-four hours.[43] Now of course, 'Abd al-Rahman was overjoyed. Marschalk, getting carried away, decided to pay for a specially designed 'Moorish' costume for the Prince—including, in true Arabian Nights fashion, a turban with a crescent and star.

As 'Abd al-Rahman and Isabella parted from their children and grandchildren with tears in their eyes, Marschalk suggested he might be able to raise a subscription, on his way to Cincinnati, for their

---

41 From the *Statesman & Gazette*, October 16th 1828, being a reprint of a handbill printed by Marschalk, criticising the free movement of Abd-al-Rahman in the United States. Hence the italics in the text. The whole is reproduced in Austin (1984), Document XXIII, 196-203.

42 Austin (1984), 128.

43 Ibid.

redemption. Ironically, Marschalk would become the most vocal critic of 'Abd al-Rahman's extensive travels in pursuit of that aim. Austin writes:

> For nearly a year, Abdul Rahahman travelled backward toward
> home. His overland march was sometimes under the care of
> the federal government, sometimes under that of American
> Colonization Society members and sympathizers, and sometimes
> under his own inclinations. It was he who proposed—on the
> basis of the scheme which freed his wife—to raise money by a
> subscription; it was he who bravely accepted invitations proffered
> by relatively poor, but free, Afro-Americans; and it was he who
> through clever rhetoric and some misrepresentation lured into his
> service his most helpful advocate, the Rev. Thomas Gallaudet.[44]

The full story of 'Abd al-Rahman's travels, and their effect, is so extensive that it could take up an entire volume on its own. For our purposes, suffice to say that 'Abd al-Rahman allowed his many audiences to gain the impression that he would help convert the Negro to Christianity upon his return, or that he supported the cause of the African Colonisation Society. This is not to say that 'Abd al-Rahman was uncritical of the blatant hypocrisy he met and experienced during his life-long ordeal. As the many documents collected by Austin show,[45] 'Abd al-Rahman challenged, like Ayyub before him, the doctrine of the Trinity and the institution of American slavery itself—comparing the latter with the Muslim practice in Futa Jallon:

> Prince speaks of the Christian religion with strong evidence of
> mature reflection. He points out very forcibly, the incongruities
> in the conduct of those who profess to be the disciples of the
> immaculate Son of God. 'I tell you,' said Prince, (an expression with

---

44 Austin (1984), 129.
45 Ibid. 133-240.

which he usually prefaces any important relation) 'the Testament very good law; you no follow it; you no pray often enough; you greedy after money.' 'You good man, you join the religion?' 'See, you want more land, more neegurs; you make neegur work hard, make more cotton.' 'Where you find dat in your law?'

On being asked if such were not the case in his own country, 'No, no' he replied with much earnestness, 'I tell you, man own slaves [in Futa Jallon]—he join the religion—he very good—he make he slaves work till noon—got to church [i.e. mosque]—then till he sun go down they work for themselves—they raise cotton, sheep, cattle, plenty, plenty.'[46]

'Abd al-Rahman travelled extensively, 'riding or walking for miles', says Austin, and sitting through:

[...] lengthy orations on colonization, on the spread of Christianity, and on the business opportunities he might originate. Throughout, he maintained the air and address of a prince as he told his story and suffered through long-winded rhetoric and well-meaning but ignorant declarations, such as: 'He was a barbarian, and a slave; ... man's victim, but nature's nobleman, [...][47]

But wherever he went, and whatever impression of himself he allowed his audience to maintain, he left the clearest indication of his position in his writings in Arabic. To almost all the recipients of these writings, he let them believe they were the 'Lord's Prayer'. In actual fact they were the verses of the first chapter of the Qur'an, the *Surah al-Faatihah*.

As we shall explain in the following chapter, the *al-Faatihah* is a dialogue between Master (God) and Slave (His creation). By writing

---

46 From one of four articles by Cyrus Griffin printed in 1828 in his newspaper the *Natchez Southern Galaxy*, reproduced in Austin (1984) document III, 137-144. The quote is from page 142.
47 Austin (1984), 129-130.

the *al-Faatihah* 'Abd al-Rahman was declaring his servitude, or slavery ('*uboodiyyah*') to Allah. He was an old man and tired, but his convictions were as strong as ever. As he travelled from one city to another, and put up with all the various men, women and organisations that sought to exploit him for their own benefit (including black leaders in New York and Philadelphia), or to entertain themselves with the novelty factor of meeting an 'African prince', he used these meetings—which his Islamic training in Africa would have taught were opportunities or 'openings' from Allah—to his benefit and the benefit of his family. His constant writing of the *Surah al-Faatihah* (the Chapter of the Opening) was a recognition of this, and a prayer, rather a conversation or dialogue, with his Lord. In this sense he was indeed writing the Lord's Prayer, and did not deceive. Moreover, the final verse of the *al-Faatihah* (asking God for protection from the Way of those who have strayed) is held, by most Qur'anic exegetes (*mufassirun*), to refer to those people who mistakenly associated partners with God amongst the 'People of the Book'—i.e. such as Trinitarian Christians. In writing the *al-Faatihah*, then, 'Abd al-Rahman was declaring that he remained, and wished to remain, a Muslim. Owning nothing as a slave, not even his own person, 'Abd al-Rahman, like so many other Muslim slaves, made use of the only property that could not be taken away from him: his education—that is, his knowledge as manifested in his character. By confronting people with an unintelligible (to them) but nevertheless powerful Arabic, personified in the verses of the *al-Faatihah*, 'Abd al-Rahman preserved his integrity as a Muslim, practised reliance only upon Allah, and managed to please his audiences enough to earn $3,400 by February 1829. This money would go towards remitting the rest of his family.

Meanwhile, on the seventh day of that same month, Isabella and 'Abd al-Rahman boarded the *Harriet* and along with 152 other passengers (including Joseph J. Roberts, the future first president of Liberia)[48] headed towards Africa.

---

48 Ibid. 130.

But Africa had changed much in the time 'Abd al-Rahman had been away. He had left Africa a young man in his mid-twenties and was returning now, at the age of sixty-six, a grandfather with lives and memories on two continents. His first act on reaching Africa was to pray to Allah and declare publicly his adherence to Islam.[49] He did not immediately make for Timbo. The news of the death of two of his brothers no doubt reached him, as did news that another brother, *Almamy* Yahya, had been deposed by a rival to the throne. He concentrated instead upon freeing his remaining family in America—at least eight of whom arrived in Liberia in December 1830 (following the death of the stubborn Mr. Foster). But only his wife Isabella was able to welcome them and some others, who may have arrived in 1835; 'Abd al-Rahman, 'Prince', son of *Almaamy* Ibrahima Yoro Pate Sori, of Futa Jallon, died in Africa on 6th July 1829. In the final days of his life, following an age-old tradition, he dedicated his manuscripts to teachers in his hometown. But he, himself, never saw Timbo again.[50]

---

49 Austin (1997), 76. Austin observes that Marschalk claimed 'Abd-al-Rahman had strictly adhered to Islam through 1828.
50 Austin (1984), 131.

9

Dialogue Between Slave and Master

In the Name of God, the Benevolent, the Merciful
Praise is proper to God, Lord of the universe,
the Benevolent, the Merciful,
Ruler of the Day of Requital.
It is You we serve, to You we turn for help.
Show us the straight path,
the path of those You have favoured,
not of those who are objects of anger,
nor of those who wander astray.

—translation of Ibrahima 'Abd al-Rahman's
writing in Arabic presented as the 'Lord's Prayer':
actually the *Surah al-Faatihah* or 'Opening' of the Qur'an.[1]

---

[1] The translation is from Cleary (trans.) (2004).

The *al-Faatihah* is eloquently and unequivocally the African Muslim response to antebellum slavery. Most surprising of all, it is a response directed not, as might be expected and is often believed, at the white Americans who practised slavery, nor at those among them who opposed it; but rather at the real and only cause of the African Muslim's enslavement and humiliation from his or her own perspective: 'In the Name of God, all praise belongs to God, both good and evil are by the will of God.'[2]

The *al-Faatihah* is one of those parts of the Qur'an which, due to its special spiritual significance, has been given several names. Its most common name is *Surah al-Faatihah*. The word *Surah* is often translated 'chapter' because of its use as such in dividing verses of the Qur'an, but it actually means 'a degree of rank', or 'a sign'[3] by which one ascends.[4] *Faatihah* itself is translated as 'Opening', but through its origins in the tri-literal Arabic root *fa-ta-ha* has connections with the idea of victory, as in the Arabic *fath*.[5] It is perhaps more correctly rendered 'Opener' in English—a meaning which is striking given the use, and effect, to which it was put by 'Abd al-Rahman. The seven verses of the *Surah al-Faatihah* are also known as the *sab'a-mathani* or 'seven oft-repeated' because they are recited in every prayer. It is also said the Prophet Muhammad described the *al-Faatihah* as the *umm-al-kitab*: 'mother of the book' and the 'Formidable Qur'an' and its greatest *surah*.[6]

The African Muslim slaves who wrote this *Surah* so often in America could have written any other verses of the Qur'an familiar to them. Indeed the *Surah al-Faatihah* is not the only portion of the Qur'an, nor the only writing in Arabic, that African slaves reproduced on the plantations. The significance of their use of the *Surah al-Faatihah* lies, however, in

---

2   Al-Badawi (trans.), Habeeb Abdullah, *The Prophetic Invocations*, (Starlatch Press, 2000), 39.

3   See for example, Penrice under the root *saa-raa*.

4   Yusuf Ali, (trans.) (1938), 13.

5   Penrice, 107.

6   Al-Badawi (trans.), Habeeb Abdullah, *The Prophetic Invocations*, (Starlatch Press, 2000), 50.

its emphasis on the relationship between the slave and his true Master: Allah. It is one of the most beautiful representations in the Qur'an of the concept of *'uboodiyyah*, and in every real sense, a declaration of man's freedom from slavery to other men, and his complete dependence upon God. It is moreover a direct and exclusive plea from the slave, *abd*, to his Lord, *Rabb*—a plea which being a part of the revelation of the Qur'an, is itself a special gift from the One who is being Petitioned, to the one who is petitioning. Moreover, it is an actual dialogue between the slave and his Master, between the servant and his Beloved, in which the Real Cause of all things—including the African's enslavement in America—is addressed directly:

> [...the Prophet said:], Allah—Exalted is He! —says: 'I have divided the prayer in two between Myself and My slave, and to My slave [I grant] what he asks.
>
> 'Half of it is Mine and half My slave's.'
>
> 'When the slave says: "All Praise belongs to Allah, Lord of all the Worlds," Allah says: "My slave praises [and thanks] Me !" When he says: "The Most Merciful, the Compassionate," He says: "My slave lauds Me !" When he says: "Master of the Day of Reckoning," He says: "My slave glorifies Me !" When he says: "You only do we worship and to You only do we turn for help," He says: "This one is between Me and My slave, and My slave shall be granted his request!" And when he says: "Guide us to the straight path, the path of those whom You have favoured, not of those who are objects of wrath, nor those who are astray," He says: "This is for My slave and My slave shall be granted his request!"'[7]

The recipients of the *al-Faatihah* in 'Abd al-Rahman Ibrahima's writing were Christians, most of whom were completely ignorant of Arabic.

---

7   Al-Badawi (trans.), Habeeb Abdullah, *The Prophetic Invocations*, (Starlatch Press, 2000), 50.

Some of them in fact supposed that 'Abd al-Rahman was writing the Lord's Prayer, not verses of the Qur'an. From Ibrahima's point of view, of course, he was indeed writing the Lord's Prayer—does not the very first line of the *al-Faatihah* begin 'Praise be to Allah, the *Lord* of all the Worlds'? But he was not writing from the Bible, and he had not, as was widely and conveniently supposed, forsaken Islam for Christianity. Neither was he, as is nowadays supposed, writing in order to impress American well-wishers and friends with the notion that he was worthy of redemption—he could after all have written any *Surah* of the Qur'an, including the shorter and also important *Surah al-Ikhlas* which all Muslims learn as infants. Or else, written something different in Arabic not related to the Qur'an at all: nobody would have known any better. But 'Abd al-Rahman, and the other slaves who wrote the *al-Faatihah*, often chose it for a specific reason: these Africans were a far cry from the docile, stupid, savage (or even 'noble savage') men of the world, that past and present discourse stemming from a European and quasi-European epistemology has attempted to make them. They were deeply learned and eloquent humans with an entirely legitimate and sophisticated understanding of the world and the events that had brought them across the Atlantic as captives of America's 'peculiar institution'. And moreover, their pleas for rescue were not addressed to the men or women who were themselves, in the Qur'anic cosmology, slaves of their own whims and desires and thus powerless to bring about harm or benefit; but rather their pleas, in the form of their writings, were addressed to none other than the One who alone had brought them to America, and Who alone could bring them back home: the *al-Faatihah* was, in short, their ransom home.

> So long as you have not contemplated the Creator, you belong to created beings; but when you have contemplated Him, created beings belong to you.[8]

---

8   Victor Danner, (trans.), *Ibn 'Ata'illah's Sufi Aphorisms, (Kitab al-Hikam)*, (Lahore: reprint 1999). Aphorism 247 page 57.

10

Bilali Muhammad and the Mysterious Orison

Here is Katie Brown, sitting in the sunny steps of her
unpainted cabin, her head swathed in a white kerchief,
her body encased in a well-worn sweater.

Her visitors have come down the coast more than fifty miles from
Savannah, crossing over to Sapelo, one of the long sea islands that
stretch along the South Carolina and Georgia Coast. Passing the
sawmill village in the center of the island, they have bounced
through woods and underbrush over winding, tree-shaded oxcart
paths to the tiny settlement on the lower end of island. Here live
the descendants of Sapelo's plantation slaves …

—Charles Joyner (*Drums and Shadows*).[1]

---

1   Savannah Unit Georgia Writers Project (1940), ix.

Katie Brown, as Charles Joyner mentions in his introduction to *Drums and Shadows*, had a great-grandfather by the name of Bilali Muhammad (also known as 'Ben Ali').[2] Bilali was a Fulbe, like 'Abd al-Rahman. Moreover he had come from Timbo, 'Abd al-Rahman's hometown, and may even have been a relative. Unlike 'Abd al-Rahman, however, Bilali would never return to Africa; instead he would lead a community of Muslims on Sapelo Island itself; and leave to posterity descendants that remembered him long after he was gone, and a manuscript shrouded in mystery.

What is known about his life is sketchy, though he was a very public and noticeable figure. His descendants on Sapelo Island speak of a pious man and his wives, who prayed regularly facing the 'east' (i.e. Mecca), and chanted words in a language that, as children, they did not understand.[3] We also know that he wore a fez and long coat in the style of Muslims in Africa and fasted in Ramadhan. He had at least twelve sons and seven daughters, all of whom bore Islamic names. He was a powerful and inspiring man, whose capabilities were recognised by his owner, Thomas Spalding. Spalding often left Bilali alone to manage his entire operation—leaving him in charge of 400 to 500 people at any one time. Bilali fulfilled his responsibilities well, saving the island and its people from disaster on at least two occasions: in 1813, during the Revolutionary War, Bilali was allowed to arm himself and 80 other men to protect the island from a British attack. Bilali promised Spalding that his fellow Muslims would defend the island, saying 'I will answer for every Negro of the true faith, but not for the Christian dogs you own.'[4]

---

2   There is in fact a great deal of uncertainty about his name. Judy chooses to refer to him as 'Ben Ali' and makes a persuasive argument for this, referring to Austin's choice of Bilali as 'fanciful'. See Judy (1993) note 1 323. Judy does however admit that 'What his actual name was is up for grabs…'. 'Ben Ali', or rather 'Bin Ali' (son of Ali) is not in itself a complete name, however. Perhaps he was Salih Bin Ali, or even Bilali Bin Ali? For our purposes the name is not as important as the significance of the presence and actions of this remarkable human being.

3   Savannah Unit Georgia Writers Project (1940), 161-162.

4   Quoted in Austin (1984), 268.

This astonishing display of prejudice and pride was all the more astonishing given that it was coming from an armed black slave, and addressed to his white, Christian master, in the only colony (Georgia) during the Revolutionary War that did not allow blacks to fight.[5] Bilali was true to his word, however, and no lives were lost. In 1824 Bilali would protect the island and its people again—this time from a hurricane that struck on 14th September. At that time Spalding was away from the island, but Bilali, taking command of the situation, '"saved hundreds of slaves" by directing them into cotton and sugar houses made of an African material …'.[6]

Katie Brown remembered that one of Bilali's wives, her grandmother (Phoebe), was from the Bahamas and that 'She speak funny wuds we didn know.'[7] She used to make a sweet cake called *Saraka* on the same day every year, and distribute it to the children of the island. This *Saraka* cake was most probably a re-enactment of *sadaqah*—voluntary alms, and a regular feature of West African Muslim society. Quoting Katie Brown, Diouf explains the significance of the tradition, found throughout African Muslim slave communities in the New World:

> The Sea Islands *saraka* and the Brazilian *saka* are the exact transposition to America of an African Muslim custom. The rice ball is the traditional charity given by West African women on Fridays. The testimonies from the Sea Islands refer to one distribution a month or a year, which indicates a lack of means in no way surprising. The Muslim women of Georgia had to accumulate, day after day, small quantities of rice and sugar—taken from their rations, gathered in the rice paddies, or brought with their limited savings. The cake is still made in West Africa in the same way that Bilali's daughter [wife?] made hers, as described by her granddaughter: 'She wash rive, an po off all duh watuh. She

---

5 Ibid. 268.

6 Ibid.

7 Savannah Unit Georgia Writers Project (1940), 161.

let wet rice sit all night, an in mawnin rice is all swell. She tak dat rice an put it in wooden mawtuh, an beat it tuh paste wid wooden pestle. She add honey, sometime shiguh, an make it in flat cake wid uh hans.' As is the case in Africa, the cakes in Georgia were given to the children, and being religious in nature, the distribution was accompanied by the traditional *ameen*. 'Duh cake made, she call us all in an deah she hab great big fannuh full an she gib us each cake,' recalled Shadrach Hall. 'Den we all stands roun table, and she says "Ameen, Ameen, Ameen", an we all eats cake.'[8]

Bilali and Phoebe were also remembered for using a rosary bead, suggesting that they engaged in the Sufi practice of *dhikr* or 'remembrance/ invocation' of Allah. Katie Brown heard from one of Bilali's many daughters, and her own cousin Cotto, that Bilali would recite the words: 'Blemambi, Hakabara, Mahamadu' on a 'long' rosary and that Phoebe would add 'Ameen, Ameen'. Bilali's words as heard by his daughter Margaret and related to Katie Brown, and then to the WPA interviewers—all of whom seem to have been ignorant of Arabic—were probably: '*Subhanallah-wa-bihamdi*' (Katie's *Belambi*); '*Allah-u-Akbar*' (*Hakabara*) and '*Muhammad-u-rasoolullah*' (*Mahamadu*). These are standard phrases in Muslim litanies, used particularly by Sufis, and mean respectively: 'Exalted is God, and Praised'; 'God is Greater'; 'Muhammad is the Messenger of God'. Diouf explains the significance of this practice with her usual eloquence:

Anybody can use the long rosary, but men and women who belong to a Sufi order and do *dhikr* (incantatory formulas that may consist of the repetition of certain names of God or Koranic excerpts) use it systematically ... The presence of these rosaries in the Americas is an indication that the Muslims who used them

---

8   Diouf (1998), 65. The quotes are from *Drums and Shadows*, Savannah Unit Georgia Writers Project. (1940), 162 and 167 respectively.

were no 'ordinary' believers but men and women deeply involved in their religion, in its most constraining and most mystic aspects. They had sought a particular type of knowledge, dispensed only to those who are deemed worthy of receiving it. *Dhikr* are passed down from *shaykh* to disciple. Without a direct transmission from a master, incantations are considered invalid and even dangerous. The passing on of *dhikr* among enslaved Muslims took place in Africa, but there is little doubt that for others the event took place in America. Enough learned men were around for this transmission to occur.[9]

It is fitting, then, that a study of the Georgia Sea Islands' slave communities should begin with mention of Bilali; and it is fitting, moreover, that that study should conjure up notions of things in heaven and earth that are barely dreamt of in our philosophy:

Katie Brown is a gracious hostess to the visitors who ply her with pipe tobacco and questions about old-time customs and beliefs. They ask her about 'sitting-up' with the dead, about conjures and spirits, about the use of drums in church services, and about animal trickster tales. 'Yeah, we hab set-ups wid duh dead,' she acknowledges, but maintains, 'I ain know bout conjuh.' As for drums in church, she recalls that they 'use to hab um long time ago, but not now on duh ilun,—leas I ain heah um.'[10]

Inspired by Melville Herskovit's attempts at establishing a connection between African cultures and tradition and slave practices in America, the *Drums and Shadows* interviewers focused their attention on folkloric, religious, and magical practices and beliefs on the Georgia Sea Islands. And as their interviews reveal, there were many stories of

---

9   Ibid. 64.
10   *Drums and Shadows* (see note above)

the 'supernatural' to be told. Within this context, the rediscovery of an unintelligible, Arabic manuscript, written by Sapelo Island's black spiritual and temporal leader, Bilali (Ben Ali) Muhammad, is noteworthy. In 1940, the year *Drums and Shadows* was published, Herskovits and Lydia Parrish (a leading authority and revivalist of Georgia slave songs and spirituals) persuaded the linguist Joseph Greenberg to take Bilali's manuscript to West Africa for translation. The Hausa 'scholars'— perhaps *marabouts* (that is 'Sufis' or 'mystics'), who examined the manuscript for Greenberg, declared that it was the wok of *jinn*—that is, creatures similar to humans, that reside on earth. Austin translates '*jinn*' or '*djinn*' as 'devils'.[11] But this is a mistake. *Jinn*, from which the word 'genie' is derived, are in fact believed to be invisible creatures, who like humans, have a choice between obeying God as Muslims or disobeying God—in which case they may be described as 'devils' or satanic. One of the earliest modern translators of the Qur'an into English, Abdullah Yusuf Ali, explains thus:

> *Jinns*. Who are they? [...] In many passages [of the Qur'an] Jinns and men are spoken of together. In [Chapter] iv. 14-15 man is stated to have been created from clay, while Jinns from a flame of fire. The root meaning of *janna, yajinnu*, is 'to be covered or hidden,' and *janna, yajunnu*, in the active voice, 'to cover or hide,' as in vi. 76. Some people say that *jinn* therefore means the hidden qualities or capacities in man; others that it means wild or jungle folk hidden in the hills or forests. I do not wish to be dogmatic, but I think, from a collation and study of the Qur'anic passages, that the meaning is simply 'a spirit,' or an invisible or hidden force ...[12]

The Qur'an is unique among religious scriptures in consciously addressing itself not only to humans, but to these, non-human, *jinn*.

---

11 Austin (1997), 90.
12 Yusuf Ali (trans.), (1938), 319 commentary on vi:100 note 929.

An entire chapter—the *Surah al-Jinn*—is dedicated to the story of a group of such creatures that heard the Qur'an being recited by the Prophet Muhammad, and became Muslims. The time of its revelation was particularly stressful for Muslims, but especially for the Prophet. The people of Mecca remained violently hostile to his message, and in the nearby town of Taif, they almost killed him. On his return from Taif the verses (*ayah* lit. 'signs') of *Surah al-Jinn* were revealed, indicating that his mission was having success among creatures and people not known to him. Two years later, a delegation of men and women from Medina would come secretly to Mecca and swear their allegiance to Islam: initiating the *hegira* or flight to Medina, and the beginning of the Islamic calendar. The beginning verses of the *Surah al-Jinn* are translated as follows:

Jinn, or the Spirits

In the Name of God, Most Gracious, Most Merciful

1. *Say: It has been revealed to me that a company of Jinns listened (to the Qur-an). They said, 'We have really heard a wonderful Recital!*
2. *'It gives guidance to the Right, And we have believed therein: We shall not join (in worship) any (gods) with our Lord.*
3. *'And exalted is the Majesty of Our Lord: He has taken neither a wife nor a son.*
4. *'There were some foolish ones among us, who used to utter extravagant lies against God;*
5. *'But we do think that no man or spirit [jinn] should say aught that is untrue against God.*
6. *'True, there were persons among mankind who took shelter with persons among the Jinns, But they increased them in folly.*
7. *'And they (came to) think as ye thought, that God would not raise up any one (to Judgement).*
8. *'And we pried into the secrets of heaven; But we found it filled with stern guards and flaming fires.*

9. *'We used, indeed, to sit there in (hidden) stations, to (steal) a hearing; but any who listens now will find a flaming fire watching him in ambush.*

10. *'And we understand not whether ill is intended to those on earth, Or whether their Lord (Really) intends to guide them to right conduct.*

11. *'There are among us some that are righteous, and some the contrary: We follow divergent paths.*

12. *'But we think that we can by no means frustrate God throughout the earth, nor can we frustrate Him by flight.*

13. *'And as for us, Since we have listened to the Guidance, we have accepted it: and any who believes in his Lord has no fear, either of a short (account) or of any injustice[...]'*[13]

We have cited these first thirteen verses of *Surah al-Jinn* for a very specific reason. For one thing, they represent an entirely different understanding of the cosmos rooted in an entirely different epistemology from the current ('Western') materialistic one. The Qur'an, without any doubt, represents the epistemological foundations of Islam, and together with the Prophet Muhammad, is the epistemology of Islam; and therefore is also the cosmological basis for Bilali's interaction with the world as *'aalim* and *dunya*. Even so much was recognised by Hodgson—or his informant, since it is by no means clear that he met Bilali himself[14]—in his address to the Ethnological Society of New York in 1859:

A biographic sketch of another Mohammedan Foolah [*sic*] slave, Bul-ali (Ben-ali) [Bilali], may be found in my 'Notes on Northern Africa' published some years ago. This Mohammedan [sic], the trustworthy servant of Mr. Spalding of Sapelo Island, Georgia, died recently, at an advanced age. He adhered to the creed and to

---

13   Yusuf Ali, (trans.) (1938), The Qur'an: (72:1–13).
14   Judy (1993), 210.

the precepts of the Koran. He wrote Arabic, and read his sacred
book with constancy and reverence. It is understood, that his
numerous descendants [...] buried him with the Koran resting on
his breast [...][15]

But the modes of discourse and the conceptual tools employed to
try to understand and decipher the so-called '*Ben Ali Diary*' have
remained secular, that is *dunyawi*. And yet, as Ronald T. Judy repeatedly
emphasises, unlike any other slave writing, the African Arabic texts—
and particularly Bilali's—are resilient to the processes of agency. Bilali's
text cannot be assigned a legitimacy acceptable within the framework of
valid slave discourse, or for that matter, within the dialectic which seeks
to represent the *Other* as inferior to the *Self*. Bilali's text is particularly
unreachable because it can hardly be read, even by those familiar with
Arabic, until and unless they become intimate with the Qur'anic
'reality' of the world, with the traditional Islamic cosmology that is most
eloquently expressed by the practice of the Sufis (*ahl at-tasawwuf*). And
the only way to do this is to transcend the *dunyawi* and enter into the
'alaami; in other words to shed all sense of *Self*, literally to disengage
with the ego (*nafs*) and enter into the domain of the *Other*. We are
deliberately employing the terminology of the Sufis here, because the
process that we are describing is no less than enlightenment. And for
the Sufis enlightenment is obtained by abasing the self, the ego (*nafs*);
by acknowledging one's slavery to Allah. We are saying unequivocally
that to understand Bilali's text you have to be enlightened. This much
should be obvious. To understand anything requires enlightenment
of a kind—but if the word ('enlightenment') itself seems odd, sounds
too 'esoteric' or decadent in our current socio-intellectual milieu, then
we must ask why. The Bilali text in particular, like African slaves, like
African Muslim slaves, lies at an isthmus where two worlds meet. When
we realise this, the response of Greenberg's Hausa 'scholars' (Greenberg

---

[15] Quoted in Judy (1993), 209.

does not give us much information about who they are) to the text becomes intelligible—contrary to our expectations, it is an enlightened response: the text itself may as well be written by '*jinn*'. As Thornton, Greenberg, and others discovered, its essential meaning is hidden (*janna, yajinnu*) by reason of its 'veils'. First, one must transcend the language barrier to access the Arabic; second, even if an Arabic reader is found, or one learns the language, one finds the orthographic signs of the text at odds with the usual orthography; third, when one transcends even this, the text seems odd, haphazard, in the sense that we cannot properly locate it within any genre. It is not an autobiography, a slave-narrative—like Frederick Douglass's work; neither is it a variation of a slave narrative—that is a diary (though it is constantly referred to as such); nor is it a letter; or a poem; or a prayer in the usual sense; or even, as Greenberg tried to assert, a legal treatise. And neither, for that matter, is it wholly unintelligible, in the sense of 'gibberish'.

> The Ben Ali manuscript is enclosed in a small leather bag, secured
> by an attached leather strap [...] The bag's color is creamy tan,
> and its untanned side is facing outward, with the tanned side
> protecting the text. There is no title page or any discernible
> declaration of a title; neither is there any signature. The text
> is written on both sides of rather thin paper. The pages of the
> manuscript are bound together by string. There is no information
> on the history of the text's binding; whether it was done by Ben
> Ali or Goulding we cannot determine. In all likelihood, it was
> done by Ben Ali or by someone who was passing familiar with
> Arabic scribal conventions, because the pagination is indicated by
> placing the first word of the subsequent page in the bottom left-
> hand corner of the preceding one [...].
>
> The ink of the manuscript is reddish brown; there are many
> blotches and the script is uneven, heavy and thick in some places
> and thin and light in others. Much of the ink has bled through
> to the opposite side on many pages. There is a very discernible

variation between the handwriting in pages '1' through '4' [...], and the handwriting in pages '5' through '13' [...]. The handwriting on the first four pages is extremely obscure and difficult to decipher, but that of the remaining nine pages is by and large legible [...].

The script of the Ben-Ali text is throughout easily identifiable as the variant of Kufic script known interchangeably as *al-khatt at-takruri*, *al-khatt as-senegali* and *al-khatt at-timbuktuti*, but there are frequent words and entire passages where standardised Arabic spelling conventions collapse.

Whether or not these graphemic displacements result from some phonic dissonance, as irregularities of spelling they are easily to follow in the manuscript [...].

When these graphemic displacements are taken into account, seven and a half of the manuscript's thirteen pages are readable [...].[16]

Bilali has effectively *janna/yajunnu* 'covered/hidden' the intelligibility of the text from anyone who reads it outside an Islamic epistemology. If a Hausa scholar says it is the work of Jinn, then to believe him, we would have to believe in Jinn—which means we would most probably have to accept the Islamic cosmology that allows for their existence, which means we could not preclude the possibility of *Surah al-Jinn* being literally true: i.e. in other words we would have to submit to the Qur'anic world view. And this is precisely the world view of the author of the text—a black slave who was buried with his Qur'an and prayer rug.

But secular epistemology, the 'materialistic' (*dunyawi*) conception of knowledge, considers itself wholly rational. If Hasusa scholars say the text is the work of *jinn*, they are obviously wrong, because there is no room for *jinn* in the secular cosmology. Not surprisingly, after hearing the opinion of these scholars, Greenberg went on to consider other possibilities.

After the requisite formulas: 'In the Name of Allah the Most Merciful, The Most Beneficent', and 'Allah's blessings upon our lord Muhammad,

---

16   Judy (1993), 237-238.

and upon his family and companions, blessings and salutations'; the text begins with: 'Verily, the master and jurist Muhammad 'Abdullah ibn Yusuf ibn 'Abd al-Qarawinidu, may Allah have mercy upon and increase his blessings, amen, said [...]'.[17] Picking up on the name 'al-Qarawanidu', Greenberg decided that the text was a copy, from memory, of the tenth century *Malikite* treatise on law—the *Risala* of Abi Zaid al-Qairawani. Judy, however, has exposed the weakness of this theory. First, the jurist mentioned in Bilali's text is *Muhammad 'Abdullah ibn 'Abd-al-Qarawinidu,* not *al-Qairawanu.* Greenberg of course recognised this, but he attempted to explain it as mispronunciation on the part of Bilali. Second, six lines of this opening epigraph and a further five and a half pages of the manuscript itself remain illegible. Moreover, whilst 'fragments of passages' from the *Risala* can be identified in the Bilali text, the order of these passages, and the sequence of chapters is not consistent.[18] Judy is right in identifying Greenberg's attempts at locating the Bilali manuscript within the acceptable genre of a mimetic reproduction, as stemming from an epistemology that values mastery over a 'book' as text, as a proof of knowledge; rather than transmission from a living master. He is also right in pointing out that in so doing, Greenberg is thereby able to portray Bilali's finished attempt as less than satisfactory due to its differences with the *Risala* and its strange orthography. In other words, he is able to call into question the strength of Bilali's education and escape an otherwise requisite admission of inability on his own part in coming to terms with Bilal's knowledge—the writing of a slave. We might say, if we are harsh, that Greenberg attempts to escape a degradation of the *Self* when faced by the formidable *Other* (i.e. an unintelligible work written by a slave); by assessing that *Other* within an invented dichotomy based on that *Other's* own intellectual sources. In other words, he is able to disguise his inability to decipher the text by attempting to apportion the blame on what he supposes is Bilali's inability to copy from memory

---

17　The translation is from Judy (1993) but without his transliteration in brackets, 240.
18　See Ibid. 245-46.

correctly. His argument, however, is only valid, if we accept that Bilali was indeed attempting to copy the *Risala* of Abi Zaid. Judy correctly points out that it is not the text itself that has primacy in the Islamic scholastic tradition from which Bilali originates, but rather it is the transmission from teacher to student that is paramount:

> By focusing on the proper name, al-Qairawani, as the cited *textual* source, Greenberg is compelled to assess Ben Ali's manuscript in terms of how accurately it reproduces that treatise. Accuracy in the mimetic reproduction of a written text is held up as the mark of scholarly mastery, which presupposes that the most important indication of authoritative knowledge is proof of individual mastery of the book. This assumes that the central relationship in the authoritative transmission of knowledge is that of scholar to text, an assumption that finds verification in the site-specific institutional knowledge of the modern university. It is not verified, however, by the mode of knowledge transmission that Ben Ali is supposed to have been engaged in. On the contrary, the most important relationship in the authoritative transmission of knowledge in the Islamic educational system of West Africa was that of student to teacher. This is not to suggest that books were not central to education; in fact, the practice of the pupil memorising a particular text on hearing it read by the master from memory which Greenberg refers to is part of the process of dictation (*imla*) that was the chief characteristic of classical Islamic learning ... Yet whilst the mastery of the curriculum was the desideratum of scholarship, the means by which this was achieved determined scholarly authority. As a fifteenth-century Egyptian treatise on education put it: 'One should not study with another who himself studied only from books, without having read [them] to a learned shaykh ...' Authoritative knowledge was, thus not transmitted from text to scholar, but from master-teacher to student.[19]

---

[19] Judy (1993), 246-247.

By the same mechanism employed by Greenberg in dealing with the problem of Bilali's manuscript; when confronted by an intelligent, authoritative, and 'civilised' Negro—personified in the African Muslim slave; white, 'civilised'—slaving America was faced with a dangerous *Other*, the existence of which exposed the faults of its own *Self*: i.e. its failure to acknowledge its own savagery. The black African Muslim, like his Arabic writings, was unintelligible as a *Negro* because his humanity could not be denied. He was therefore, because of his Arabic writings, portrayed as an *Arab* or a *Moor*—and thus made intelligible as a 'noble savage', in the same way that Bilali's text could be made intelligible as a work which showed an incomplete, but nevertheless promising, education.

Thus, 'Abd al-Rahman and other Muslim slaves could be exploited as a means of evangelising, or colonising Africa for 'civilisation's' sake. And writers like Blyden, before his own conversion (to Islam), could hope that the conversion of Africa to Islam 'might herald its ultimate conversion to a purified Christianity.'[20] For this reason, rendering assistance to these slaves, allowing them to become 'drivers' or 'managers' on the plantations, or helping them return home could be justified—and sometimes became necessary, even in the opinion of those who were amongst the strongest supporters of America's peculiar institution.

---

20 Blyden (1887), xiv. Blyden's conversion to Islam has been debated, though he prayed in Mosques and became the target of attacks from some of his fellow Christian missionaries.

II

Bilali's Key to Emancipation

There are more things in heaven and earth, Horatio,
Than are dreamt of in your philosophy.

—Hamlet (Act I, Scene V)[1]

Take another look at the thirteen signs (*ayah*), or 'verses' of *Surah al-Jinn*, quoted in the previous chapter. The Hausa scholars who examined the thirteen pages of Bilali Muhammad's (Ben Ali's) manuscript—the so-called *Ben Ali Diary*—said it was the work of *Jinn*. This much, we have already mentioned in the previous chapter. We pointed out, albeit briefly, that these verses were revealed to the Prophet Muhammad at a time when the Muslims were going through a particularly brutal phase of persecution in Mecca; but shortly after their revelation, this situation was radically altered when a delegation from Medina accepted the Prophet's message. The *hegira* or flight to Medina followed. We also mentioned that the response of the Hausa 'scholars' to

---

[1]   Shakespeare, William, *Hamlet*, Watts, Cedric (ed.) Wordsworth editions (1992).

the Bilali text was—contrary to our expectations—an enlightened one. How is this so?

Let us remember that the response of these Hausa scholars to the Bilali text is the only significantly 'original' statement that has been made by the few Muslims ever to examine it. As Muslims, these men shared the same epistemology as Bilali Muhammad. But men like Greenberg, who were the recipients of this response, were epistemologically within the same tradition as Bilali's slavemaster, and as all slavemasters in America: that is, they were from a *dunyawi* tradition. This same epistemology, through its philosophers, intellectuals, and leaders, was able to portray the Negro as savage: that is 'wild', 'primitive', 'barbarous'. The word 'savage' is connected, among other things, to the Latin '*silvaticus*': meaning, 'of woodland'. As Abdullah Yusuf Ali mentions in his commentary and translation of the Qur'an, this is precisely one of the meanings attributed to the word '*Jinn*': '... Some people say that jinn therefore means the *hidden qualities or capacities in man*; others that it *means wild or jungle folk hidden in the hills or forests* [emphasis added] ...'[2]

In telling Greenberg that the Bilali text was the work of *Jinn*, these Hausa 'scholars' were in effect indicating, intentionally or otherwise, that this is the work of a man or men, *who in your perception*, are '*jinn*'—that is, wild savages, that dwell in the jungles of Africa—i.e. '*Negroes*'. At the same time, they may have been saying that it is the work of a man with 'hidden qualities' or 'capacities': a reference perhaps to the fact that they recognised Bilali's work as an esoteric Sufi or *marabout* text, such as a *gris-gris* or charm; or that they recognised that Bilali (Ben Ali) was an initiate of a Sufi order. Or else, they may have been saying that Bilali, as a *Negro*, was assumed to be a *savage*, but like all black men and women in the Americas, he had talents and capacities that were deliberately hidden: in other words they were drawing attention to a kind of 'mask of Sambo' in the Wyatt-Brown sense (mentioned in Chapter 8 in the context of 'Abd

---

2   Commentary on Surah 6:100 of the Qur'an by Yusuf, Abdullah Ali, (trans.) (1938), 319 note 929.

al-Rahman Ibrahima). Or, of course, they may well have been saying that this was the work of invisible creatures called *Jinn* as understood in the traditional sense (creatures made of a kind of 'smokeless fire' invisible to humankind in this world, but visible to them after death). It may well be that these Hausa men of learning knew exactly what the text Greenberg had shown them was, but that they were not prepared to reveal its secrets to Greenberg for a number of predictable reasons. They may, however, have left us with some important clues in their remarks to Greenberg.

The fact that parts of Bilali's text are similar to the *Risala* of Abi Zaid is also interesting when considered in the context of the *Surah al-Jinn*. The *Risala* was a legal text, dealing therefore with the believer's interaction with the *dunya*, that is the outward (*dhaahir*) aspects of the world: buying and selling, detailed injunctions on cleanliness and ritual ablutions, property rights, etc. The *Maliki(te)* school of law (of which the *Risala* is a principal text) is also called the *Medina* school because of its emphasis on the Prophet's community of *Medina* as the model community for understanding the workings of Islamic Law. As we have mentioned, the *Surah al-Jinn* was revealed in a particularly distressing time during the *Meccan* phase of Muslim history, when a spiritual community was being prepared inwardly (*baatin*) preceding its flight (*hegira*) to Medina where an outwardly visible (*dhaahir*) community would be established, and when many of the legal rulings of the Qur'an would be revealed. The encounter with these hidden forces of the *Jinn* coincided with a low point in the early history of Islam—when the survival of the Muslims, let alone the establishment of a 'community' as such, was in question. The *Surah al-Jinn* in this sense can be seen as the threshold or turning point for the early Muslims. The point of transition from the overwhelming majesty (*jalaal*) represented by Mecca to the overwhelming beauty (*jamaal*) of Medina: that is from the pure reality of Mecca, to the pure *shari'ah* of the Medinan state. The Muslim's abasement in Mecca was complete— i.e. their slavery (*'uboodiyyah*) had been perfected, and they were ready to be the guardians, to use a biblical phrase, of 'the kingdom of God'.

The success of the Prophet's message in the hidden realms of the *jinn*, as testified by the *Surah al-Jinn*, would now translate to success in the apparent realms of humankind. The Jinn themselves express uncertainty about what awaits these humans: 'And we understand not whether ill is intended to those on earth, Or whether their Lord (Really) intends to guide them to right conduct' (*Surah al-Jinn* verse 10). They are also aware of the belief among some of their kind, in a trinity—the same belief that differentiated the Abrahamic tradition of the Muslim slaves from the Pauline (or 'quasi-Abrahamic') tradition of their Christian masters (see *Surah al-Jinn* verses 2 and 3).

Is it possible that Bilali was preparing his Muslim community on Sapelo Island for a transition from being a persecuted slave community, to becoming an emancipated *Medinan* society? Perhaps his manuscript was a kind of *gris-gris* or supplication (*du'a*), or invocation (*ruqya*) for the success of that community, or as a precursor to its foundation. *Gris-gris*, after all, are supposed to be unintelligible except to those Sufis who are initiated into their use. They are written on a small piece of paper and bound in a leather pouch to be worn around the neck. But there is no reason why they should not be written in the form of a book—or thirteen pages—and placed in a leather 'bag' like the Bilali manuscript. An early description of the use of *gris-gris* is given by Richard Jobson—a British trader—who was in the Gambia in 1623:

> The Gregories bee things of great esteeme amongst them, for the
> most part they are made of leather of severall fashions, wounderous
> neathly, they are hollow, and within them is placed, and sowed
> up close, certaine writings, or spels which they receive from their
> Mary-bukes [marabouts], whereof they conceive such a religious
> respect, they do confidently believe no hurt can betide them, whilst
> these Gregories are about them.[3]

---

3   Quoted in Diouf (1998), 128-129.

Diouf points out that *gris-gris* were used in Muslim-slave communities throughout the Americas. As in Africa, even non-Muslim Africans in the New World made use of *gris-gris* composed by the Muslim *almaamys* and *marabouts* among them.[4] As Diouf points out, some commentators have questioned the use of Qur'anic verses in this way. But most Muslim scholars of the past—including the same Ibn Abi Zaid al-Qairawani whose *Risala* Bilali was supposed to have copied in his text (according to Greenberg), strongly defended the practice![5] The paper, the type of ink, the form of writing, the subtle changes of letters, the irregular use of orthography, the time of writing—all of these are important factors in the proper composition of a *gris-gris* and are also features that typify the enigmatic quality of the Bilal Muhammad (Ben Ali's) text. If the Hausa scholars that Greenberg consulted in the 1940s really did tell him that the Bilali text was the work of '*Jinn*', they were perhaps giving us the key to unlocking some of its mysteries.

Our preconceived notions, however—stemming from an epistemology different from that of the African Hausa scholars, and from that of the Muslim slave Bilali—can lead us to find fault in the Other, to find *ignorance* or *stupidity*, where instead we might discover the answers for which we have been looking. Perhaps, this, after all, is the true meaning behind Bilali Muhammad's (Ben Ali's) writing: the mystical, literary, and spiritual composition of a Negro slave, that no 'slave owner' can understand.

And Allah alone knows best.

---

4   Ibid. 128-134.
5   Ibid. 129.

IV

Meem

The Endless Sea

In this concluding part of the study we revisit the themes with which we began and consider how aspects of the writings and lives of the slaves mentioned in Part 3 continue to surface in modern day America.

Most importantly we suggest that the lives and legacy of the African Muslim slaves who came before us present an important message for us in modern times. A message that calls for us to critically examine our *Selves* in the light of the *Other* ...

12

Irony and Meaning

What concerns us is not what the historical facts
*which appear at this or that time **are**, per se, but what*
they signify, what they point to, by appearing [...]

— Oswald Spengler, *The Decline of the West*[1]

On 23rd August 2010, at International House in Berkeley, California, a group of fifteen students, family, friends, guests and scholars gathered together for the inaugural convocation of the first Muslim liberal arts college in the United States. The opening speech of the convocation began with the first two *ayahs* of the *Surah al-Faatihah* and referenced the long history of Muslims in America. 'We can't speak of Islam in America,' said Dr. Hatem Bazian, 'without knowing who Job Ben Solomon is, Prince 'Abd al-Rahman, Bilali Muhammad, Umar ibn Saeed [...]'

What does Zaytuna College mean to the American Muslim community? In reality, Zaytuna College should be thought of as a culmination of a long, complex and sometimes painful Muslim

---

1 Spengler (2000), 6.

199

encounter with America both in the past and in the present ...
Muslims and Islam itself have been part of this country before
America became America.[1]

Dr. Bazian, one of the three co-founders of this historic institution of
learning, also prefaced his speech with a comment about the completely
unplanned for, but welcome, 'coincidences' surrounding the inaugural
convocation itself:

> What a blessed and joyous beginning for Zaytuna College ... and
> to open its doors nonetheless in the middle days of the month of
> Ramadhan. By Allah we did not plan it that way! We were not
> thinking about Ramadhan when we planned for the opening
> of the classes. With a full moon upon us tonight or tomorrow
> while singing *tala-al-badru-alayna* [i.e. *the White Moon rose over
> us* ... a poem sung by the first Muslims to welcome the Prophet
> Muhammad into Medina thus inaugurating the first-ever Muslim
> community] ... You cannot plan for all these things to fall into
> order as they have for the opening of Zaytuna College.[2]

But there is a great deal more to the opening of Zaytuna College that
even Dr. Bazian did not mention. The other two co-founders of America's
only accredited liberal arts Muslim college are Imam Zaid Shakir—
an African-American Muslim scholar; and Shaykh Hamza Yusuf—a
white American Muslim scholar who studied Islamic scholarship in the
traditional way at the feet of Africans in the deserts of Mauritania. In
other words, Shaykh Hamza Yusuf studied with the same pedagogy,
with many of the same texts, and in much the same manner as Job Ben
Solomon, Salih Bilali, and Salih Ben Ali, Umar Saeed, and the other
learned African Muslim slaves that we have mentioned in this study.

---

1   Zaytuna College Inaugural Convocation 23rd August 2010, Berkeley, California.
       The convocation can be viewed at https://youtu.be/75R4N0E4_X8 .

2   Ibid.

And he did so in Africa. That the names of these African Muslim slaves should be invoked more than 200 years later in the very country that had enslaved them, by American Muslim freemen at the inauguration of a historic American Muslim educational institution that can trace its epistemological roots back to African Islamic scholarship, is a thing of great wonder; and a mighty testimony to the power of their prayers and the strength of their tradition.

That this institution should, moreover, be founded by an African-American Muslim who is a descendant of slaves; together with a white American Muslim (who therefore shares the same race as the proponents of the slave trade) who studied and transplanted the Islamic liberal arts tradition from Africa to America; and an Arab-American Muslim who, at the inaugural address of that institution, rightly traced the roots of Muslim interaction in the Americas to Africa, invoking the names of those very slaves, is extraordinary, as it not only testifies to the unifying power of Islam, but also the great potential for transformation in America itself. Dr. Bazian is right: 'You cannot plan for all these things to fall into order ...'

Dr. Bazian went on to mention other great African-American Muslims: Warith Deen Muhammad, Malcolm X, Betty Shabazz, and Muhammad Ali. Muhammad Ali began his early life as a Muslim with the Nation of Islam (NOI)—a movement which may well have origins in African Muslim slave retentions. Of course, together with Malcolm X, Muhammad Ali soon distanced himself from that movement's racist and un-Islamic teachings. Warith Deen Muhammad was also instrumental in trying to lead the NOI away from its heretical practices and beliefs. In a moving ceremony meticulously planned by Muhammad Ali himself, and executed by his family and friends when he died, Imam Zaid Shakir led the funeral prayers and facilitated the many speeches and tributes that were given by some of those who were touched by Muhammad Ali's generosity and noble character. These people included African-Americans, Muslims, Jews, Christians, Buddhists, Native Americans, men, women, students, celebrities, and even a former president of the

United States. Once again, a Muslim, African-American descendant of slaves was demonstrating a new way to look at the world and showing us the latent possibilities in America: the potential for a harmonious co-existence. And he did so in the spirit of his faith.

But not long before his death another potentiality in America reared its ugly head once again: this time in the form of Republican presidential nominee Donald Trump, who, among other things, openly called for a ban on Muslims entering the United States in his presidential campaign of 2016. He thereby echoed a call made many centuries ago by papal edict at the beginning of the European exploitation of the New World, and one since repeated several times by powerful elites worried about what effect the Muslim *Other* with a world view focused on the *Divine* might have on their hegemonies (see Chapter 6 above). In response to Donald Trump's many disturbing views, the rival democratic nominee, Hilary Clinton, brought another Muslim voice to the public discourse: the father of a Muslim-American soldier who gave his life defending his country in Iraq. The Gold Star father, Khizr Khan, publicly challenged Donald Trump (and by extension all those Americans who share his views) at the Democratic National Convention, with the question: 'Mr. Trump. Have you read the United States constitution?' Adding, 'I'll gladly lend you my copy.'[3] Khizr Khan's comments at the convention and later in newspaper articles, interviews and even in an advert for the Clinton campaign, raises an important question about American identity. Speaking of his son, Captain Humayun Khan, Khizr said: 'He was 27 years old, and he was a Muslim American. I want to ask Mr. Trump, would my son have a place in your America?'[4]

There was a clear parallel in the Democratic campaign's use of Muslim voices to further its objectives in modern times, with abolitionist and Christian missionary attempts—in antebellum times—to manipulate African Muslim slaves by bringing their stories to the public discourse

---

3   Democratic Convention, Philadelphia, July 2016.

4   *Gold Star father Khizr Khan questions Donal Trump's stance on American Muslims in Hilary Clinton ad*, Independent, 21/10/2016.

in order to serve their own political agendas. After winning the 2016 Presidential election the Trump regime worked hard to implement its agenda of ethno-nationalism—acting in ways to define America not only as a white Christian nation, but as a white Christian nation according to the beliefs of a particular group of right-wing Christian fundamentalists trying to bring about Armageddon, and with it, the second coming of Christ.[5]

The chief ideologue of the Trump campaign was Steve Bannon, an individual trapped in a medieval fantasy world in which the Judeo-Christian West is struggling for survival against the dark forces of the East. Perhaps Bannon sees himself as a latter day Charles Martel who in popular Orientalist mythology saved Europe from Islam when he successfully defeated a small Umayyad army outside Poitiers in 734 CE. Bannon conveniently ignores the fact that the Muslims and Christians in that part of Europe also fought together to defend themselves against Martel.[6] In any case his definition of the American (Western) *Self* as 'Judeo-Christian' has not prevented him from allying with the worst anti-Semites on both sides of the Atlantic. In fact he has stated unequivocally that he agrees with all of the policies of some of the worst anti-Semites,

---

5   For more on this see Clark, Victoria, *Allies for Armageddon: The Rise of Christian Zionism*, Yale University Press, (2007).

6   See Bannon's comments in a Skype address given to a conservative Catholic group meeting at the Vatican in 2014. He explicitly references the Battle of Poitiers referring to Martel, and others, as 'our forefathers'. The address is embedded in the New York Times article by Scott Shane entitled *Stephen Bannon in 2014: We Are at War With Radical Islam*, New York Times, 1st February, 2017, available at https://nyti. ms/2k19iNs (accessed 08/04/2019). The myth of Martel being defender of the West against Islamic expansionism was perhaps most famously articulated by Edward Gibbon in his *Decline and Fall of the Roman Empire*. Such myths conveniently recreate the past in the shadow of the present. Martel's forces were repelled at the siege of Narbonne in 737 CE when its Muslim and Christian citizenry successfully defended themselves from Martel's expansion further south. See Chapter 6 above. See also James T. Palmer's article for the Washington Post: *The fake history that fueled the accused Christchurch shooter*, Washington Post, https://www.washingtonpost.com/ outlook/2019/03/18/fake-history-that-fueled-accused-christchurch-shooter/?utm_ term=.e0df5b70a2b3 (accessed 08/04/2019).

racists and Islamophobes in Europe: 'Please listen and write this down,' Bannon said in an address at the Oxford Union. 'I support Orban and I support Salvini, one hundred per cent … I agree with what they're trying to accomplish.'[7] The greatest irony in all of this, is perhaps, that Bannon himself seems to have been powerfully influenced in at least some of his thoughts by René Guénon—a French philosopher and convert to Islam who saw Sufism as a saving force for European civilisation and culture.[8] In fact Guénon believed Islam was the only 'religious world practically accessible to Westerners' and that Islamic practice was more compatible with Western life than, for example, Hinduism with which he also had a fascination.[9] He argued that Islam was the last living tradition of humankind that could save Western civilisation from disaster. He was initiated into the Shadhili order of Sufism, took on the name Abdal Wahid Yahya and devoted his life to Islamic spirituality. His very last word before he died was 'Allah'.[10] Guénon, among others, remains one of most important intellectual founders of the so-called 'Traditionalist School' among whom Julius Evola remains a leading intellectual figure for the far-right.[11]

On 3rd January 2019 another African Muslim made headlines in America when she became the first African-American, Muslim, female

---

7   Steve Bannon addressing the University of Oxford's Oxford Union, 16th November 2018. See https://youtu.be/8AtOw-xyMo8 at 48:38.

8   For some brief glimpses into this aspect of Bannon see Joshua Green's excerpt from his book, *Devils Bargain*, for Vanity Fair entitled *Inside the Secret, Strange Origins of Steve Bannon's Nationalist Fantasia*, (https://www.vanityfair.com/news/2017/07/the-strange-origins-of-steve-bannons-nationalist-fantasia accessed 06/04/2019).

9   Furlong (2011), 45.

10   Chacornac (2005), 98.

11   Both Guénon and Evola were deeply concerned with what they saw as the crisis of modernity that was destroying the West. However whereas Guénon turned to Islam and Sufism as the remedy, Evola turned to Hinduism and fascism. He described himself as a 'super-fascist' and remains an intellectual hero for the far-right. This is an important discussion which merits detailed examination in a future work. The interested reader may wish to listen to a short lecture by University of Cambridge professor, T. J. Winter, accessible at https://youtu.be/6n3y2GckR_k (accessed 08/04/2019).

member of the House of Representatives. Twenty-three years earlier Ilhan Omar had come to America as a refugee escaping the civil war in Somalia. In her hegira to America she was following a now well-established tradition of people escaping strife in the old world for a new life in the 'land of the free and the home of the brave'. Also making headlines was the first ever Palestinian-American Muslim female member, Rashida Tlaib, and the first ever native American women in Congress: Deb Haaland and Sharice Davids. In all these cases, Muslims in America—slaves or Gold Star generals, African-Americans or Asian-Americans—politicians, intellectuals, activists, and ordinary folk, alongside their fellow 'Others', are yet again playing a major role in the development of the American sense of *Self*. Earlier in this study we suggested that

> [...] the *Other* in every case bears a message which challenges or
> confirms the Observer's cultural self-perception. With its close ties
> to Christianity and its historical role in Spain and in the renaissance,
> Islam has always been European civilisation's greatest '*Other*'. It
> is the Christian world's close brother, the secular West's obstinate
> spiritual neighbour to the East, and the constant mirror in which
> it finds its own self-image. Perhaps for this reason, when Muslim
> slaves were brought to antebellum America, some of them, at least,
> were able to show their slave masters a humanity in the African
> that the usual justifications of slavery worked so carefully to deny.
> At times—as we shall see—the Muslim slave exposed the savagery
> of the slave-master; always he demonstrated the evil of antebellum
> slavery as an institution. But in most instances the slave master
> responded by admitting, in part, the Muslim slave's civility or
> humanity but denying, in turn, his Africanness and his blackness.[12]

In the contemporary discourse only one element seems to have changed here. Where before the undeniable humanity of the African Muslim was

---

12   See Chapter 4 above.

explained away by questioning their *African-ness*, the undeniable humanity of present-day American Muslims is explained away by attempting to deny them their *Muslim-ness*. As if to say that any good we see in Muslims cannot be a product of their faith, but rather in spite of their faith. What else can explain the fact that the absurd question 'Is Islam a Religion of Peace?' is now considered a reasonable matter for debate?[13]

The way the two sides argue this question is revealing: the principal tactic of those who argue that Islam is a religion of violence is to list a catalogue of violence perpetuated by Muslim fascist groups at random times in the twentieth and twenty-first centuries. When this argument is countered by listing countless examples of Muslim peace activists throughout history—including in the last two centuries; the response is to claim that 'of course there are "good Muslims". But their goodness does not come from Islam, but from living in the West or from Western values.'[14] For people holding this view, the actions of Capt. Khan are the result of his American values, not his Islamic values. What they would make of Muslim leaders such as Khan Abdul Ghaffar—the non-violent pacifist Muslim spiritual leader and close friend of Gandhi—who spent his entire adult life resisting British colonialism through preaching non-violence from the Qur'an and *Sunnah* (i.e. from the life-example and teachings of the Prophet Muhammad), remains unknown. But what is clear is that Abdul Ghaffar (whose name means 'Servant of the All-Forgiving') derived his non-violence from within the Islamic tradition itself. In the 1890s, when Khan Abdul Ghaffar Khan was born, America was still recovering from the aftermath of a bloody civil war, in which the

---

13 A topic of debate, it seems, on both sides of the Atlantic. See for example the Oxford Union debate in 2013, 'This House believes Islam is a religion of peace,' and a US debate at the 92nd Street Y on 5th October 2010 entitled 'Is Islam a religion of peace?' In both debates those seeking to persuade the audience that Islam was a 'religion of violence' relied more or less entirely on examples of acts of violence perpetrated by fringe Muslim groups, much in the same way that proponents of slavery referred to acts of sabotage or violence among Africans to justify that they were 'savages'.

14 See Oxford Union debate 'This House believes Islam is a religion of peace' (Thursday 23rd May 2013). See https://youtu.be/Jy9tNypo3Mo (accessed 09/04/2019).

legitimacy of keeping human beings as chattels had been a major cause of violence. In a sense, the US is still coming to terms with this darker aspect of its history: disproportionate police violence against African-Americans remains a pressing problem for modern day America. And despite all of the random acts of gun violence—including school shootings and high-school massacres—a culture of violence is glorified in games, movies and popular entertainment; firearms are readily available to purchase; and the 'right to bear arms' has its strongest defenders in areas that were the last to give up slavery.

What is clear, however, is that for those who see the *Muslim* as *Other*, a 'good' Muslim is more American than *Muslim*, whereas a 'bad' Muslim is clearly too much Muslim and not enough *American*. So Muslims become a special case, justifying, for some, secret trials, torture, extra-judicial killings and even drone attacks—all things that are anathema to the mainstream American values of liberty, freedom of expression, and rule of law. In other words, to justify actions that are contrary to the collective moral conscience of America, i.e. contrary to the moral values which inform the American sense of *Self*, the victims of those actions have to be de-humanised, i.e. made to seem *Other*, and the actions themselves have to be made to seem necessary in order to (1) defend those very values and (2) to help reform the *Other* and integrate 'it' into the human *Self*. And so in the words and deeds of today's Islamophobes we hear clear echoes of the words of Ulrich B. Phillips in his justification of antebellum slavery and all the horrors that its victims had to endure as they were snatched away from their homes in Africa and thrown into a life of slavery—*it was all for their own good*: '… slavery in the Old South had impressed upon the African savages and their native-born descendants the glorious stamp of civilisation.'[15] Specifically, Phillips argued:

> 1. A century or two ago the negroes were savages in the wilds
> of Africa. 2. Those who were brought to America, and their

---

15 Phillips (1918), see Chapter 2 above.

descendants, have acquired a certain amount of civilization, and are now in some degree fitted for life in modern civilized society.

3. This progress of the negroes has been in very large measure the result of their association with civilized white people.[16]

As we mentioned at the outset of this study, the presence of literate, pious, intelligent, and articulate black slaves in Africa—many of whom were Muslims—directly challenged this notion and exposed such justifications of slavery as a lie perpetuated to deal with the cognitive dissonance between what white slaving-America claimed to be its values, and what its actions actually represented. In such cases those slaves had to be portrayed as 'not black', but as 'Moors' that needed to be very quickly returned to their homelands to avoid attracting attention. In the same way, in our age those who claim to uphold the highest values of the West must paint the victims of their actions as medieval savages desperately resisting modernity, who must be liberated at all costs. Now, as then, the presence of literate, pious, intelligent, and articulate Muslims in America (and elsewhere) poses a problem to demagogues: exposing them for what they really are—peddlers of hate and enemies of the very values they claim to cherish. Of course not only Muslims but Latinos, Native-Americans, and other minorities in modern day America are also to be found on the receiving end of this sort of bigotry.

We began this study by pointing out in Chapter 2 that '… that bigotry is still with us. Or at least the demons of that racist past continue to haunt us intellectually and morally as a civilisation.' We have not as yet been able to free ourselves from its poison. The legacy of African Muslim slaves directly challenges that bigotry because to this very day we have access to their own writings, written in their own hands, and in their own language. We also have, alongside this material, the writings, speeches and records of the white well-wishers, friends and helpers who came into contact with the slaves and attempted to fashion the slaves'

---

16   Phillips (1968), 83. See also Chapter 2 above.

writings (through the 'translations' they offered); and the slaves' presence (through the interpretations and explanations they gave) according to their own designs. But because of the very fact that these African Muslim slaves were firmly rooted in their own African faith, culture, and tradition they were able to escape all these processes of agency and leave us with one enduring message. At the risk of falling into the same trap as those very friends and well-wishers they met in their lives, it is not for me to definitively state what that enduring message is. It has rather been the attempt of this study to call us all to revisit their lives, their writings, and their legacy and to ask what it might mean for us today. My contention is that the significance of these men and women—what their encounter with the evil of American slavery and the good of those Americans who became their allies in their personal quests for liberty means—can only be properly understood if we have recourse to the world view, traditions, and culture of the slaves themselves. But we can only have recourse to that if we are able to do two things: suspend our own prejudices and consider the world through *their* epistemology, through *their* cosmology, through *their* faith and spirituality and through *their* defining texts. And moreover, that we do so knowing full well that as we look into the eyes of the *Other* we look into a mirror that shows us our *Self*. If we can manage this as individuals, as intellectuals, as Americans, as Africans, as Muslims, as Christians, as Westerners, as Easterners, as men and as women; then what we will find, no doubt, is an ongoing struggle—a *jihad*—for liberty, and an emancipation that is yet to come.

Postscript

Then and Now

The viewer of television, the listener to radio, the reader of magazines, is presented with a whole complex of elements—all the way from ingenious rhetoric to carefully selected data and statistics—to make it easy for him to 'make up his own mind' with the minimum of difficulty and effort. But the packaging is often done so effectively that the viewer, listener, or reader does not make up his own mind at all. Instead, he inserts a packaged opinion into his mind, somewhat like inserting a cassette into a cassette player. He then pushes a button and 'plays back' the opinion whenever it seems appropriate to do so. He has performed acceptably without having had to think.

Mortimer Adler, *How to Read a Book*[1]

This work began as a thesis submitted a few weeks before the September 11th attacks on New York City in 2001. The original manuscript of the book had been written at the same time. In fact the thesis was a summary of the book itself. But the manuscript was

---

[1]   Adler and Van Doren (1972), 4.

lost shortly after the attacks—as if buried in the rubble of the world that changed on that day, never to be quite the same again. But over the subsequent years, between then and now, it was reborn. This rebirth came, as it were, at the persistence of the very men whose lives it recollects and whose meanings it seeks to make intelligible. For a long time I actively resisted finishing the book, thinking others, better qualified and more erudite, would make these meanings plain in the fullness of time. But as the years went by and the post-9/11 world seemed to plunge from one dark episode to another, the African Muslim slaves I had been writing about persisted in reminding me, like ghosts from the past, of my unfinished project.

The most pressing reminder came from Ayyub bin Suleiman himself. It was 2009, and a friend researching the history of Islam in Britain handed me an A4 card from the National Portrait Gallery. The card was part of an appeal launched by the Gallery for support to acquire 'William Hoare's compelling and moving portrait of Ayuba Suleiman Diallo (1733), thus saving from export Britain's earliest known portrait of a black African Muslim and a freed slave.'[2] The portrait was printed on the other side of the card. I sat staring at Ayyub bin Suleiman's dignified face, his Koran hanging round his neck; and I remembered how I had felt sitting in a room in the British Library, some years earlier, with the letter Ayyub had written to Nathaniel Brassey in my hands. The letter begins with Arabic writing followed by what claims to be an English translation, but is more likely Job's English dictation to a scribe:

[In Arabic:]

Composed by Ayyub bin Suleiman

In the Name of God, The Benevolent, the Merciful

---

2   From the National Portrait Gallery's printed campaign literature (National Portrait Gallery, 2009).

Honourable Mister Brassey, Member of Parliament Lombard Street

Peace be with you. Praise and thanks is proper to God, Lord of the universe—abundant praise. Mister Brassey, all of the Muslims of Zagha—men and women—wish you much good. By God, [they wish you] good. You are Mister Brassey. [This] is composed by Ayyub bin Suleiman of Zagha. Praise and thanks is proper to God, Lord of the universe.

[In English:]

A translation of the above writing from Job's mouth.

Honourable Sir,

After my humble service presented to you these few lines may inform you that I am at present, in good health and that I arrived safe (praise be to God for it) at James Fort in the River Gambia, where I met with very kind usage from Gov. Hull and likewise the rest of the Gentlemen. all [sic] the musulman of my acquaintance pray for your health long life and prosperity for many good services you have done me. I sent my messengers up into my country with … when I was the river, waited a considerable time, but had no return of an answer. This day I arrived at James Fort and found a vessel ready to sail in a few minutes. I hope all your good family is well, convey my respects to all friends especially to the young lady Miss Gray.

Your most obedient humble servant

Job B. Solomon

I hope I shall have an opportunity to write again in a little time.[3]

---

3   Job Ben Solomon Letters to Nathaniel Brassey and John Chandler: British Library Add. 32556 folios 235, 237b, 239.

As I held that letter in my hand, I knew I was holding the very same piece of paper that, so many hundreds of years before, Ayyub himself had held somewhere in Africa (see Chapter 7). In a real, tangible way—albeit in a very small way—the paths of our lives had intersected across time. For Ronald T. Judy the complete dissonance between the Arabic and English texts of the letter would become cause for deep analysis, as we have discussed already. For Gates, whom Judy critiques, this was the beginning of African-American literature. But for me, the real questions were: what does this intersection of Ayyub's life with mine mean? What does this signify for me? And then by extension what does this signify for us? The 'us' here referring to all of us—to us *moderns*.

But I had put these thoughts aside and was getting on with my life. I had tried over the years to forget about this book, fragmented and broken as it was after the digital disaster that resulted in the loss of the original manuscript; coinciding with the human catastrophe of a world committed to a war against undefined enemies. But here it was: a copy of Ayyub's portrait in my hands. And his life's adventures were once again—in the twenty-first century no less—causing an international controversy as various actors (including states) struggled to acquire ownership of his portrait; just as, once upon a time, they had struggled to acquire ownership of him. (The portrait now resides in Qatar, but is loaned out to museums around the world.)

In 2012 the (British) National Portrait Gallery was able to borrow Ayyub's portrait for a tour around Britain. The poet Ben Okri accompanied the tour and shared his feelings about Ayyub's life and the effects of the portrait on him. He also composed a poem in response to Ayyub's story and performed it publicly in front of the painting.

Who can read the riddle of life in this portrait of mine?
I am one on whom providence has worked its magic reversals
Behind me are silent stories like a storm
I have worn history around my neck like chains
Freedom is a difficult lesson to learn.

> I have tasted the language of death till it became the water of life.
> I have shaped, a little, my canvas of time
> I have crossed seas of fires and seen with these African eyes
> the one light which neither empires
> nor all the might of men obscure.
> Man is a sickness, God the cure.[4]

Ordinary members of the public took part in workshops where they composed their own poetic responses to Hoare's painting of Ayyub. And I marvelled at how Ayyub, through this medium, was looking at them even now across the centuries—still evoking emotion, admiration, and wonder in the Englishmen and women of today. Except those men and women now include black people, and, of course, Muslims too. In some very real ways, his life had made that transformation of the English identity possible ...

Meanwhile, across the Atlantic, another portrait of another African Muslim slave—this time by Charles Wilson Peale—was having an equally profound effect on James Johnston, an American lawyer and historian. Peale had painted some of the greatest white men in American history—George Washington, Benjamin Franklin, and Alexander Hamilton among them. He had also painted a portrait of Yarrow Mamout—an African Muslim who had survived 44 years of slavery in Maryland and Virginia before his manumission in 1796. Yarrow had gone on to purchase land in Georgetown, build a house, invest in the Columbia Bank, and become a financier for black and white local merchants. Peale's portrait was painted in 1819 when Yarrow was 73 years old. In 1822 another portrait of him was made by James Alexander Simpson, who went on to become professor of art at Georgetown. This painting hangs in the Georgetown Public library and fascinated James Johnston: 'I was surprised to see a portrait of a poor black man at the Georgetown library.

---

4   The poem and further information is available at the National Portrait Gallery's website: https://www.npg.org.uk/whatson/diallo/home [accessed 09/04/2019].

After all, Georgetown's whole image is rich and white.[5] Eight years of research later, Johnston published a book about Mamout's life entitled *From Slave Ship to Harvard: Yarrow Mamout and the History of an African American Family*. (One of Mamout's descendants, it turns out, graduated from Harvard University in 1927.)

> It was Mamout's leap from an enslaved person to landowner and entrepreneur that most stirred Johnston's curiosity. Even for white Americans of the labouring class at the time, that level of success was barely attainable. So how did Mamout do it? The main secret to his success seems to have lain in his faith and persistence.

According to Johnston,

> [...] a remarkable part of this story is that he wasn't freed until he was 60 and immediately has enough money to invest, which he loses. He starts over again and earns another $100 and loses that too—both times because of the actions of the men holding the money for him ... He sets out to earn money again, but now he's learned from his experience. He has enough savvy to know about corporations and puts his money into a bank to keep it safe. He goes on to loan money to white merchants, which would have been risky at the time but by then he understands the system and has the confidence to use it ...
>
> Understanding the system was no small feat—an enslaved person couldn't come by this knowledge easily. In Mamout's case, it's likely that his personal intellect combined with the Qur'anic education he received as a young man in Guinea prepared him for a lifetime of learning. In short, he was able to recognize valuable information when he heard it [...][6]

---

5 Velotti (2016), 27.
6 Ibid., 28.

Yarrow Mamout was a Fulani and probably arrived as a slave in Maryland around the same time as Ayyub bin Suleiman. He is one of the 75 African Muslims mentioned by Austin (see Chapter 1). Like Ayyub he remains famous to this day because of his personality, devotion to his faith, and ability to overcome greatest misfortunes: '… he enjoyed a "good temper" even when local boys teased him and was known for his "sobriety and a cheerful conduct," his Muslim prayers in the streets, and his jocular way with local businessmen.'[7]

One of those streets where he was known to pray publicly was 3324 Dent Place NW. This is where Mamout built his house. In an article on Yarrow Mamout, Ramin Vellotti introduces this part of the world as follows:

> 3324 Dent Place NW is a narrow lot in the middle of one of
> the many stony streets in the Georgetown neighbourhood of
> Washington D.C. It lies fallow, sandwiched and fronted by the
> stately brick-and-clapboard town homes for which the area is
> known. Jackie and John F. Kennedy lived across the street as
> newlyweds. Donald Rumsfeld lived on the street and … today
> Secretary of State John Kerry makes his home just blocks away.
> In the early 1800s, lawyer Francis Scott Key, author of the poem
> that would become America's national anthem, lived less than a
> kilometre away … [8]

Yarrow Mamout could not have known that the land he chose to purchase and build his house on, the streets where he would pray—publicly and in open defiance of the naysayers and bigots—would one day host some of the most significant men in modern American history. As I have said, this work began as a thesis submitted a few weeks before September 11th, 2001. That day left a wound on America whose pain is now felt, in some way or other, by the entire world. Americans, Africans, Muslims, and

---

7   Austin, (1997), 32.
8   Velotti (2016), 27.

everyone else in between have all somehow or other suffered as a result. In many respects, some of the modern residents of 3324 Dent Place, NW, Washington D.C. have been instrumental in directing America's response to the events of that day. Donald Rumsfeld is certainly one of the chief architects of this unfolding tragedy …

So, I began to reassemble this book from its scattered fragments. Occasionally friends and colleagues who knew of the book would ask me about it, urge me to finish it, or request a copy of the manuscript to read. Remarkably in those long fifteen years or so, as this book has re-emerged from scattered fragments of notes, from annotations in books, from memories—prompted by tragic affairs on the world stage and the cajoling of friends and colleagues—the message that I originally hoped to convey has not changed. Rather it has grown in its urgency. The meaning that, for me, so powerfully emerges from a study of the lives of these men and women—African Muslim, men and women—has only become more amplified by the times we live in now. As I completed the writing of this work the United States had just elected Donald Trump to be its president. Muhammad Ali, the famous boxer, philanthropist and people's champion, had died; and Native Americans had won an historic first battle in their struggle to prevent an oil pipeline being built through their sacred waters.

Muhammad Ali's funeral brought the diversity of America(ns) to the attention of the world. Following his own immaculate planning before his death, Muhammad Ali deliberately brought on to the stage and gave a common voice to American Muslims, Hollywood actors, Muslim Imams, Christian Priests, Jewish Rabbis, Buddhist monks, Native Americans, academics, and—most importantly of all—ordinary Americans, men, women, young and old. All had been touched in some deep way by the life of this extraordinary African-American Muslim whose ancestors had suffered through slavery. His ceremony began with the *Surah al-Faatihah* of the Qur'an and ended with the Qur'an. He was an intensely spiritual person who had consciously set himself on a path of service in the light of the teaching of the Prophet Muhammad:

The best of humankind are those that serve humankind.[9]

Imam Zaid Shakir—one of the founders of Zaytuna College—was chosen by Muhammad Ali and his family to preside over the ceremony. A little while later he was at Standing Rock, Dakota. Native American tribes and allies had gathered together to peacefully protest and resist the construction of an oil pipeline that would desecrate sacred land, poison the water supply for future generations, and violate treaty rights between the United States and Native peoples.[10] In a powerfully symbolic gesture Imam Zaid Shakir handed over to one of the Native American leaders water from the Sacred Well of Zamzam in Mecca. A gift of sacred water from Mecca to the Water Protectors of the American future; an exchange between African Muslims and Native peoples reminiscent of the African Muslim and Native American exchanges in antebellum times and earlier (see Chapter 1).

Meanwhile a national registry for Muslims, internment camps, extra-judicial killings (in the form of drone attacks), and mass surveillance have become realities in contemporary American life; as an American president quite unlike any other sits in the White House tweeting away on social media. What does this situation mean for us? And what does this have to do with the African Muslim slaves whose lives refuse, even now, to become lost in the rubble of history?

In this work I have tried to answer both these questions. And I deliberately arranged the work in a way that points to meanings beyond the surface text. Meanings that can only be discovered when they are consciously sought out using the epistemology of the Qur'an and the Islamic tradition itself. This is what the African Muslim slaves seemed to have been doing quite consciously in their writings. But the quest to search out these meanings may not suit everyone. Ultimately, it was perhaps this recognition that held me back from completing this book.

---

9   A well known saying of the Prophet Muhammad.
10 The Dakota Access Pipeline (DAPL).

But then I came across two statements that most powerfully point the way and have made it easier to explain the message of this book. The first came from Salih Bilali (Chapter 10), who like Ayyub bin Suleiman, Yarrow Mamout, and the others, still finds ways to make us remember him—this time through the words of another of his descendants: Cornelia Walker Bailey. A younger relative of Katie Brown's, she wrote a moving, magical work on life growing up on Sapelo Island and memories of her ancestors, entitled *God, Dr. Buzzard and the Bolito Man*. 'Bilali is watching us', she says …

> Bilali is watching us. He has become the father of us all … The
> spirits will watch over us and over the island through the dark night
> as we search for the first rays of light in the sky at day-clean. They
> will keep on watching in all the days to come, they will watch until
> Gabriel blows his horn and everyone rises facing the East. This I
> believe, because it's what the old people believed.[11]

That Cornelia's words echo something of the mystery and wonder of her great African Muslim grandfather's own writings should not surprise us. His memory and spirit live on in her, and in her efforts to keep the Sapelo Island community together.

The second statement came from Phenocia Bauerle, Director of Native American Student Development at UC Berkeley and a member of the Absakola Nation. Speaking at a discussion on the non-violent actions of self-styled 'Water Protectors' resisting the Dakota Access Pipeline, she spoke of the deeper meanings behind what they were doing:

> Native world views, not unlike other indigenous world views across
> the world, often have very specific relationships with the land, in
> that we are not in a hierarchical relationship. We are all parts of
> the same environment, which I think is very different from this

---

11   Bailey (2001), 334.

Western world view of hierarchy. So that those tribal members and people who have taken on this idea of being Water Protectors—it's their right to stand up and be Keepers of the Land versus 'this is our land and we have the right to decide what happens here'. I mean that is the language of sovereignty from the United States; but really what is going on, on the undercurrent, is that they are reaffirming this right to have a world view in opposition with what we are brought up to believe. For me that is where so much of this has been so powerful, and it becomes so personal for so many native people and indigenous people across the world.[12]

Ultimately the African Muslim slaves who found themselves in America were not just affirming their right to have a world view different from that of their Western slave masters. In their actions, their speech, their prayers, their writings—and even in the paintings of their portraits which they permitted—they went beyond merely affirming their right to a different world view. Rather they exercised that right to the fullest capacity that God had given them.

In our age it is no longer so simple to talk about *their* world view and *our* world view. Because they are *us* and we are *them*. This is no longer a cliché. This is what Muhammad Ali's life demonstrated and his death showed us in the voices of all those people who spoke of him with such affection at the time of his departure. This is why we remain so fascinated by the lives and legacies of these African Muslim slaves. They remind us of ourselves—our better *selves*.

For them jihad meant the pursuit of liberty and freedom to worship Allah. In other words—*dear reader*—we are free to the extent that we ourselves define who we are. They wrote it then. I write it now.

Praise is proper to God—Lord of the Universe.

Only the faults are ours.

---

[12] *Solidarity in Difficult Times #Standing Rock*, Zaytuna College, Berkeley, California., Thursday November 17, 2016. The full event is available to view at https://youtu. be/_LnkHVXXAEA (accessed 09/04/2019). The quote is from 23:46.

بِسْمِ ٱللَّهِ ٱلرَّحْمَٰنِ ٱلرَّحِيمِ

الٓمٓ ﴿١﴾

ذَٰلِكَ ٱلْكِتَٰبُ لَا رَيْبَ ۛ فِيهِ ۛ هُدًى لِّلْمُتَّقِينَ ﴿٢﴾

In the name of Allah, the Most Compassionate, Most merciful

1. Alif. Laam. Meem.

2. That is the Book without doubt
Wherein is guidance for those who ward off evil

—The Qur'an 2:1–2

Bibliography

Qur'an Translations

Ali, Abdullah, Yusuf, (trans.), *The Holy Quran: Text, Translation and Commentary*, (Dar Al Arabia, Beirut-Lebanon: 1938).

Cleary, Thomas, (trans.), *The Qur'an: A New Translation*, (Starlatch, 2004).

Pickthall, Marmaduke, (trans.), *The Glorious Qur'an*, (Reprint. Istanbul: Cagri Yayinlari, 2008).

Other Works

'Abd-ar-Rahman, Aisha (trans.), *The Meaning of Man: The Foundations of the Science of Knowledge by Sidi 'Ali al-Jamal of Fez*, (Norwich: Diwan Press, 1977).

'Abou Bekir Sadiki, Alias Edward Doulan, 'Documents', *Journal of Negro History*, XXI (July 1936), 52-55.

Adler, Mortimer J., and Doren, Charles Van, *How to Read a Book*, (New York: Simon & Schuster, 1972).

al-Badawi (trans.), Habeeb Abdullah bin 'Alawi al-Haddaad (original comp.), *Adhkar As-sbaah wa-l Massaa*, Mostafa al-Badawi (trans.) as The Prophetic Invocations, (Burr Ridge: The Starlatch Press, 2000).

Alford, Terry, *Prince Among Slaves: The True Story of An African Prince Sold into Slavery in the American South*, (New York: OUP, 1977).

Al-Qushayri, Abu-l-Qasim Abd-al-Karim bin Hawazin, *al-Risala*, Rabia Harris (trans.), *The Risalah: Principles of Sufism*, (Great Books of the Islamic World, 2002).

Aptheker, H., *American Negro Slave Revolts*, (1943).

Astley, Thomas (comp.), 'The Remarkable Captivity and Deliverance of Job Ben Solomon, a Mohammedan Priest of Bûnda, near the Gambra, in the year 1732 …', *A New General Collection of Voyages and Travels, etc.*, vol. 2, 1745.

Ata-Malik Juvaini, *Ta'rikh-i-Jahan-Gusha*, J. A. Boyle (trans.), *Genghis Khan: The History of the World Conqueror*, (Manchester: 1997).

Austin, Allan D., *African Muslims in Antebellum America: A Sourcebook*, (New York: 1984).

—*African Muslims in Antebellum America: Transatlantic Stories and Spiritual Struggles*, (New York, London: 1997).

Bailey, Cornelia Walker with Bledoe, Christina, *God, Dr. Buzzard, and the Bolito Man: A Saltwater Geechee Talks About Life on Sapelo Island, Georgia*, (New York: Anchor Books, 2001).

Beoku-Betts, Josephine A., '"She Make Funny Flat Cake She Call Saraka": Gullah Women and Food Practices Under Slavery' Quarters' in *Working Toward Freedom: Slave Society and Domestic Economy in the American South*, ed. Larry E. Hudson (New York; University of Rochester Press, 1994), 211-231.

Blassingame, John W., *The Slave Community: Plantation Life in the Antebellum South*, (New York and Oxford: OUP, 1979).

Bluett, Thomas, *Some Memoirs of the Life of Job, the son of Solomon*, Richard Ford, (London: 1734).

Blyden, Edward, *Christianity, Islam and the Negro Race*, 1887. Reprint. (Edinburgh: 1967).

Cook, Bradley J. (ed.), *Classical Foundations of Islamic Educational Thought: A Compendium of Parallel English-Arabic Texts*, (University of Chicago Press, 2011).

Chacornac, Paul, *The Simple Life of Rene Guenon*, (Sophia Perennis, 2005).

Chomsky, Noam, *Year 501: The Conquest Continues*, (South End Press, 1992).

Cornell, Vincent J., (trans)., *The Way of Abu Madyan*, The Islamic Texts Society, (Cambridge: 1996).

Creel, Margaret Washington, *"A Peculiar People": Slave Religion and Community-Culture Among the Gullah*, (New York, London: NYU Press, 1988).

Curtin, Philip D., *Africa Remembered: narratives by West Africans from the era of the Slave Trade*, (University of Wisconsin Press: 1967).

—(et al.). *African History*, (London: Hutchinson, 1978).

—*Cross-Cultural Trade in World History*, (Cambridge: CUP, 1984).

—*The Rise and Fall of the Plantation Complex: Essays in Atlantic History*, (Cambridge: CUP, 1990).

Cyrus, Griffin, 'The Unfortunate Moor,' *African Repository* (Feb. 1828), pp. 365-367.

Davis, Angela, *Women, Race and Class*, (London: The Women's Press, 1982).

Danner Mary Ann K., (trans.), *The Key to Salvation: a Sufi Manual of Invocation*, (Cambridge: The Islamic Texts Society, 1996).

Diouf, Sylviane A., *Servants of Allah: African Muslims Enslaved in the Americas*, (New York, London: NYU Press, 1998).

Donnan, Elizabeth, *The Slave Trade into South Carolina Before the Revolution*, The American Historical Review, Vol. 33, Issue 4, July 1928.

Durkee, et al., (trans.), *Al-Madrastu-sh-Shadhdhuliyyah, Vol. One: Orisons*, (Alexandria: 1991).

Elkins, Stanley, *Slavery: A Problem in American Institutional and Intellectual Life*, (Chicago: University of Chicago Press, 1969).

Fisher, Allan G. and Humphrey J., *Slavery and Muslim society in Africa: The Institution in Saharan and Sudanic Africa and the Trans Saharan Trade.* (London: C. Hurst & Co., 1970).

Franklin, J. H., et al., *Runaway Slaves: Rebels on the Plantation*, (Oxford, New York: OUP, 1999, 2000).

Friedmann, Yohanan, (trans.), *The History of al-Tabari Vol. XII: The Battle of al-Qadisiyyah and the Conquest of Syria and Palestine A.D. 635-637/A.H. 14-15*, (State University of New York Press, 1985).

Furlong, P., *Social and Political Thought of Julius Evola*, (Routledge, 2011).

Genovese, Eugene, D., ed., *The Slave Economy of the Old South: Selected Essays in Economics and Social History*, (Baton Rouge: Louisiana State University Press, 1968).

—*Roll Jordan, Roll: The World the Slaves Made*, (New York: Vintage, 1974).

Gomez, Michael A., 'Muslims in Early America', *The Journal of Southern History*, vol. 60, Issue 4 (Nov. 1994), 671-710.

Grant, Douglas, *The Fortunate Slave: An Illustration of African Slavery in the Early Eighteenth Century*, (London: OUP, 1968).

Gray, John, *Al Qaeda: And What it Means to be Modern*, Faber (2003)

Guillaume, A., *The Life of Muhammad: A Translation of Ishaq's Sirat Rasul Allah*, (Oxford University Press: Karachi, 1978 reprint).

Haley, Alex, *Roots*, (New York: Doubleday, 1976).

Herskovits, Melville, *The Myth of the Negro Past*, (Boston: Harper & Brothers, 1941).

Hirtenstein, Stephen, *The Unlimited Mercifier: the spiritual life and thought of Ibn 'Arabi*, (Oxford: 1999).

Ibn Ata'illah, *Kitab al-Hikam*, trans. Victor Danner as *Sufi Aphorisms: Kitab al-Hikam*, (Lahore: Suhail Academy reprint 1999).

Immanuel Kant, *Observations on the Feelings of the Beautiful and Sublime*, trans. John Goldthwait (Berkeley: University of California Press: 1960)

Job Ben Solomon, *Letters to Nathaniel Brassey and John Chandler*. Held at British Library. Add. 32556 folios 235, 237b, 239.

Joyner, Charles, *Down by the Riverside: A South Carolina Slave Community*, (Chicago: University of Illinois Press, 1985).

Judy, Ronald T., *(Dis)Forming the American Canon: African Arabic Slave Narratives and the Vernacular*, (Minneapolis: University of Minnesota Press, 1993).

Keller, Nuh Ha Mim, (trans.), *Invocations of the Shadhili Order*, (Abul Hasan Books, Amman, 1998).

Kolchin, Peter, *American Slavery, 1619-1877*, (New York, Hill and Wang: 1993).

Kubick, Gerhard, *Africa and the Blues*, (University Press of Mississippi: 1999).

Levine, Lawrence, *Black Culture and Black Consciousness: Afro-American Folk Thought from Slavery to Freedom*, (Oxford: OUP, 1977).

Levtzion N. and J.F.P. Hopkins (eds), *Corpus of Early Arabic Sources for West African History*, (Princeton: Markus Wiener Publishers, 2000).

Lewis, Bernard W., *The Muslim Discovery of Europe*, (Phoenix Press: 2000).

Lings, Martin, *Muhammad: His Life Based on the Earliest Sources*, (Islamic Texts Society, 3rd New edition, 1991).

Lomax, Alan, The Land Where the Blues Began, (The New Press: 1993).

Michener, James A., 'Roots, Unique in its Time', *New York Times Book Review*, February 26, 1977, 41.

Mollien, Gaspard Theodore Comte De, *Travels in the Interior of Africa, to the sources of the Senegal and Gambia*; performed by the command of the French government, in the year 1818. (London: H. Colburn & Co. 1820).

Moore, Francis, *Travels into the Inland Parts of Africa*, (London: 1738).

Niane, D.T., (ed.), *UNESCO General History of Africa IV*, (California: 1984).

Oliver, Paul, *Savannah Syncopators: African Retentions in the Blues*, (Studio Vista: 1970).

Parrish, Lydia, *Slave Songs of the Georgia Sea Islands*, (1942), reprint. (Athens: University of Georgia Press, 1992).

Penrice, John, *Dictionary and Glossary of the Kor-an with copious grammatical references and explanations*, (London: Henry S. King & Co., 1878).

Phillips, Ulrich Bonnell, "The Plantation as a Civilizing Factor", Sewanee Review (July 1904), 258. Also cited in Davis (1982,3). The original text is archived at https://archive.org/stream/ jstor-27530631/27530631_djvu.txt accessed 1st October 2019 17:47.

— *American Negro Slavery: A survey of the Supply, Employment, and Control of Negro Labor as Determined by the Plantation Regime*, (New York and London: D. Appleton, 1918).

— *The Slave Economy of the Old South: Selected Essays in Economic and Social History*, edited by Eugene D. Genovese (Baton Rouge: Louisiana State University Press, 1968).

Power, Steve, *The Memento: Old and New Natchez 1700–1897*, (1897).

Public Records Office: T, 70: 93: 243; T, 70/93: 243; T, 70/302: 68; T, 70/1424: 18.

Raboteau, Albert, *Slave Religion: the "Invisible Institution" in the Antebellum South*, (New York, Oxford: OUP, 1978).

Roberts, Nancy, (trans)., *The Jurisprudence of the Prophetic Biography*, (Dar Al Fir: Damascus, 2007).

Said, Edward W., *Orientalism*, (Penguin: 1995).

Savannah Unit Georgia Writers Project, Work Projects Administration, *Drums and Shadows: Survival Studies Among the Georgia Coastal Negroes*, (Athens, London: 1940).

Spengler, Oswald, *The Decline of the West Volume I: Form and Actuality*, (Der Untergang Des Abendlandes), Atkinson, Charles Francis (trans.), (Alfred A. Knopf, New York: 2000).

Sufi, Abdalqadir, *The Way of Muhammad*, (London: Madinah Press, 2002).

Trimingham, J. Spencer, *Islam in West Africa*, (Oxford: OUP, 1959).

Velotti, Ramin, 'Yarrow Mamout: Freedman', *Aramco World*, vol. 67 no.4, Aramco Services Company (July/August 2016).

White, Deborah G. *Ar'n't I a Woman?*, (New York: W.W. Norton & Co, 1985).

Windley, Lathan A., *Runaway Slave Advertisements: A Documentary History from the 1730s to 1790s*, (Westport, CT: Greenwood Press: 1983).

Winter T.J. (trans.), (ed.), Al-Ghazali on Disciplining the Soul & on Breaking the Two Desires: Books XXII and XXIII of the Revival of the Religious Sciences, (Cambridge: the Islamic Texts Society, 1997).

Wood, Peter H., *Black Majority: Negroes in Colonial South Carolina from 1670 through the Stono Rebellion*, (Alfred A. Knopf, New York: 1974).

Wyatt-Brown, Bertram, 'The Mask of Obedience: Male Slave Psychology in the Old South', in Society and Culture in the Slave South, ed. J. William Harris, (London: Routledge, 1992), 128-161.

Index

'*aalam* (abode of signs) 32, 43, 117, 118,
182
abd (slave) 29, 34, 37
abolitionists 99, 103–4, 107, 131*n*, 202
Abraham, prophet 73, 192
Absakola Nation 220
Abyssinia 19*n*, 67, 71, 72, 73–4, 77, 79,
80, 81*n*, 82, 83, 86, 87–8
acupuncture 61
adab (etiquette) 32, 38, 153
Adahu 62
Adam (great ancestor) 32
Adams, John Quincy 154, 157
adhan (call to prayer) 54, 69
Adler, Mortimer J.: *How to Read a Book*
xiii, 211
Africa *see individual nation name*
African-Americans xv, 6, 7, 54, 100, 105,
107, 126, 200, 201, 202, 204, 205,
207, 214, 218
African House, London 132, 140
African Repository, The 156, 157–8, 162–3
Alfa, Karomoko 151
Alfa of Bambuk 115
Alfa of Damga 115
Alford, Terry 155, 155*n*, 159, 160*n*
Ali, Abdullah Yusuf 43*n*, 116*n*, 121*n*,
127*n*, 128*n*, 180, 182*n*, 190
Ali, Muhammad 201, 218, 219, 221

Allah 7, 24, 27, 33, 35–6, 37, 38, 39, 43,
46, 56, 61, 69, 70, 94, 124, 125, 126,
136, 150*n*, 154, 161, 162, 169, 170,
173, 174, 178, 183, 185, 186, 193,
200, 204, 221, 223
al-Lat (Arabian goddess) 84
Almoravid dynasty 86–7
alms:
sadaqah (voluntary alms) 28, 177
zakah (obligatory alms) 54–5
Al Qaeda 56–8
al-Uzzah (Arabian goddess) 84
America *see* United States of America
American Civil War (1861–5) 206–7
American Colonisation Society (ACS) 156,
157–8, 162–3, 167
American Revolutionary War (1775–83)
176, 177
amulets of protection 24, 25
Andalusian civilisation 61, 62, 92
Angola 93
Annapolis, Maryland 123, 128
anti-Semitism 203–4
Aptheker, Herbert: *Slave Resistance in the
United States* 21*n*, 26, 27
Arabella (ship) 119, 122–3, 124
Arabia 71, 80, 82, 84
Arabic xiii, 3, 8, 19*n*, 20, 24, 25*n*, 32, 38,
38*n*, 41, 42, 43, 54, 58, 67, 70, 73,

82, 85, 113–14, 115, 118, 126, 127,
131, 136, 137, 138, 151, 152, 153,
154, 154*n*, 156, 164, 168, 169, 171,
172, 173, 174, 178, 180, 183, 184,
185, 188, 212, 214
asalaamualaikum ('peace be with you') 54
Ashanti kings 24
Astley, Thomas: *A New General Collection
of Voyages and Travels volume II* 102,
108, 111, 112, 113
Atkins, John 103
Austin, Allan D.:
*African Muslims in Antebellum America:
A Sourcebook* xvi, 5, 7, 8–10, 11, 20,
62*n*, 70–1, 105, 110–11, 151*n*, 153*n*,
154*n*, 156, 157, 158, 160*n*, 161*n*,
162, 166*n*, 167, 168*n*, 170*n*, 176*n*,
180, 217
*African Muslims in Antebellum America:
Transatlantic Stories and Spiritual
Struggles* 10, 22*n*, 23*n*, 68*n*, 71*n*,
105*n*, 106*n*, 107*n*, 109*n*, 111*n*, 142*n*,
152*n*, 158*n*, 160*n*, 161*n*, 162*n*, 170*n*,
180*n*, 217*n*

Bahamas 177
Bailey, Cornelia Walker: *God, Dr. Buzzard
and the Bolito Man* 220
Bakr, Abu 84, 114
balaagha (rhetoric) 153
Bambuk 115, 115*n*, 116, 117
Bannon, Steve 203, 203*n*, 204, 204*n*
Barbot, John 103
Bauerle, Phenocia 220–1
Bazian, Dr. Hatem 199–200, 201
Beoku-Betts, Josephine 28, 69
Berbers 65, 66, 82, 91–2
Berger, Morroe 7
Bey of Tunis 139
Bible 22, 25, 25*n*, 135, 156, 174
Bilali, Salih 20, 69, 70, 100, 176*n*, 200, 219
Biographie Universelle 109
blackamoors 62
'blackness', associating Muslims with
64–6, 108, 205

Blassingame, John 16
Bluett, Thomas: *Some Memoirs of the Life of
Job, the son of Solomon* 102, 104, 105,
106, 107, 108, 109, 111, 112–13,
114, 114*n*, 115, 115*n*, 118*n*, 120*n*,
121*n*, 122, 124, 125, 128, 129, 130,
131–2, 133, 134, 135–6, 138, 139,
141–2, 143–4
Bogdani, William 138
Bondu (*Bunda*) 104, 109, 110, 112, 114,
114*n*, 115, 115*n*, 116, 118*n*, 119,
120, 122, 126, 142, 145, 151
Borno 90
Brassey, Nathaniel 138–9, 212, 213
British Library 8, 212
Brown, Katie 175, 176, 177, 178, 179,
220

Caroline, Queen 137, 142, 144
Catechetical Instructions in Arabic 136–7
Catholicism 61, 63, 64, 92, 203*n*
Caxlitus III 63
Chalmers, Alexander 109
Chandler, John 37
Cherokee 94
Chesapeake Bay 123
China 59, 60, 66
Christianity 7, 18–19, 19*n*, 22, 25, 25*n*,
26, 27, 36, 38, 43, 58, 59, 60, 61, 62,
63, 64, 65, 66, 72, 73, 74–5, 77, 78,
79, 80, 82, 86*n*, 92, 100, 103, 104,
106, 113, 130, 135, 136, 155, 162,
167, 168, 169, 173, 174, 176, 177,
188, 188*n*, 192, 201, 202, 203, 203*n*,
205, 209, 218
Christian missionaries 27, 64, 100, 112,
113, 188*n*, 202–3
civil rights movement 6
Clarkson, Thomas 103, 130–1
Clay, Henry 165–6
Clinton, Hilary 202
colonialism 6, 37, 42, 43, 51, 52, 53,
56–60, 62, 91, 100, 109, 123, 206
Columbia Bank 215
Columbus, Christopher 59, 61

Conner, James 146
Conquistadores 61
Cox, Dr. 162–4, 163*n*, 166
Creator (*Khaliq*) 33, 35, 174
Creel, Margaret: *A Peculiar People* 13
Curtin, Philip D. 21, 37, 59*n*, 61*n*, 62,
    89*n*, 90*n*, 110, 113, 114*n*, 115*n*,
    116*n*, 117*n*, 118*n*, 119*n*, 125*n*, 145*n*

Dakota Access Pipeline 219*n*, 220
Damasensa 120, 143
Dar-al-Islam ('Abode of Peace') 54
Dar-al-Kufr ('Abode of Infidelity') 54
Davids, Sharice 205
Davis, Angela: *Women, Race and Class* 16,
    28, 152*n*
'day-to-day' slave resistance 26–7
'de-Africanisation' 106, 152
deen ('life-transaction') 78
Democratic Party, U.S. 202–3
Denianke dynasty 115
Denton, Vachell 123, 126, 127–8
de Valleca, Father Francisco 64
dhikr ('remembrance/invocation' of Allah)
    178–9
Dibbalemi, Mai Dunama 90, 91
Diouf, Sylviane: *Servants of Allah: African
    Muslims Enslaved in the Americas* 10,
    11–12, 17*n*, 19*n*, 21*n*, 27, 36, 37, 38,
    57*n*, 62*n*, 63, 71, 72, 78, 87*n*, 88,
    89*n*, 90, 91, 153, 177, 178–9, 192*n*,
    193
Dolphin 142–3
Donnan, Elizabeth 93
Douglass, Frederick 41, 68*n*, 184
Dramane 117
du'a (supplication) 192
dunya (world) 26, 32, 34, 40, 43, 117,
    118, 182, 183, 191
dunyawi (secular/earthly) 41, 42, 183, 185,
    190

East Africa 71, 72 *see also individual nation
    name*
Egypt 62, 90, 137, 187

Elkins, Stanley: *Slavery: A Problem in
    American Institutional and Intellectual
    Life* 6, 15–16, 17*n*, 18, 19, 20, 21,
    27–8, 126, 155, 159
Ethnological Society of New York 182
ethno-nationalism 203
Evola, Julius 204

Faleme river 114, 116–17
fascism 86*n*, 204, 206
Fezzan 90
fiqh (law and jurisprudence) 153–4
Florida 92–3
Foster, Sarah 160–1
Foster, Thomas 160, 161, 164, 165, 166,
    170
France 86, 93, 109, 116, 117, 119, 141,
    204
Franklin, Benjamin 215
Fulbe 112–13, 114, 120, 122, 124, 138–9,
    149, 150, 151, 157–8, 160, 162,
    163*n*, 176
fuqaha (jurisprudence) 56
Futa Jallon (Guinea) 21, 91, 149, 150,
    151, 157, 161, 162, 163*n*, 167–8,
    170, 216
Futa Toro or Tukulor 114, 115, 118*n*,
    142

Gabriel, angel 33, 154, 220
Gadiaga 114*n*, 115*n*, 117, 119
Gagnier, John 127
Gambia 94, 102, 109, 116, 117, 118, 119,
    121, 123, 124, 126, 131, 140, 141,
    142, 158, 159, 163*n*, 192, 213
Gandhi 206
Gawth, Abu Madyan al- 82, 83*n*
Geladio, Samba 115, 121, 124
Geladio, Satigi 114–15
General Biographical Dictionary 109
Genovese, Eugene 16; *Roll Jordan, Roll:
    The World the Slaves Made* 18–19, 22
Gentleman's Society of Spalding 106, 109,
    138, 176
Georgetown, Washington D.C. 215, 217

Georgia 12, 13, 68*n*, 94, 127, 130, 175,
176*n*, 177, 178, 179, 180, 182
Sea Islands 13, 175, 177, 179–80
Ghaffar, Khan Abdul 206–7
gold 62, 89, 109, 116–17, 140, 141, 158,
163, 163*n*
Gold Coast 20, 54, 94, 116
Gomez, Professor Michael: 'Muslims in
Early America' 5, 10, 12, 71, 91*n*,
92–4, 150*n*
"good Muslims" 206, 207
Grant, Douglas: *The Fortunate Slave: An
Illustration of African Slavery in the
early
Eighteenth Century* 101*n*, 103, 104, 105,
106*n*, 108, 109*n*, 110, 111, 112,
119–20, 121, 122*n*, 123*n*, 127*n*, 130,
131*n*, 136, 137, 138*n*, 139, 141
Gray, Professor John 56*n*, 57, 58*n*
great pilgrimage (*al-Hajj*) 55
Greenberg, Joseph 180, 183–4, 185, 186,
187, 188, 190, 191, 193
Green, Thomas 102, 113, 180
Griffin, Cyrus 152, 153*n*, 154*n*, 156–7,
159, 161, 165, 166, 168*n*
gris-gris (amulets) 24, 25, 192–3
Guénon, René 204
Gulf of Guinea 91
gum trade 109, 116–17, 141, 146–7
Gurley, Ralph R. 156, 157, 159
Gutman, Herbert 16

Haaland, Deb 205
hadith literature 34*n*, 35*n*, 70*n*, 81, 82,
118*n*
Hajib, Ibn Amir 89
Haley, Alex: *Roots* 6–7, 8
Hall, Gwendolyn Midlo 93
Hamilton, Alexander 215
Harriet 169
Harris, Joel Chandler 68, 68*n*
Harun, Aaron 68
Harvard University 9, 216
Hausa 90, 180, 183–4, 185, 189–90, 191,
193

Hayes, Charles 131
Hegel, Georg Wilhelm Friedrich 107, 118
hegira (flight) 52, 71, 72, 83, 86, 181, 189,
191, 205
Henderson, Reverend Mr. 128
Herskovits, Melville 18, 19, 21*n*, 22, 180
hilaawatul-Imaan (sweetness of faith) 56
Hinduism 204
Hizb al-Bahr ('Litany of the Sea') 24–5
Hoare, William 212, 215
Holden, Samuel 132, 142, 144
House of Representatives, U.S, 205
Hui people 66
Hume, David 107, 108
Hunt, William 119, 121, 123, 126, 127,
128, 130, 131, 132, 133, 139
Huraira, Abu 70

ibaadah (worship) 34
Iberian Peninsula 59, 61, 86, 87, 92
Ibibio 94
ibn Aamir, Rib'ee 31
Ibn Abi Talib, Ja'far 75–6, 79, 80
ibn Fuhayrah, Amir 84
ibn Said, Umar 20, 199, 200
Ibrahima, 'Abd al-Rahman (Abraham
the Slave of the Merciful/'Prince of
Natchez') 3, 21, 26*n*, 28, 35, 35*n*,
38, 39, 40, 41, 42, 65, 82, 99, 100,
149–70, 171, 172, 173–4, 176, 188,
191, 199
Ibrahima, Isabella 162, 166, 169, 170
Igbo 94
ijaza or (permission to make use of text
and teach it) 154
'ilm (knowledge) 32, 118
'ilm-ut-tajweed (Qur'anic recitation) 153
Imams (or *almaamy*) 23, 24, 42, 114, 115,
116, 121, 124, 133, 134, 137, 139,
141, 193, 218
Inca people 61
Innocent XI, Pope 137
Inquisition 61, 64
International House, Berkeley, California
199

invocation (*ruqya*) 192
Iraq 202
Ishaq, Ibn 80, 81*n*
Islamic education model/system 21, 36,
    42, 57, 58, 87, 91, 153, 187
Islamic law 62, 63, 69, 69*n*, 153–4, 82,
    87, 191
Israelites 22, 23–4, 25–6

Jahl, Abu 80–1
Jamaica 10, 11
James Fort, Gambia 123, 142, 144, 145,
    213
Janissary guards 62–3
Jay, Lamine 120, 121, 122, 123, 141
Jesus 22, 73, 76, 77, 78, 79
jihad 221
jinns 33, 180–2, 184, 185, 189, 190, 191,
    192, 193
Joar 119, 122, 126, 144
Jobson, Richard 192
Johnson, Maurice 138
Johnston, James 215–16; *From Slave Ship
    to Harvard: Yarrow Mamout and the
    History of an African American Family*
    215–16
Journal of Southern History 10
Joyner, Charles 26*n*, 94*n*, 175, 176
'Judeo-Christian', definition of the
    American (Western) *Self* as 203
Judy, Ronald T.: *(Dis)Forming the
    American Canon* xv, 12, 39–40, 41,
    42, 107*n*, 108*n*, 111, 113, 114*n*,
    126*n*, 176*n*, 182*n*, 183, 185*n*, 186,
    187, 214
Juvaini, Ata-Malik: *Ta'rikh-i-Jahan-Gusha*
    (*History of the World Conqueror*) xi,
    120*n*

kaafir ('concealer of the truth') 33–4,
    158
Ka'bah (Islam's most ancient building)
    55, 60
kalaam (scholastic theology) 153
Kanem, near Lake Chad 90

Kant, Immanuel 40, 45*n*, 46, 107, 108, 118
Kanuri 90, 91
Ka-ur 119, 143, 145
Kebe, Lamine 20, 91
Keita 88
Kennedy, John F. 217
Kent County, Delaware 112, 124, 125
Kent Island 123
Kerry, John 217
Key, Francis Scott 217
Khan, Captain Humayun 202, 206
Khan, Khizr 202
kidnappings 62
Kiri (or Ki) 88
Kolchin, Peter 15*n*, 22

La hawla wa la quwwata illa billah
    ('there is no power or authority save
    God') 36–7
Lake, Sir Byby 132
Lawalo 88
Leach, Miss 68
Leopold I, Holy Roman Emperor 137
Liberia 156, 169, 170
Lings, Martin 73–4
literacy 21, 26, 91, 105, 106, 150,
    151
Louisiana 93, 94

Madajeros (Spanish Muslims) 91
madhaahib ('Schools of Law') 56
Maghreb 61, 63, 71, 82, 86, 87, 92
makhluq (His creation) 35
Malcolm X (al-Hajj Malik Shabazz) 7, 15,
    201
Mali 85, 87, 88–90
Malikite 186
Malinke 117, 118–19, 120, 121
Mamluks 62, 89, 90
Mamout, Yarrow 20, 215–17, 220
Mandingo people 7, 88, 89, 92, 118*n*,
    120, 121, 124, 158, 160
mantiq (logic) 153
marabouts (African Muslim Sufis) 11, 23,
    24, 78, 180, 190, 192, 193

Maracci 137
Marschalk, Andrew 156–7, 164, 165–7,
170*n*
Martel, Charles 86*n*, 203
Maryland 37, 109, 123, 124, 141, 215,
216
Mauritania 24, 200
Mecca 55, 56, 60, 71, 75, 77, 79, 80, 83,
89, 176, 181, 189, 191, 219
Medina 77, 83, 181, 189, 191, 192, 200
Medina school 191
Michener, James A. 7
Middle Passage 25, 123, 159
Mississippi River 68
Mongol armies 62
Moore, Francis: *Travels into the Inland
Parts of Africa … with a Particular
Account of Job Ben Solomon* 102, 103,
104, 105, 106, 108, 109, 110, 111,
112, 113, 119, 120*n*, 122*n*, 123*n*,
142–7, 147*n*
Moors xvi, 24, 54, 62, 63, 64–5, 68, 82,
91–2, 152–3, 155, 157, 161, 165,
166, 188, 208
Morocco 11, 99, 164–5
Moses 22–6
Muadhdhana ('to proclaim') 67, 68
Muezzin 46, 52, 54, 67, 68, 69, 70, 83,
88
Muhammad, Bilali (Ben Ali) 20, 22, 23,
24, 27, 28, 39–41, 69–70, 83, 84, 88,
100, 153, 175–93, 199, 200, 219–20
Muhammad, Phoebe 177, 178
Muhammad, Prophet 31, 35, 69, 70, 71,
72, 73, 74, 75, 77, 79, 80, 82, 83,
84, 88, 89, 101, 115, 125, 129, 136,
153, 154, 172, 181, 182, 185, 189,
200, 206
Muhammad, Warith Deen 201
Musa, Mansa, King of Mali 85, 88, 89–90,
91, 150
Muslim fascist groups 206

nahw (grammar) 153
Napoleon Bonaparte 62

Narbonne, France 86, 203*n*
Natchez, Mississippi 9, 149, 155, 157,
159, 163, 164
Natchez Southern Galaxy 156–7, 161*n*,
168*n*
National Portrait Gallery, London 212,
214, 215*n*
Nation of Islam (NOI) 7, 201
Native Americans 11, 92, 94, 201–2, 205,
208, 218, 219, 220
'Negro' 11, 15, 16*n*, 17, 25*n*, 26, 41, 44,
45*n*, 65, 75, 82, 86, 93, 94, 102, 105,
106, 107, 108, 109, 118, 122, 125,
126, 127, 131, 133–4, 138, 152, 153,
155, 157, 159, 161, 163*n*, 164, 167,
176, 188, 190, 193, 207, 208
Negus, The (King of Abyssinia) 67, 72,
73–4, 75, 76–7, 78–80, 82, 87–8
neo-conservatives 59
New Testament 136
Newton, Sir Isaac 106, 138
Nicholas V, Pope 63
Nichols, John 109
Niger Bend 87
Niger Delta 20
Nigeria 21, 87, 94
9/11 xiii, 7, 44, 59, 211–12, 217
'noble savage' 18, 65, 103, 133, 135, 174,
188
North Africa 61, 63, 65, 71, 82, 86, 87,
88, 89, 92
North America 5, 9, 11, 21
import of African Muslim slaves into
antedates arrival of the English
93–4
percentage of African Muslim slaves in
slave population of 21

Ogelthorpe, James 127–8, 130, 131, 132,
137, 140, 144, 146
Okri, Ben 214
Old Testament 22, 25
Old World 59–60
Omar, Ilhan 205
Orban, Viktor 204

Orientalism xvi, 17, 72, 113, 135, 136, 203

Other xvi, 12, 17, 40, 41*n*, 42, 45–6, 66, 108, 111, 116, 118, 135, 183, 186, 188, 193, 197, 202, 205, 207, 209

Ottoman Empire 60, 61, 62–3

Oxford Union 204, 206*n*

Parrish, Lydia 180; *Slave Songs of the Georgia Sea Islands* 13*n*, 180

Pauline (or 'quasi-Abrahamic') tradition 192

Peale, Charles Wilson 215

Pennsylvania 124–5

Percival, Mr. 93

philanthropists 60, 100, 218

Phillips, Ulrich B. 16, 17, 18, 107, 126, 152, 155, 207–8

Pike, Captain 119, 121, 122, 123, 124, 126, 127, 143

plantations 6, 7, 16*n*, 19, 26, 27, 57, 63, 68, 93, 104, 123, 130, 159, 160, 161, 166, 172, 175, 188

poisoning food 26

Pope, Alexander 106, 138

Portugal 61–2, 63, 64, 91, 92, 116, 119, 120

prisoners of war 95, 104, 118

Prophethood, Muslim concept of 77

Qadariyya 154

Qairawani, Abi Zaid al-: *Risala* 186, 187, 191, 193

Quakers 68, 130

Qur'an:
   2:1–2 32, 223
   2:186 149
   3:96 55
   12:56 ix
   19:93 31
   28:52–55 80–1
   30–41 53
   38:41–44 101, 112, 147
   'ilm-ut-tajweed (Qur'anic recitation) 153

Surah al Faatihah or 'Opening' (lit. 'Opener') 3, 37, 38, 39, 42, 44, 100, 155, 168–9, 171–4, 199, 218

Surah al-Ikhlas 174, 189

Surah al-Jinn 181–2, 185, 189, 191, 192

tafsir (Qur'anic commentary) 153

Qur'anic 'melodies' 13

Quraysh 73, 74, 76–7, 78, 79

Raboteau, Albert 24

racism 6, 16, 17, 152, 201, 204, 208

Ramadhan 54, 133, 176, 200

Register, James: *Jallon: Arabic Prince of Old Natchez* 152

Renaissance 66

Roberts, Joseph J. 169

Royal African Company (RAC) 101–2, 112, 113, 127, 130, 131, 132, 139, 140, 141, 142, 144, 145, 146, 163*n*

Royal Family, British 106, 138–9, 140–1, 142, 144

Rumsfeld, Donald 217, 218

runaway slave adverts 12–13, 94

Sacred Mosque (*Masjid al-Haram*), Mecca 55, 60

Sacred Well of Zamzam, Mecca 219

sadaqah (voluntary alms) 28, 177

Sahara 71, 85, 87

Said, Edward 17

Said, Nicholas Ben 9

salatul-jumu'ah (Friday congregational prayer) 139

Sale, George 136, 137–8

Salvini, Matteo 204

'Sambo' stereotype 15–16, 18, 19, 20, 21, 26, 70, 115*n*, 163, 190

sanad 154

Sapelo Island 12, 22, 100, 175, 176, 180, 182, 192, 220

Schwabes, J.J.: *Allgemeine Histoire der Reisen* 108

'Sea of Darkness' 25*n*, 54

'Sea of Oppression' (*Bahr al-Dhuloom*) 25

secular epistemology/'materialistic'
   (*dunyawi*) conception of knowledge
   41, 42, 183, 185, 190
secular world culture (*novus ordo seclorum*)
   59
Senegal 62, 64, 86, 87, 91, 94, 109, 114,
   116, 117
Senegambia 20, 21, 64, 93, 94, 116, 117
Shabazz, Betty 201
Shadhili order of Sufism 24, 25, 204
Shakespeare, William:
   Hamlet 189
   Othello 64–5
Shakir, Imam Zaid 200, 201, 219
shar'iah (Islamic Law) 87
shiatsu 61
Sierra Leone 20, 21, 94
silsilah 154
Simpson, James Alexander 215
slavery:
   existing studies on African Muslims
      enslaved in the Americas 5–46
   contemporary United States, importance
      of the lives and legacies of African
      Muslim slaves to xiv, 197, 199–221
   Islam and 31–46
   narratives of African Muslim slaves xiv,
      99–193
   origins of the slave trade and colonialism
      in relation to Islamic history,
      overview of xii–xiv, 51–95
   study of African Muslim slavery, value of
      xv–xvi, 5–13
Sloane, Sir Hans, Duke of Montague 106,
   137–8, 140–1, 142, 144, 146
Snelgrave, William 103
Society for the Promotion of Christian
   Knowledge 136–7
Society for the Propagation of the Gospel
   112
Solomon, Job Ben (Ayyub bin Suleiman)
   7, 8, 22, 28, 36–7, 41, 65, 74–5, 95,
   99, 101–47, 155, 199, 200, 212–15,
   216–17, 219
Songhay people 87

Sori, Ibrahima Yoro Pate 149, 150–1,
   163*n*, 170
South America 10–11, 12
South Carolina 11, 20, 21, 93, 94, 175
Spain 61, 62, 63–4, 66, 82, 86, 91, 94,
   120, 149
   decree forbidding the movement of
      Muslims into the New World
      (1543) 92–3
   expulsion of Muslims from (1492) 92
Spelman College 5
Spengler, Oswald: *The Decline of the West*
   5, 60, 199
State Department, U.S. 164, 165–6
St. Domingo, massacre of (1804) 157
St. Simon's Island 12, 20, 69
Sufism 11, 13, 23, 24–5, 44, 60, 78, 82,
   83*n*, 154, 174*n*, 178, 180, 183, 190,
   192, 204
suicide 94, 150*n*
Suleiman, Ibrahim bin (*Hibrahim*) 104,
   114, 114*n*, 119
Sunjaata 88, 90
sunnah/ahadith (critical examination of
   traditions concerning the life of
   the Prophet Muhammad and his
   companions) 24, 56, 153, 206

tafsir (Qur'anic commentary) 153
Taif 181
Takrur 86, 87, 88
Tambucane (Fort Saint Joseph) 117
Tancrowall 119, 120
tawhid (oneness and unicity of God) 55,
   135
3324 Dent Place, Washington 217–18
Timbuktu 54, 63, 87, 88, 115*n*, 149, 150,
   151, 157, 159, 164, 170
Tlaib, Rashida 205
Tolsey, Mr. 123, 124, 125–6
Tower of London 138
Traditionalist School 204
Trinitarian Christians 73, 169
Trump, Donald 92*n*, 202, 203, 218
Turks 36, 65, 66, 135, 136

uboodiyyah (the state or 'station' of
    worship) 34–6, 37, 169, 173, 191
UC Berkeley 220
Uighur people 66
Umari, Ibn Fadl-Allah al- 85*n*, 89, 90*n*
Umayyah 83–4, 203
ummah (unity of mankind) 55
UNESCO: *General History of Africa* 85,
    86–7, 88–9
United States of America:
    ban on Muslims entering, Trump calls
        for 92*n*, 202
    Civil War (1861–5) 206–7
    contemporary, importance of the lives
        and legacies of African Muslim
        slaves to xiv, 197, 199–221
    narratives of African Muslim slaves in
        antebellum xiv, 99–193
    origin of slavery in antebellum xiii–xiv,
        51–95
    Presidential election (2016) 203
    Revolutionary War (1775–83) 176, 177
Uriel, Captain George 128–9

Vellotti, Ramin 217
Voss, Antonio 119–20

wa-alaikum-as-salaam wa rahmatullah
    ('and with you be peace and the
    mercy of God') 54
Wardjabi, King 87
Washington, George 215

Water Protectors 219, 220–1
West Africa 20, 24, 54, 61–2, 71, 72,
    82–3, 85–95, 114, 117, 153, 154,
    177, 180, 187 *see also individual
    nation name*
White, Deborah Gray: *Ar'n't I a Woman?*
    28
Whydah 93
Wikraminayake, Marina: *The Free Blacks in
    Antebellum South Carolina* 11
William 128–9
Windley, Lathan A. 12
Wolof language 125
Works Projects Administration (WPA) 12,
    27, 178
    Georgia Writers Project: *Drums and
        Shadows: Survival Studies Among
        the Georgia Coastal Negroes* 12–13,
        26*n*, 94*n*, 175, 176, 179–80
*World Displayed, or, A Curious Collection of
    Voyages and Travels, The* 102, 110
Wyatt-Brown, Bertram: *The Mask of
    Obedience* 149–50, 151–2, 155, 158,
    160, 190–1

Yahya, Abdal Wahid 204
Yamina 120
Yusuf, Shaykh Hamza 200

Zaytuna College, Berkeley, California
    199–201, 200*n*, 219

www.ingramcontent.com/pod-product-compliance
Lightning Source LLC
Chambersburg PA
CBHW032001050726
47590CB00006B/2000